MW01630172

IN THE SHADOW OF VELÁZQUEZ

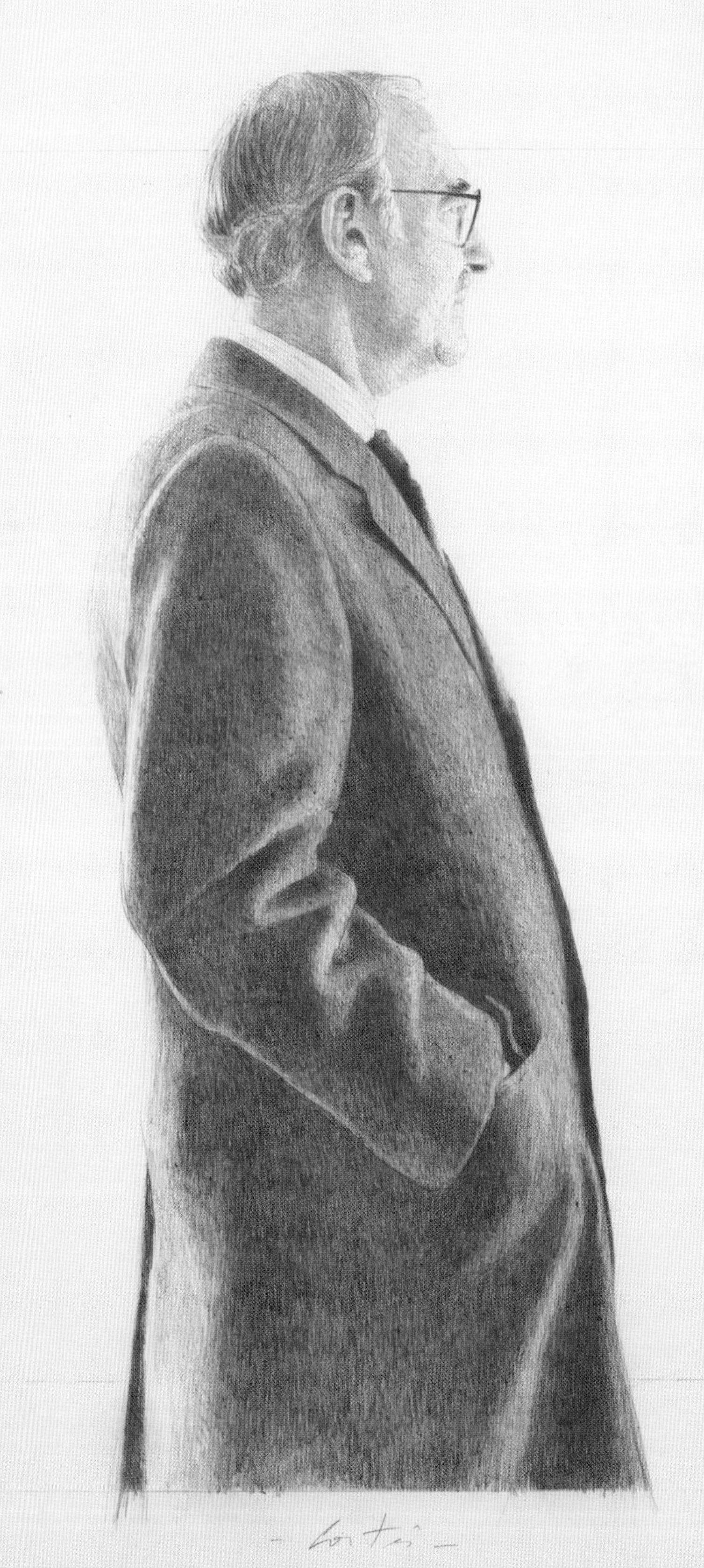

IN THE SHADOW OF
VELÁZQUEZ

A LIFE IN ART HISTORY

Jonathan Brown

Yale University Press • New Haven and London

TO BENNY, LEO, AND JAKE,

A *RECUERDO* OF GRANDPA.

Designed by Emily Lees
Printed in China

Library of Congress Cataloging-in-Publication Data

Brown, Jonathan, 1939–
[Speeches. Selections]
In the shadow of Velázquez : a life in art history / Jonathan Brown.
pages cm
Includes bibliographical references and index.
ISBN 978–0–300–20396–7 (hardback)
1. Brown, Jonathan, 1939– 2. Art historians – United States – Biography.
3. Hispanists – United States – Biography. 4. Art, Spanish – Historiography. I. Title.
N7483.B76A5 2014
709.2 – dc23
[B]
2013042759

A catalogue record for this book is available from the British Library

Frontispiece: Hernan Cortés, portrait of Jonathan Brown.
Image on p. vi: Photo montage of *Las Meninas* with Jonathan Brown as Velázquez (detail).

CONTENTS

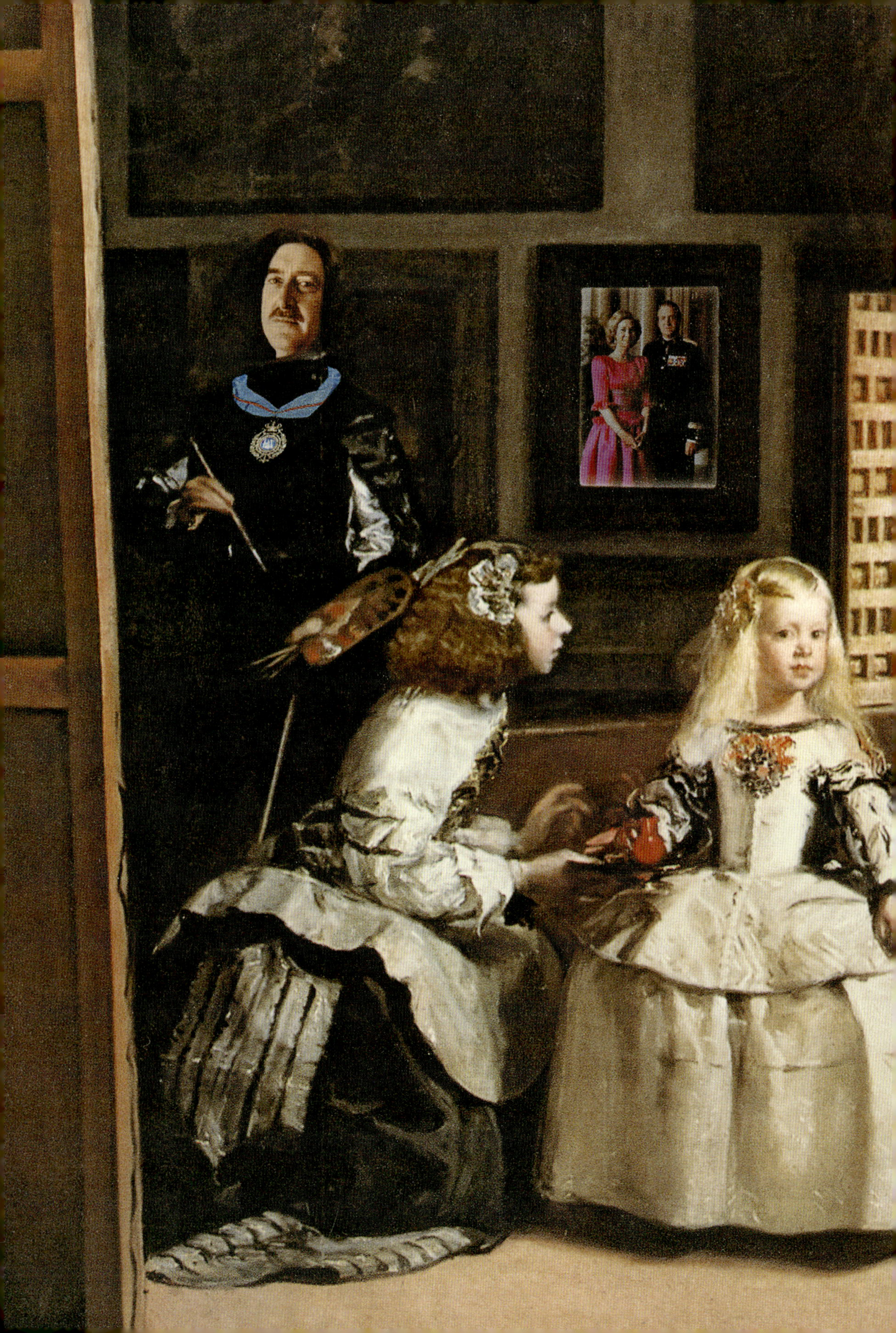

ACKNOWLEDGMENTS

I am very grateful to the Patronato del Museo Nacional del Prado for inviting me to occupy the Cátedra del Prado in 2012. An equal dose of gratitude is owed to Miguel Zugaza, director, and Gabriele Finaldi, vice-director, both of whom were the most gracious hosts. Mar Nogal took charge of the practical arrangements with unparalleled efficiency. I have to say that this experience was one of the high points of my career and one of the most rewarding.

The English edition is indebted to the support of Gillian Malpass, Yale University Press, London. We have worked together on several projects since 1983, that is to say, for three decades. I believe that no one would argue with my opinion that she is the best art-history editor in the business. This handsome book was designed by Emily Lees. Hannah Jenner is responsible for the picture research – a long, inevitably frustrating task, which she has performed without ever losing hope or patience.

This seems like the right moment to thank the librarians and staff of the Marquand Library, Princeton University, where I have spent nearly half my waking hours reading in that incomparable library of art history.

My daughter Claire played a decisive role as I worked on the final revisions. She was hired as an assistant and performed as a collaborator, not only sparing me a wrestling match with the computer but making cogent editorial suggestions all along the way.

Over the past few years, I have toyed with the idea of writing an autobiography. During the course of fifty years as an art historian, I have had dealings with many outstanding scholars. My stint as Director of the Institute of Fine Arts, New York University (1973–78), brought me into contact with bankers and industrialists and the senior officers of several art foundations. There were moments when I was deeply involved with the top echelon of the Spanish government in modernizing the Prado Museum. The chance to experience these realms from the inside made a deep and lasting impression and certainly sharpened my understanding of life outside the cloister. Most importantly, I was afforded an insight into how financiers and politicians conducted their business, and how radically different was their vision of the world as compared with mine. Surely this would make a compelling story.

Looking for models on which to base my writing, I came across one that was decisive. The author had met many important people inside and outside the art world and had participated in a much-debated decision affecting a major collection of art. As I turned the pages, it dawned on me that the book was boring. Many of the people cited by the author might not even remember meeting him. A big event in the autobiographer's career could well have passed almost unnoticed by others who were involved. As far as I can tell, an autobiography can be of general interest only if the author has been in the public eye (for example, politicians, celebrities, athletes) or is a compelling writer who is willing to share his/her inner life. The history of art is and has always been an interest of a minority of the population (despite the growth of the audience which has occurred over the last thirty years). As a consequence, I did not expect that the potential readership for the autobiography of Jonathan Brown would be very large.

Still, the tug of my ego was too powerful to restrain. To quiet the urge to share aspects of my professional career, I came up with a framework which would allow me to intertwine episodes of my personal history as they related to my work. In the event, the opportunity arose to translate my thoughts into action. This arrived in the form of an invitation to deliver the six lectures attached to the Cátedra del Prado, an honorific appointment made by the Patronato (Trustees) of the Museo Nacional del Prado. The *catedrático* is obligated to deliver the lectures and to lead six seminars for advanced graduate students. The lectures were given in two installments, in May and October, 2012. The Director of the Prado, Miguel Zugaza, had

Jonathan Brown lecturing, Prado 2012.

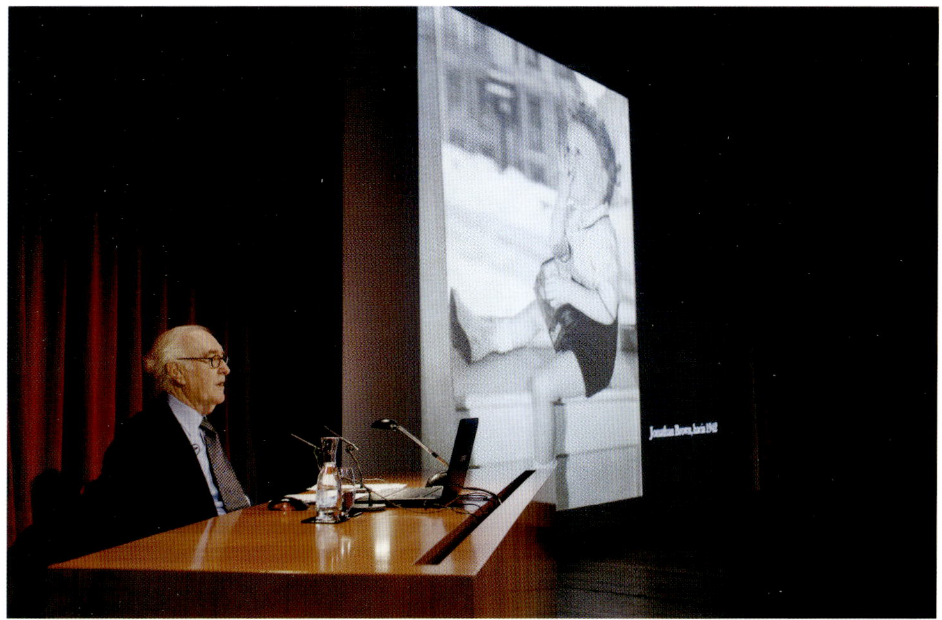

suggested that I choose a topic that would interest the general public as well as the art historians in the audience. He insisted on this approach once I had sent him the proposed title: "Autobiography as Historiography." Although this title accurately described the theme of the lectures, Miguel was worried that few would understand what I planned to talk about. He was right, of course, as I should have known from my experience as Slade Professor, Oxford, and Andrew W. Mellon Lecturer at the National Gallery of Art, Washington, which are intended for a similar hybrid audience.

The Prado lectures were written to be published soon after they were delivered. I thought it might be more engaging to maintain the somewhat informal tone of the lectures rather than to convert them to a full-blown scholarly text. In keeping with this decision, I have kept footnotes to a minimum both as to number and length.

Conspicuously absent from the narrative is my wife, Sandra. Given that the emphasis here is on my public career, this oversight is intentional, although a marriage that has endured for forty-seven years and added three children (Claire, Michael, and Daniel) to the world population should forestall any unfavorable conclusions that might be drawn from this omission. My focus here is on my work as a scholar and teacher of Hispanic art. Still, I do recognize that it cannot always be rewarding to be married to a spouse who loves to work, and especially to write. Despite this hardship, Sandra has never failed to provide me with love and support. I have to add that there is a tremendous advantage to being married to an experienced psychoanalyst, one who has always been there to provide what I call "on-site therapy."

PRINCETON, NOVEMBER 2013

x

The cycle of lectures that formed the basis for this book was deliberately unconventional. Instead of focusing on the Golden Age of Spanish painting from a strictly historical vantage point, I chose to mingle personal history with art history. In the course of nearly fifty years as a professional art historian, I noticed in my own work, and in the work of others, that the pursuit of plausible interpretations to events that happened in the past was inevitably tinged by factors that lay outside the library, the archive, and the art gallery. For want of a better word, I use the word "personality" to name a decisive factor in the production of art historical knowledge. Who we are determines what we think and do. Or, to cite W. B. Yeats's memorable line, "How can we know the dancer from the dance?" Since the 1970s, the world of art history has been in a constant state of flux; art historians have chosen to work on material that was considered of little interest to the canon of artists established in the late nineteenth century, when German scholars inserted art history into the university curriculum. In addition, we have become aware of how the history of art rides the waves of current events. As each generation asks new questions about the role played by politics, religion, and society in artistic production, historians forge new tools in their attempt to shape their conception of the past.

In this book, I try to bring this wide spectrum of personal experience and external events to light and to demonstrate the complex responses that people have invented in their pursuit of the knowledge of the Golden Age of Spanish painting. The first two chapters explicitly discuss these methodologies by reference to my personal history and to the evolution of the study of Spanish painting in the second half of the twentieth century. The following three chapters are case studies that concern first the workshop practices of El Greco and Ribera. The workshop, the low road of art history, has lately been repositioned and is now considered an object worthy of serious study. The fourth chapter addresses the rising importance of court studies and how the flurry of writings on the Spanish Habsburg court has enriched the historical image of early modern Spain. These studies demonstrate that Spain was at the center, not the periphery, of important aspects of artistic life in the seventeenth century. Velázquez, arguably the greatest European painter of his time, is the acme of Spanish painting. In the fifth chapter, I attempt to summarize the recent approaches to Velázquez and concentrate on a few of the attributions that have recently been put forward and the ensuing debates about authenticity. The problem and perils of making attributions to great painters is a leitmotif of the narrative. And, foolhardy though it may be, I take another stab at the interpretation of *Las Meninas*. The cycle ends with an introduction to painting in New Spain (Mexico) as an example of the challenges that lie ahead for understanding the processes of diffusion and differentiation of Spanish art in the various territories of its global empire.

1

CURRICULUM VITAE

THE FORMATION OF A HISPANIST

"The one duty we owe to history," wrote Oscar Wilde in 1891, "is to rewrite it." Wilde delighted to "épater la bourgeoisie" and perhaps this outrageous observation is designed to accomplish that purpose. Suppose, however, we decide to take it seriously. Wilde is perversely expressing a phenomenon experienced by all historians, including historians of art. History is malleable and moveable and, up to a point, we are constantly revising historical events to fit the needs and circumstances of the moment. Otherwise the story of the Spanish Civil War would require but a single book and one, moreover, that would never need to be revised. A single monograph on Velázquez would satisfy our need for information and attributions once and for all. Universities could hire only a fraction of those who fill the ranks of History Departments.

Perhaps the discipline should be renamed "histories," thus taking into account the ways in which the present seeps into the past and vice versa. With these brief observations, I intend to clear the ground for the basic premise of this book, which is partly autobiographical. My plan is to interweave the story of my personal life and my public career as a Hispanist in the belief that the latter cannot be understood without the former.

All historians are persons; there is no other way to express this platitude which nonetheless makes a good operating premise. Life transpires as if it were a novel written on the fly. Personal circumstances, accidental events, unforeseen changes form the character of a historian, even down to the choice of field of study. To cite a specific example, a good friend was drafted into the US Army in 1943 and sent to the Philippine Islands, where he participated in many skirmishes and saw the "Disasters of War" at close range. In due course, he became one of the leading military historians of our time. My friend and co-author Sir John Elliott has often made the point that the parallels he perceived between the history of the Spanish Empire in the seventeenth century and the England he knew as a young man – both empires in decline – influenced the choice of Spanish history as his field of interest. A scholar who is dedicated to the Dark Ages is unlikely to feel attracted to the period of the Enlightenment. With the proper training or guidance, an individual could probably retrace the path that led to where he is today. I would only say that all of us construct a personal narrative, which we constantly revise as some doors open while other doors close. However this may be, I have chosen to take a personal approach to some of the questions that have interested me in my five decades as a Hispanist, attempting to demonstrate how I chose the subject of my researches and writings and how personal factors interacted, if not determined, the approaches I used and the mistakes that I made.

I was born in Springfield, Massachusetts, on July 15, 1939 (pl. 1). My father, Leonard, was in the insurance business, which provided our family with a comfortable life. He had had the benefit of a university education, which was rather uncommon in the 1920s. He graduated from Brown University in 1930, just in time to encounter the Great Depression. For many of his generation, the Depression was a soul-searing event, but my father never talked about it at all. He was a stylish man (pl. 2) – he was generous, well-dressed, and had a wonderful, wry sense of humor. He was a bon vivant, who liked to eat and drink good food and wine and developed a refined palette. In a move that seemed the height of sophistication, he commissioned the first built-in wine cellar in Springfield. Outside work and family, he dedicated his time to playing golf, a sport in which he had an obsessive interest. Once the sun had set and his clubs had been stored away, he and my mother would often go to concerts, especially during the season at Tanglewood, the summer home of the Boston Symphony Orchestra. Unfortunately, my father died at the early age of 61. It was as if somewhere in the heavens, a decision had been made to take away the life of a man who truly loved being alive.

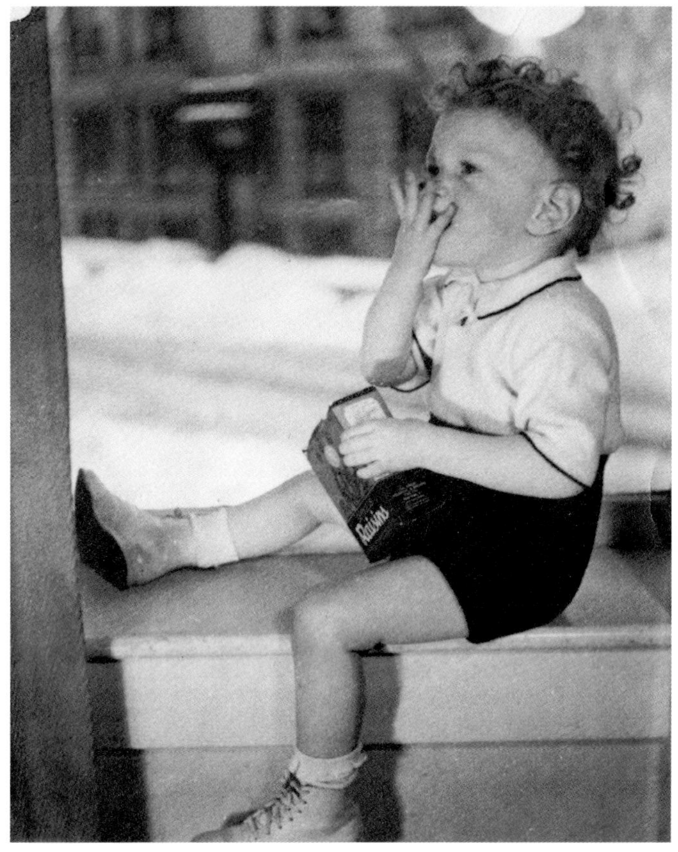

1   The author, age 3.

My mother, Jean Brown, was denied all the privileges enjoyed by my father (pl. 3). She was born in the tenements of lower Manhattan, the last of five children. Her father was an occasional presence, leaving his immigrant wife to fend for herself in very difficult conditions. My grandfather's one saving grace was his vocation as a rarebook dealer, and it was he who introduced my mother to the infinite pleasures of the world of books. She completed high school and then went to look for work, a quest that brought her to Springfield. She was employed by the local library, where she met my father-to-be. Despite the lack of a university education, my mother had a brilliant mind, which finally found an outlet in the later years of her life.

To all outward appearances, we were a typical provincial family of the upper middle class. (The family was completed by the birth of my brother, Robert, in

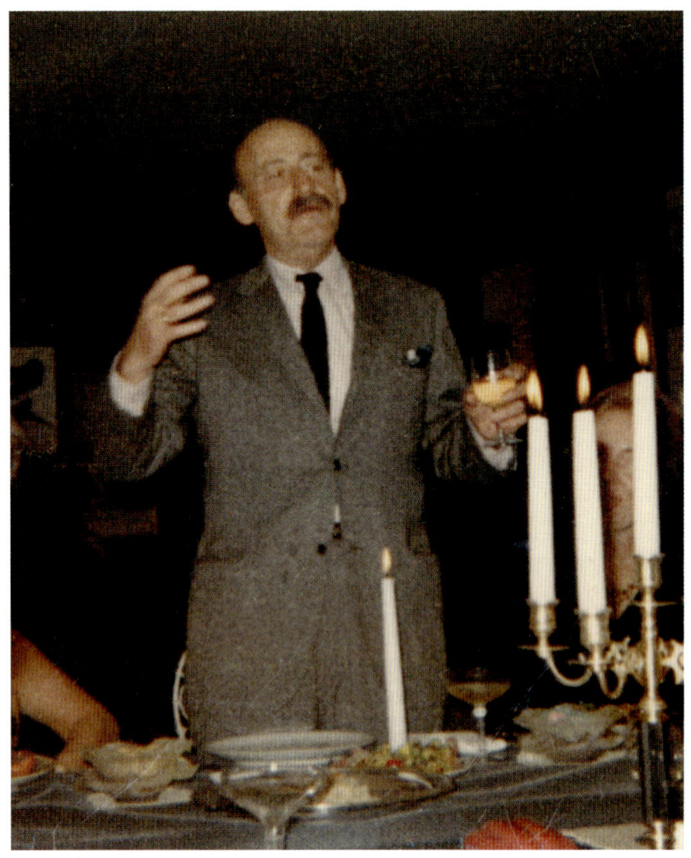

2   Leonard Brown, offering a toast.

1942.) In one important respect, however, my parents were very different indeed – they were avid collectors of contemporary art. I'm not entirely certain how they found their way to the leading New York artists and dealers of the 1950s. As best as I can recall, the agent of their interest was a painter who ran a studio for beginners in one of the local museums. He was an abstract painter who was on the margins of the New York art scene and finally moved to the hills just to the north of Springfield. I was young at the time and cannot remember the mechanics of my parents' collecting practices. On occasion, they would go to New York for a few days and return with the new acquisitions. Their taste was unerring. During the 1950s, they bought works by Jackson Pollock, Franz Kline, Mark Rothko, Willem de Kooning, Philip Guston, Ad Reinhardt, just to mention the names that have

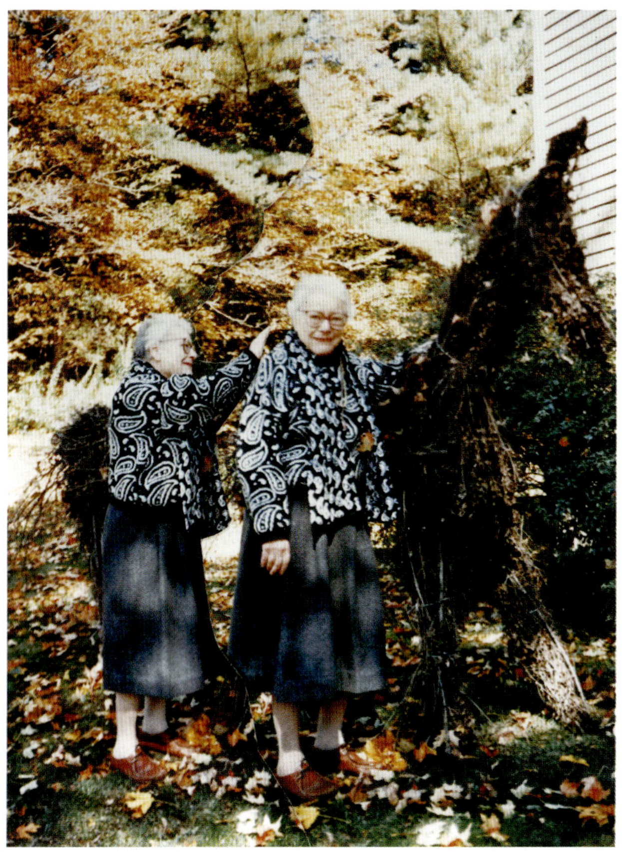

3   Surrealist portrait of Jean Brown.

come to be counted as the leaders of Abstract Expressionism. These works, mostly small in scale, were proudly displayed on the walls of a large, drafty, shingle-style house located in an area that was once the home of Springfield's elite but was then being invaded by charitable institutions, which chopped up the once-noble spaces into office cubicles. As the collection grew, so did the scorn of their friends, who could not come to grips with paintings without discernible subject matter or evidence of craftsmanship. The heat generated by these arguments often threatened to reach boiling point, not entirely unwelcome in the house of a thousand drafts.

In 1958, my father suffered a serious heart attack. In those days, physicians prescribed long periods of rest as the best way to repair the damage. As my father's health improved, so did his boredom increase. In a moment of inspiration, my

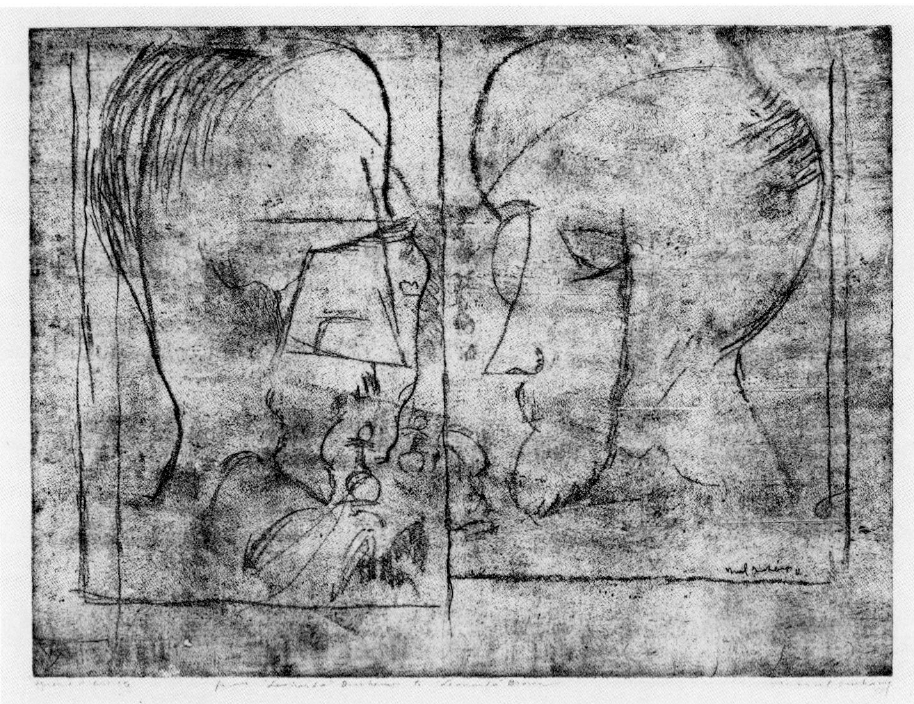

4   Marcel Duchamp, *Chessplayers*, with dedication to Leonard Brown.

mother acquired a copy of Robert Motherwell's anthology *The Dada Painters and Poets* (1951). My parents were enthralled by the book and decided to start to collect the documents and publications of Dada and Surrealism, which was just as well because they had been priced out of the market for contemporary art. They noted that the bibliography had been compiled by Bernard Karpel, librarian of the Museum of Modern Art, and made an appointment to meet him. Then, or soon thereafter, Karpel became the advisor of their collection. This material was difficult to locate, particularly papers related to Dada. Most were to be found in Paris, to where my parents traveled every winter. They were able to cultivate the interest of a few Parisian antiquarian booksellers, the only ones who specialized in the period. They attempted to track down the survivors of the movement and met Philippe Soupault and, above all, Tristan Tzara. I have a dim recollection of going with them to the apartment of Tzara. It looked like nothing had been moved since the living room was photographed in the 1930s.

The real star of my parents' Dada universe was Marcel Duchamp. At a time when Duchamp was just starting to be recognized as one of the most influential artists of the twentieth century, he had already been installed as our household god. My mother, in particular, revered him and spoke of him incessantly. She considered him to be the Leonardo da Vinci of our time. Duchamp, of course, was then living in New York and proved to be easy to contact. A relationship was formed, the best testimony of which is a print inscribed by the artist and dedicated to my father, "To Leonardo Brown from Leonardo Duchamp" (pl. 4). On one occasion, in the autumn of 1966, Sandra, my wife, and I attended an exhibition of Duchamp at the Cordier & Ekstrom Gallery on Madison Avenue. Photographs were taken (pl. 5) and if you look carefully you can see us in the background, looking on with bemused expressions.

Dada was a short-lived movement and furthermore had endorsed the destruction of art as a principal tenet. The possibilities of enlarging the collection were thus limited. It was in the late 1960s that my mother and father discovered the descendants of Dada, of whom the most conspicuous was George Maciunas, self-appointed

5   Marcel Duchamp sitting for Andy Warhol's screen test, Cordier & Ekstrom Gallery, New York, 1966. Photograph by Nat Finkelstein.

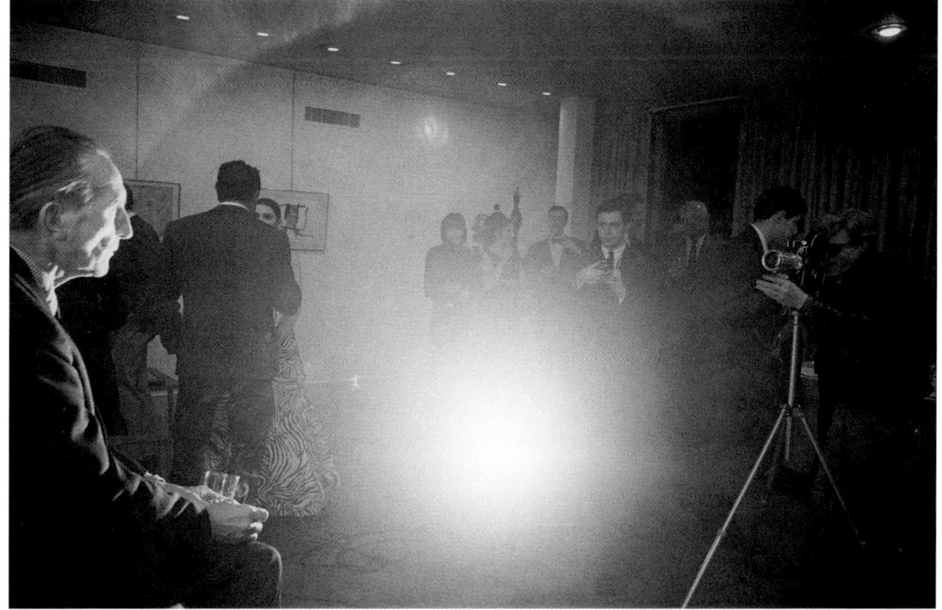

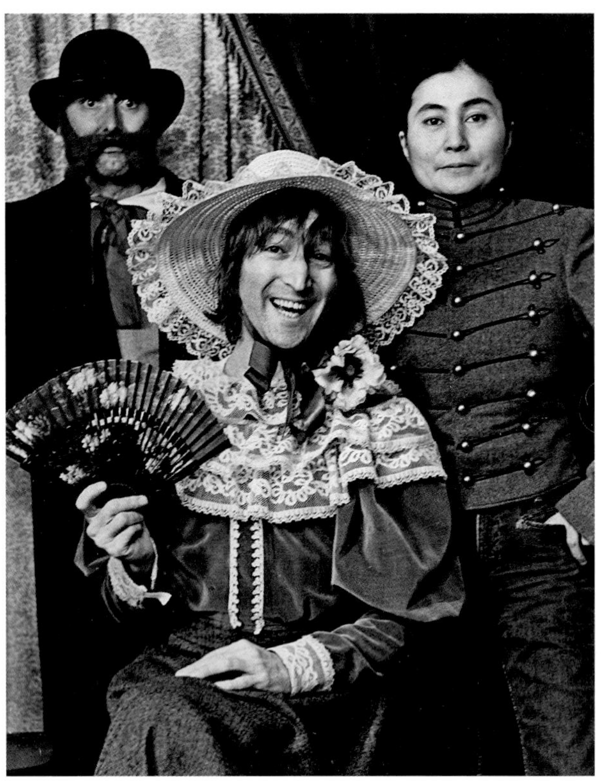

6   George Maciunas, John Lennon, and Yoko Ono –
visitors to the Shaker Seed House.

ringmaster of Fluxus (pl. 6). Over time, the friendship with George deepened and my mother became one of his principal supporters. In the late 1960s, my parents had purchased a small house in the hills of western Massachusetts. It is known as the Shaker Seed House because it had once been part of a nearby Shaker settlement (pl. 7). (The Shakers were a Christian sect that flourished in the nineteenth and early twentieth century and supported themselves by the cultivation of seeds and other mercantile products which were famous in their day.) Following my father's death in 1971, my mother made the unexpected decision to move her permanent residence to the Seed House and to devote her life to collecting books and objects made by "anti-artists," artists who shunned the art world establishment by using unconventional materials and who sought to bridge the gap between art and texts. Over the next fifteen years, my mother, through her collecting activities, became instrumental in building an international network of various movements that shared this point of view. In fact, I believe that my mother fostered a sense that these seemingly unconnected practitioners were part of a larger phenomenon. The artists must have agreed because they began to visit the Seed House to study the collection, much of which was kept in a wall-sized filing cabinet designed by Maciunas. Eventually my mother was overwhelmed by the increasing demand to do research in the collection and decided sell it. In 1985, she transferred ownership to the Getty Research Institute in Los Angeles. If you are interested in seeing her collection, you can find it on the Getty Research Institute website, where it is displayed in an organized fashion quite unlike anything my mother was able to achieve in the Seed House. The collection had been assembled in part to console my mother for the loss of her husband, and once the collection disappeared, her spirits began to flag. She died in May 1994 and is buried in the town cemetery, her resting place marked by a monument based on Man Ray's *Metronome*, which we commissioned from a local artist.

The question immediately arises as to how someone who was raised in an environment saturated with liberal politics and contemporary art came to be a student of Hispanic art of the early modern era. I have often pondered this question. Perhaps

7   Shaker Seed House, Tyringham, Massachusetts.

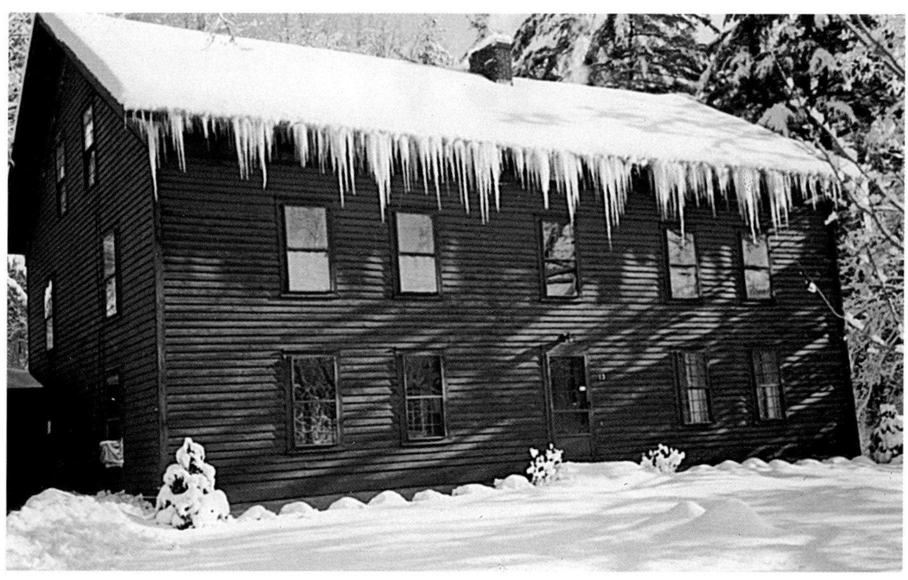

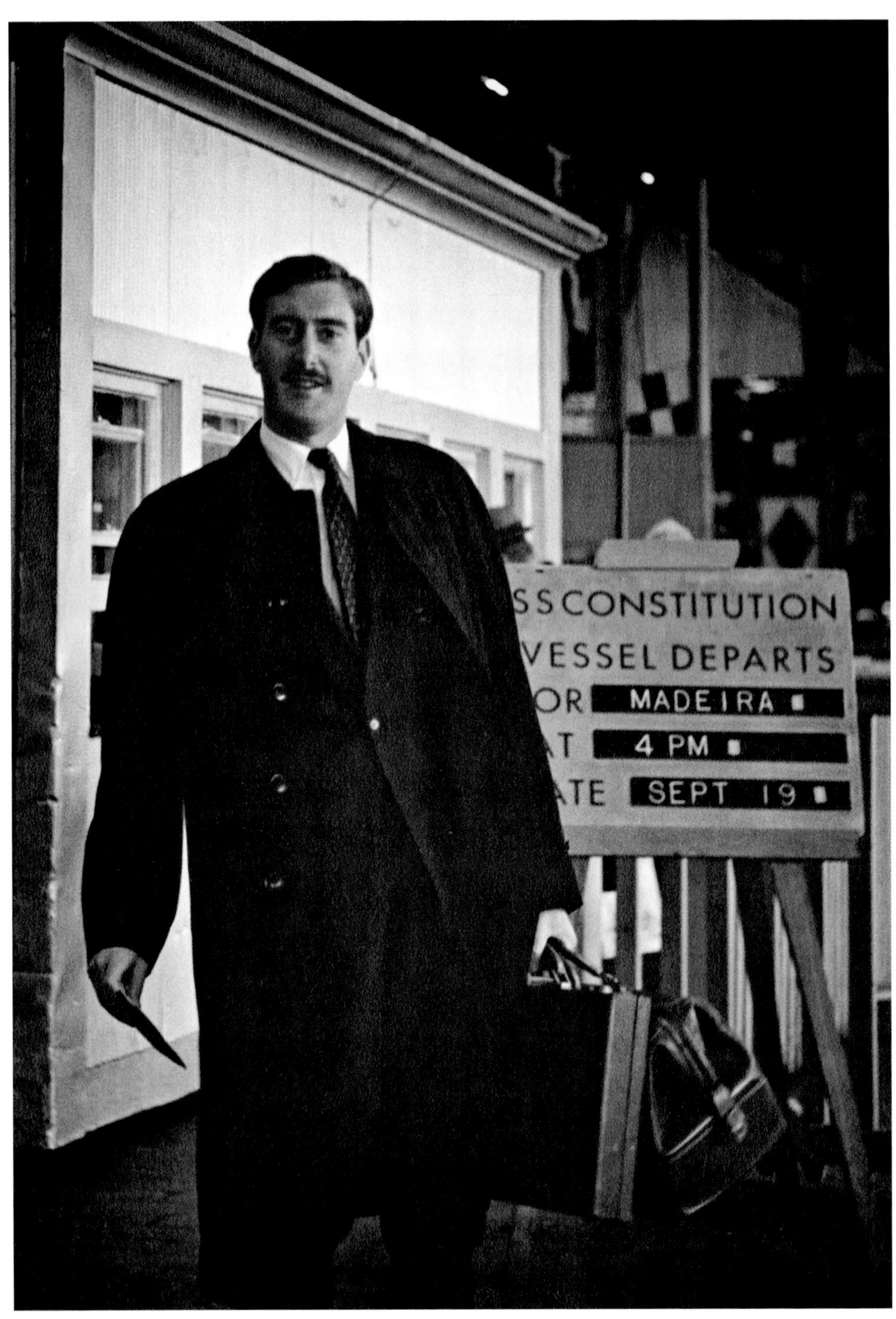

8   Jonathan Brown, departing for Spain, 1958.

my interest can be attributed to a sort of post-adolescent rebellion which occurred at a time when the options for rebellious behavior were very limited. Spain in the 1950s was still regarded as a pariah state by the liberal democracies of Europe and the United States. If I was looking for a melodramatic way to declare my independence from the comfortable life I lived at home, a year in Franco's Spain was made to order. However, the most logical and convincing explanation of my decision to become a scholar of Hispanic art is the impact of the year I spent in Madrid in 1958–59 (pl. 8).

Allow me a moment to go back first to the year 1956, when I matriculated at Dartmouth College. For me this choice was strange. Dartmouth is located in the village of Hanover, New Hampshire, and even today is difficult to reach. The nearest large city is Montreal. This remote location was not the biggest drawback; that distinction was shared by two factors – the long, harsh winters and the absence of female students. The psychological effects of this enforced isolation were mitigated by the excessive consumption of alcohol. To a person of my experience, Dartmouth seemed like a high-end gulag. I overstate, but it is true that between December and March, there was no way out. I am not certain where I discovered a temporary reprieve, the Junior Year Abroad.

At the time, academic programs, which are now universally known as Junior Year or Semester Abroad, were few and far between, except for those located in the major capitals of western Europe and the city of Florence. Only one American college offered a Junior Year in Spain, Smith College, and that of course was limited to female undergraduates. However, in that very year, New York University was launching its first study abroad program, and the chosen site was Madrid. After overcoming a hundred bureaucratic obstacles, New York University agreed to accept me, and Dartmouth to give me full credit for the year I would be away.

Hopes were high when the Sabena four-propeller plane touched down at Barajas. The airport was surprisingly quiet, except for the chatter of people at the bar and terrace. A favorite pastime of madrileños was going to watch the planes as they landed and took off. More surprises waited although it took a while to process them. One was the virtual absence of private automobiles (pl. 9). If you had a car, you could park it right in the middle of the Plaza Mayor with plenty of space to spare. The omnipresence of police officers amazed me; it was a vivid introduction to the machinery of a military dictatorship. Another amazing sight was the number of priests and nuns, whose vocations may have been determined more by hunger than by faith. Signs of poverty were everywhere; in addition to the multitude of beggars,

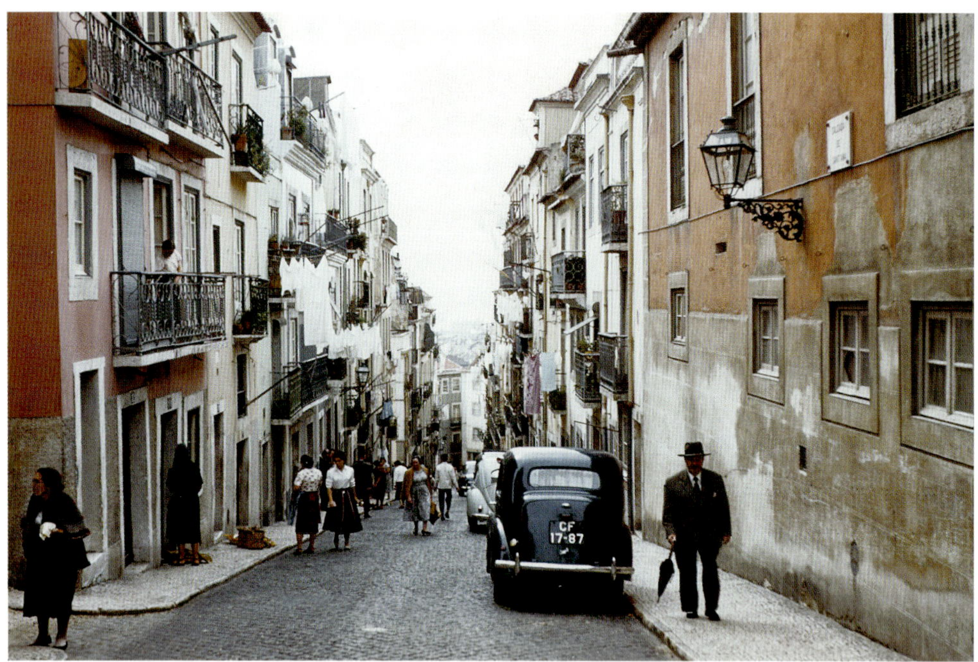

9   Street scene, Madrid, 1958–59.

many of them wounded in the Civil War, there were the blind sellers of the ONCE lottery tickets, who stood on the street corners, shouting at the top of their lungs, "Sale hoy! Sale hoy! Cinco tiras iguales para hoy."

Even more impressive to a young American college student was the campus of what was then called the Universidad de Madrid. As I soon found out, the university had been the site of one of the most bitter battles of the Civil War. Signs of this conflict were easy to see – buildings partially in ruins, bullet holes in the walls of structures that had remained standing, broken windows waiting to be replaced, although the war had ended almost twenty years earlier. For a moment, I longed for the pastoral beauty of the campus of Dartmouth College.

The Facultad de Filosofía y Letras, where we attended classes, had been heavily damaged in the Battle of Madrid. It had been rebuilt by the time I arrived. Despite the quality of the architecture, the Facultad was a gloomy place (pl. 10). Each classroom was adorned by a statue of the Crucified Christ, a symbol of the alliance of Church and State that had characterized Spanish history from the Catholic monarchs to General Franco.

Surprisingly, our professors were all *catedráticos* and some were scholars of distinction. I imagine that they had been offered significant financial inducements that were paid on condition that they, and not their beleaguered assistants, would impart the lectures. As an intended Spanish major at Dartmouth, I had never taken a class in art history. At the time, the faculty of the Art Department at Dartmouth left much to be desired. To fill the gap, I elected to take two courses in Madrid, one taught by Diego Angulo Iñiguez, the other by Francisco Sánchez Cantón, director of the Museo del Prado. Of Diego Angulo I will have more to say in the next chapter.

Sánchez Cantón was among the small group who ruled the world of art history in Spain. He had served as subdirector of the Prado faithfully, even as he watched the directors come and go. By tradition, the Director of the Prado was a practicing painter – that is the explanation for Picasso's brief tenure in the post. However, everyone who cared knew that the Prado was in the hands of Sánchez Cantón. He had to wait until 1960 before justice was done and he was handed the directorship.

10   Jonathan Brown in class photo, University of Madrid, 1958–59.

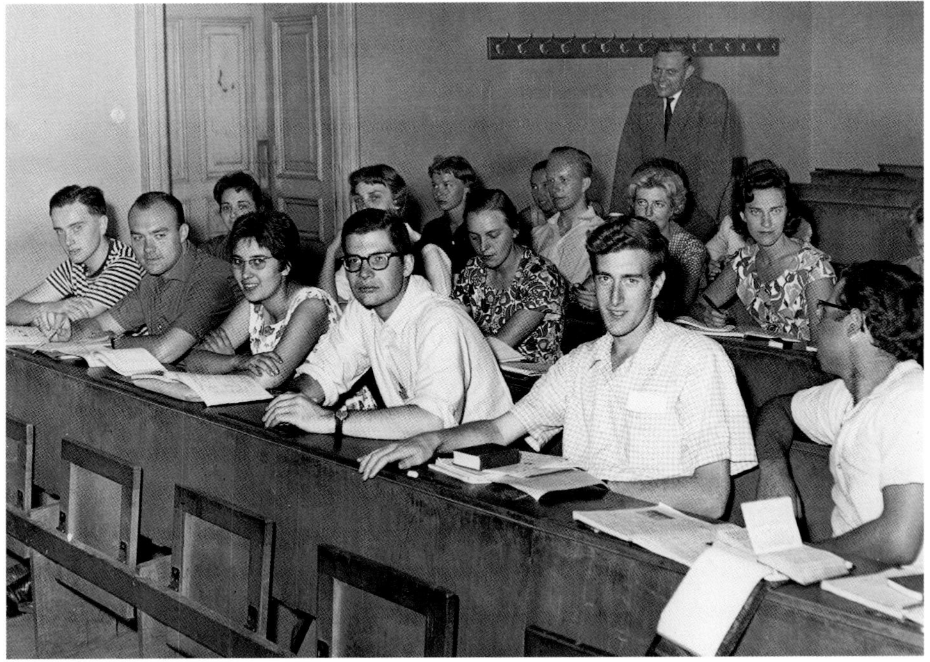

In appearance and demeanor, Sánchez Cantón seemed a mild, unassuming man, although he had a very brusque manner. He habitually wore a black suit which was adorned, if that is the word, with a black necktie. More than anything, Sánchez Cantón resembled a Jesuit, a resemblance reinforced by his deep devotion to the Catholic faith. I had already visited the Prado on several occasions, but this informal course truly opened my eyes.

Perhaps it is now time for a few remarks about the Prado as experienced by a youthful American student. As might be imagined, my parents were habitual museum-goers. Although the Art Museum of Springfield was of no special distinction, the city was not far from larger collections easily reached by driving an hour or so. I mention a few – the Worcester Art Museum, the Wadsworth Atheneum in Hartford, Connecticut, the Smith College Museum of Art in Northampton, Mass., and the Clark Institute in Williamstown. Needless to say, I had also been brought to the Metropolitan Museum of Art, although for some reason or lapse of my memory, never to MoMA. No matter the size, these museums were well-kept and well-lighted. To one degree or another, they had public events, including exhibitions and educational programs. Obviously the increase of interest in art museums over the last thirty years has transformed these institutions in ways that nobody could have predicted. Nonetheless, at the time the comparison between the Prado and these wealthy American museums was not favorable to Spain. Indeed, as I traveled through the country it was obvious even to my untrained eye that the great cultural patrimony was threatened with devastating losses through neglect and decay. (I hasten to add that this situation has now been remedied.)

But to return to the Prado of 1958–59, as I say, I was struck by the absence of visitors, except on Sundays. As Professor Sánchez Cantón led our small group around the museum, we never had to jockey for space, nor did we impede the sightline of members of the public. The lighting was dismal; I eventually learned to visit the eastern galleries in the morning and then switch to the western galleries to catch the afternoon sun. As for amenities, there was a cafeteria at the southern end, near the Puerta de Murillo. The space was small and cramped, with a limited menu (although I must say that the cooks made a delicious tortilla de patatas). The rather dingy impression made by the collection was a consequence of surfaces and paintings that had not been cleaned and walls that had not been painted within recent memory. One happy consequence of the inertia was that the pictures were never moved. Until recently, when the installation changes with some frequency, I could locate by memory where all the pictures were hanging during my student days.

Part of the problem stemmed from the fact that the Prado had few if any curators. I was not then in a position to analyze the administrative structure of the museum. A few years later, a visit to the Director's office revealed the presence of one curatorial staff member, the subdirector. The problem with the Prado was easy to identify; it was starved of money. To visitors from abroad, the museum looked like a warehouse of masterpieces of western European painting. To my innocent eyes, it was heaven, so much so that I came to the decision to make the study of these pictures my life's work. Ironically, my post-adolescent rebellion was determined by my parents' passionate love of contemporary art. As I stood as close as I could in front of *Las Meninas* and focused on almost any part of the canvas, I could see an immediate resemblance to Jackson Pollock. Such is the folly of youth. Upon reflection, this reaction is not as misguided as it may appear, if you are willing to accept Velázquez as a gestural painter of the seventeenth century; I will develop this notion in the fifth chapter.

I returned to Dartmouth for a final year, concentrating on Spanish literature, there being no one at the College who knew about the art of Spain. I do, however, wish to acknowledge the influence of Professor Robert Russell, the noted scholar of the novels of Pérez Galdós. Bob may have physically inhabited the Hanover Plain, but his head was always on the meseta of Castile. He gave me the confidence to think that I might be able to make a mark in the academic world. When it came time to choose a graduate school, I saw that enthusiasm could carry me only so far. There were then three senior Hispanists teaching in American universities – Harold Wethey, University of Michigan; George Kubler, Yale; and José López-Rey, at the Institute of Fine Arts. Thanks to the copious scholarship of Chandler Post, Harvard had a reputation for the study of Spanish art and an excellent photo archive that Post had bequeathed to the Fogg Museum. However, when he retired, he was not replaced. I applied for admission to all but Michigan, which seemed too far away. And for some reason, I made an application to Princeton, which of course had a renowned department of art history but lacked a Hispanist. The results were not heartening. Both Yale and Harvard rejected my applications; the Institute of Fine Arts accepted me as a provisional student – the same outcome as my application to Princeton. Having heard that López-Rey was a fine scholar but an impatient advisor, I threw my lot in with Princeton.

In 1960, when I matriculated as a Ph.D. candidate in the Department of Art and Archaeology, Princeton was a small town with a decidedly rural character. Just beyond the city limits was a large dairy farm, which asserted its presence when the wind came from the east, delivering a pungent cloud smelling of cows and manure that enveloped the town. Potato farms were another feature of the area. To a native of New England, Princeton had a southern flavor. Having once experienced student life in a small town, it may seem perverse that I elected to repeat the mistake I had made in going to Dartmouth. There was this difference – Princeton was an hour's train ride from New York.

The Department of Art and Archaeology was one of the oldest art history departments in the USA and was particularly noted for its achievements in the field of medieval art. The department was small; only six or seven Ph.D. candidates were admitted every year. By the time I arrived, the department's interests were broadening but not to the extent of including Spanish art. It is a matter of fact that I never studied Spanish art during my graduate school years, except for a stimulating course on Spanish Baroque architecture offered at Columbia University by that blithe spirit, René Taylor, who was there for a year as a visiting professor. The menu of seminars I sampled was diverse indeed. I participated in Erik Sjoqvist's seminar on Pompeian wall painting. With John Rupert Martin, we investigated the Carracci brothers and their patronage by the Farnese family. Renssaeler Lee's course on Watteau was an extraordinary experience; Lee came to art history with a Ph.D. in English literature and I believe he had memorized all the plays of William Shakespeare and had a quotation from the bard to suit every occasion. He was a keen student of artistic theory, one of the last in the line of humanist scholars whose origins dated back to Renaissance Florence. Most compelling of all was the medievalist Kurt Weitzmann (pl. 11), who had been the favorite pupil of Adolph Goldschmidt, a universally admired professor of art history at Berlin. In seminars on Carolingian Bible illustrations and twelfth-century ivories, Weitzmann embodied rigorous Germanic scholarship. Every graduate student was required to participate in one of Weitzmann's seminars; some survived, some perished, and a few escaped with only bruises.

Hovering over the department was the professor of art history at the Institute for Advanced Study, which has always been independent of the university. This was Erwin Panofsky, the most influential art historian in the world (pl. 12). Panofsky taught a seminar at Princeton from time to time; I shudder to think that I did not enroll simply because I was scared to death. Even when absent, however, Panofsky's text-based method was omnipresent and had seeped into the mental world of everyone associated with the department.

I forged a connection of a less formal sort with the rising young star of the department, Robert Rosenblum (pl. 13). In 1963, I was appointed as his assistant

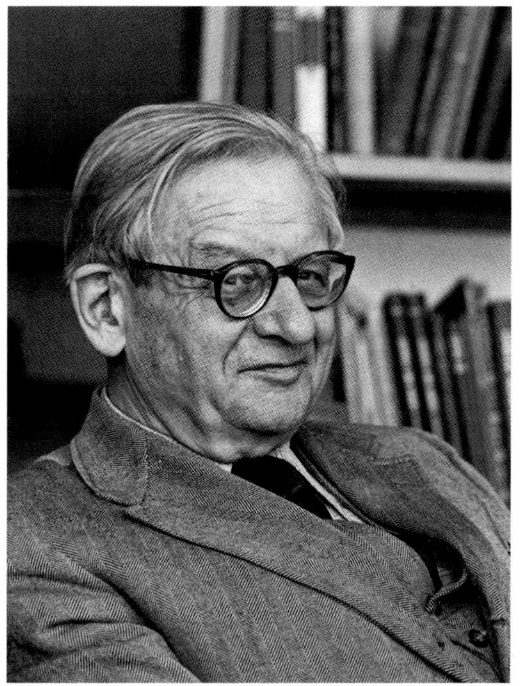 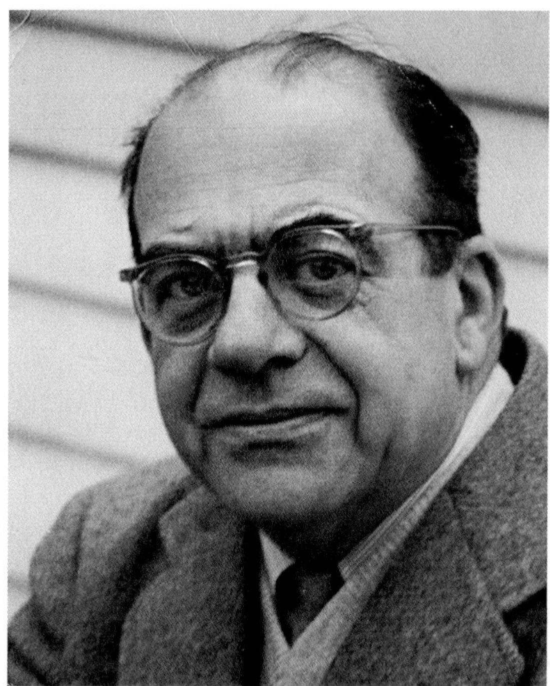

11   Kurt Weitzmann.   12   Erwin Panofsky.

in a lecture course on the history of modern painting. Rosenblum was the most facile lecturer I have ever heard. He spoke rapidly, as if reading a text at high speed, never missing a beat. However, it was all improvised from notes. As his assistant, I spent a lot time in his company and could study an innovative scholar at first hand. He was then working on his ground-breaking book *Transformations in Late Eighteenth Century Art* (1970), in which, among other things, he demonstrated his characteristic admiration for art outside the mainstream of Europe and the United States. He was responsible for bringing Caspar David Friedrich and the German Romantics to the attention of the English-speaking world. At the same time, he was one of the early supporters of Andy Warhol. For this reason, he was an aficionado of Spanish painting, all of which, it seemed to him, was eccentric, non-normative, and slightly outrageous. He was one of the few American art historians who knew and admired the sculpture of Francisco Salzillo. Seeing the art of Spain through the somewhat jaded eyes of this inimitable art historian provided an unbelievably liberating effect on the study of my subject of interest.

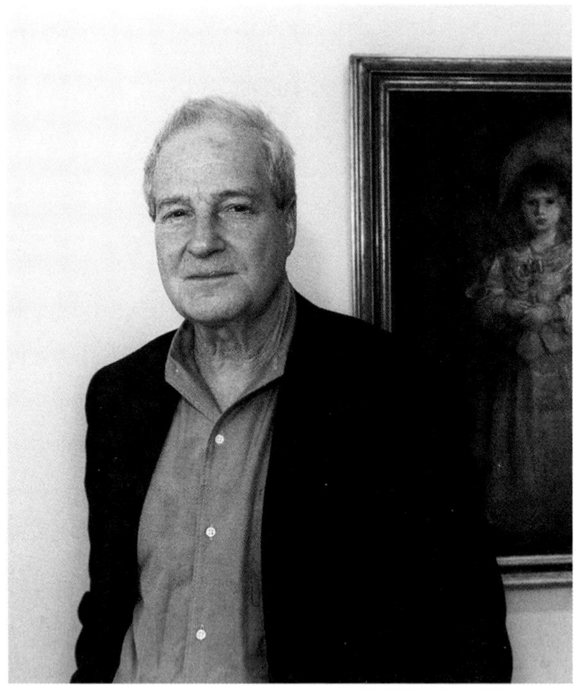

13   Robert Rosenblum.

Looking back on my graduate education, I am still struck by the apparent lack of a coherent scholarly agenda. Later on, I could see that despite the chaos of my course of study, I had profited from the experience of working with excellent, disciplined scholars, who offered encouragement at every turn. Princeton provided another advantage, which was the emphasis on clear expository prose, a necessary tool for the kind of narrative art history I was suited to practice. As time passed, the language of art history was infiltrated by the extensive use of jargon and neologisms. As I hoped to expand the audience for my studies of Hispanic art, the technique of clear narrative exposition was the best strategy to accomplish this goal. The virtual absence of formal study of Spanish art liberated me from the prevailing doctrines; or to put it differently, it provided a place to stand outside the mainstream and observe the complex web of art history as practiced in Spain.

In 1965, I accepted the appointment of assistant professor in the Princeton department, where I remained happily until 1973, when, at the age of thirty-four, I was offered the directorship of the Institute of Fine Arts of New York University.

Blinded by the prestige of the Institute, I accepted without fully realizing the challenges of the position. In fact, the Institute was a semi-autonomous branch of New York University, located in a magnificent mansion on the corner of Fifth Avenue and 78th Street. It had been founded by the distinguished Hispanist Walter Cook and originally staffed by many art historians fleeing from the rise of the Nazis. A famous quotation from Cook is still repeated today. "Hitler shook the apple tree and I gathered up the apples."

The Institute was self-funded; its operating expenses were derived from tuition fees and the income of a small endowment. In 1973, the USA experienced a severe recession, which was magnified in New York. At the first meeting of our Board of Trustees, Brooke Astor, then known to have a fortune of $100,000,000, worried that she would become penniless. As I soon discovered, the Institute was in a truly perilous financial condition. Fortunately, at just that moment the great financier John L. Loeb agreed to accept the chairmanship of our Board. Working closely with Mr. Loeb, we extricated the Institute from its endangered position, increasing the endowment, restoring the Duke House to its glory, and building a new physical plant for our Conservation Center. The connection to Mr. Loeb put me in contact with some of the leading citizens of New York, the bankers of Wall Street, whose way of looking at the world provided me with an invaluable perspective on my chosen profession of art historian. Most salient was the different approach to the template of leadership. Academia was governed by consensus, a slow, time-consuming process. The world of affairs was ruled by command and accordingly moved at a much faster pace.

After five years, I found that the pressure of the job left me little time for my scholarship; it was time to make a choice between administration and research and teaching. In 1978, I resigned the directorship and turned my attention to my major goal, which was to increase interest and knowledge of Spanish art in the English-speaking world. The Institute was the perfect platform – it was a graduate institute, open only to Master's and Ph.D. candidates, which gave the faculty the freedom to choose its own courses. From 1978 on, except when on leave, I taught four courses per year, all on Spanish, and later Latin American, art from 1500 to 1800. From my perspective, there were numerous gaps that I set out to fill with my own work and that of my students. In other words, I undertook the challenge of "field building." In this endeavor, I was inspired by a former colleague at Princeton, Professor Wen Fong (pl. 14), a leading scholar in the field of Chinese painting. At the time, Chinese painting was laboring under the same conditions of neglect as prevailed in the study

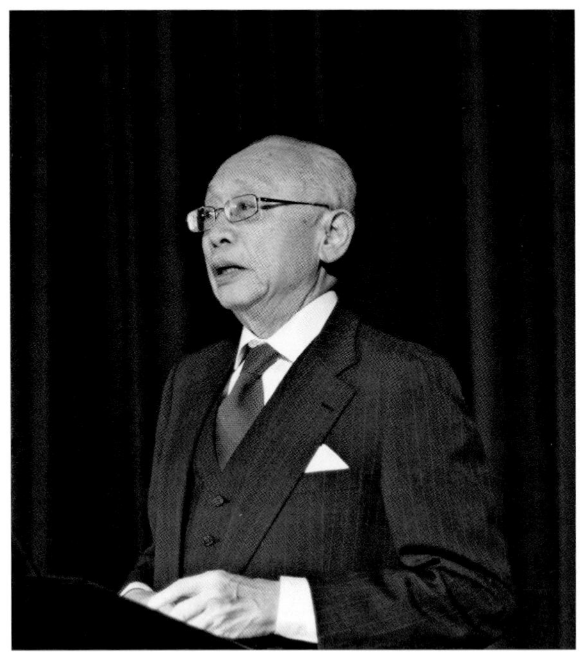

14   Wen Fong.

of Spanish painting. Mao Tse Tung was Francisco Franco writ large. Professor Fong's multi-pronged attack to improve this situation provided an example to follow. It involved training specialists, publishing his own work, helping his students to find jobs, and organizing exhibitions and symposia. Eventually, he was appointed chairman of the department of Asian Art at the Metropolitan Museum of Art and revived the dormant status of this section of the collection. The magnitude of his achievements was beyond my reach. Nonetheless, I did succeed in advancing the field, using his template. I have supervised over thirty doctoral dissertations; my former students now occupy professorships and curatorial posts throughout the USA and Canada; two have important posts in Madrid. I also formulated a Visiting Scholars Program, which has made it possible for more than a dozen younger Spanish art historians to spend time at the Institute and to experience the methods of art history as practiced in the United States. The pace of change in art history accelerated in the USA in the 1970s, and the times were propitious for my approach to the field. That said, the most important event by far occurred in 1975, when General Franco died. The stage was set for the Spanish miracle to begin.

2

"SCIENTIFIC AND RIGOROUS"

It is sometimes said that art historians always find the answers to their questions. Upon reflection, this is no surprise, since we carefully frame the questions we are asking. During the time that I was writing my doctoral dissertation (1964), there was a consensus that all questions had definitive answers. It was simply a matter of finding the correct text or image that could "solve the problem." Debates tended to center on who had produced the most conclusive evidence – a battle of the texts. The prolonged debate about the meaning of *Las Meninas,* in which I was an active participant, is an excellent case in point. There must be a few dozen recent essays that claim to have cracked the "secret code" of this masterpiece. Needless to say, fresh attempts appear with regularity. I will to return to this painting and its problems in a later chapter.

In the 1970s, certainty went up in a cloud of tear gas. One cause of the change in paradigm was strictly demographic. In the United States, the "baby boomers" began to flood the market place. With a whiff of revolution in the air, these young art historians demanded new intellectual spaces to occupy, sometimes including the office of the university's president. The social revolution that began with the events of 1968 inevitably had a major impact on interpretive strategies deployed by art historians. In the English-speaking world, newly fledged art historians looked to thinkers in France and England for guidance and began to appropriate their ideological frameworks. Marxist interpretations, and social theory in general, became a major strategy. Michel Foucault, the leading post-structuralist thinker, examined the structure of hierarchical power and how it had insidiously come to dominate western culture. Deconstruction, as articulated by Jacques Derrida, analyzed the shifting meaning of texts, attempting to demonstrate that they had no fixed significance; they could be interpreted in several ways, depending on who the interpreter was. Entirely new approaches entered the discourse. Gender studies, marked especially by feminist art historians, became a major force in the field, gradually spawning gay and lesbian studies. One by one, groups that had been sidelined or neglected by "mainstream" art history, made their voices heard. The "new" art history invaded the field and began to colonize it.

No one observed these changes with greater skepticism (mingled with a certain dose of trepidation) than art historians. For the sake of brevity, allow me to introduce two sets of dichotomies that epitomize the fault lines of these new, earth-shaking developments – theory versus empiricism and university versus museum. Let me hasten to say that art historians – and I am one of their number – remained true to their faith in empirical evidence. However, they did introduce new lines of inquiry that involved the novel use of documents and primary sources. The hope for renewal was found in areas such as patronage studies, including the fertile topic of art at the European court, and art as seen from the perspective of religious, political, and economic vantage points. Even the bedrock of art history, the monograph, gathered strength from the emergence of increasingly sophisticated instruments for technical evaluation. The voice of the conservator added new strength to the empiricist camp.

In Spain, these new approaches had little resonance. Anyone who, for any reason, had stopped reading publications on the history of Spanish painting in 1960, would have had no difficulty in picking up in 1980 where he left off. I hasten to add that the "new" art history was not just a fad or fashion. Because it was generated by profound changes in the social and political order, the new art history could not be simply dismissed by empirical art historians. Works of art have always been a vehicle for social and political expression and therefore interpretation is inherently mutable, as are the social and political institutions themselves.

I provide this sketch of the recent evolution of art historical inquiry in order to aid an understanding of my perception of art history in Spain in the years 1965–85. Another theme that is developed in this chapter is competition and rivalry as fundamental factors in the production of art history. I will discuss this phenomenon in greater detail in a later chapter. Here I wish only to acknowledge this presence as I survey my own experience in the world of Spanish art history.

I returned to Spain for the academic year 1964–65, having defended my dissertation in August 1964. The less said about that bit of work, the better. Fortunately, the defects soon became apparent to me and I wisely refrained from publishing it, in drastically revised form, until 1978. Entitled *Images and Ideas in Seventeenth Century Spain*,[1] the premise of the book is a thinly veiled critique of the prevailing norms of Spanish art history, specifically painting of the seventeenth century, and a demonstration of the possibilities of contextual or interdisciplinary art history. In the span of time between 1964 and 1978, I had filled the gaps in my reading and first-hand knowledge of Spain's cultural patrimony. In 1965, I was appointed as Assistant Professor at Princeton, where, for several years, I taught courses in everything except Spanish art. The paucity of interest in my field was alarming, and I wanted to find out why this was so and how the situation could possibly be improved. Eventually the problems came into a fuzzy focus, if not into total resolution.

At the top of the list was the political situation in Spain. There was an international antipathy to the Franco dictatorship. People of liberal political convictions – like my parents, for instance – avoided visiting Spain, which was regarded as showing support for General Franco.

Spain was a poor country, although the economic conditions slowly improved, especially after 1953, when the government of the USA began to provide financial assistance in return for the right to establish military bases in places like Torrejón, Zaragoza, and Rota. Another pillar of the economy was the tourist industry, which cornered the market for cheap holidays.

Still, there was not enough money to go around and university education was not a priority of the government. The field of art history was quite small by comparison to the various branches of science, medicine, and law. When I started my career, there were no more than eight or nine departments of art history in the Spanish university system. For the most part, the faculty and students studied the art of the region where they were born and raised. They stayed at home not for lack of curiosity but for lack of money to fund travel grants even to nearby countries.

While there was a steady stream of scholarly publications, most were done on a shoestring. The quality of design and production was poor, as were the illustrations; the pages had to be slit open with a knife or letter-opener. Color reproductions were just coming into fashion in Europe and the United States, but this ornament of art history monographs was beyond the reach of Spanish budgets.

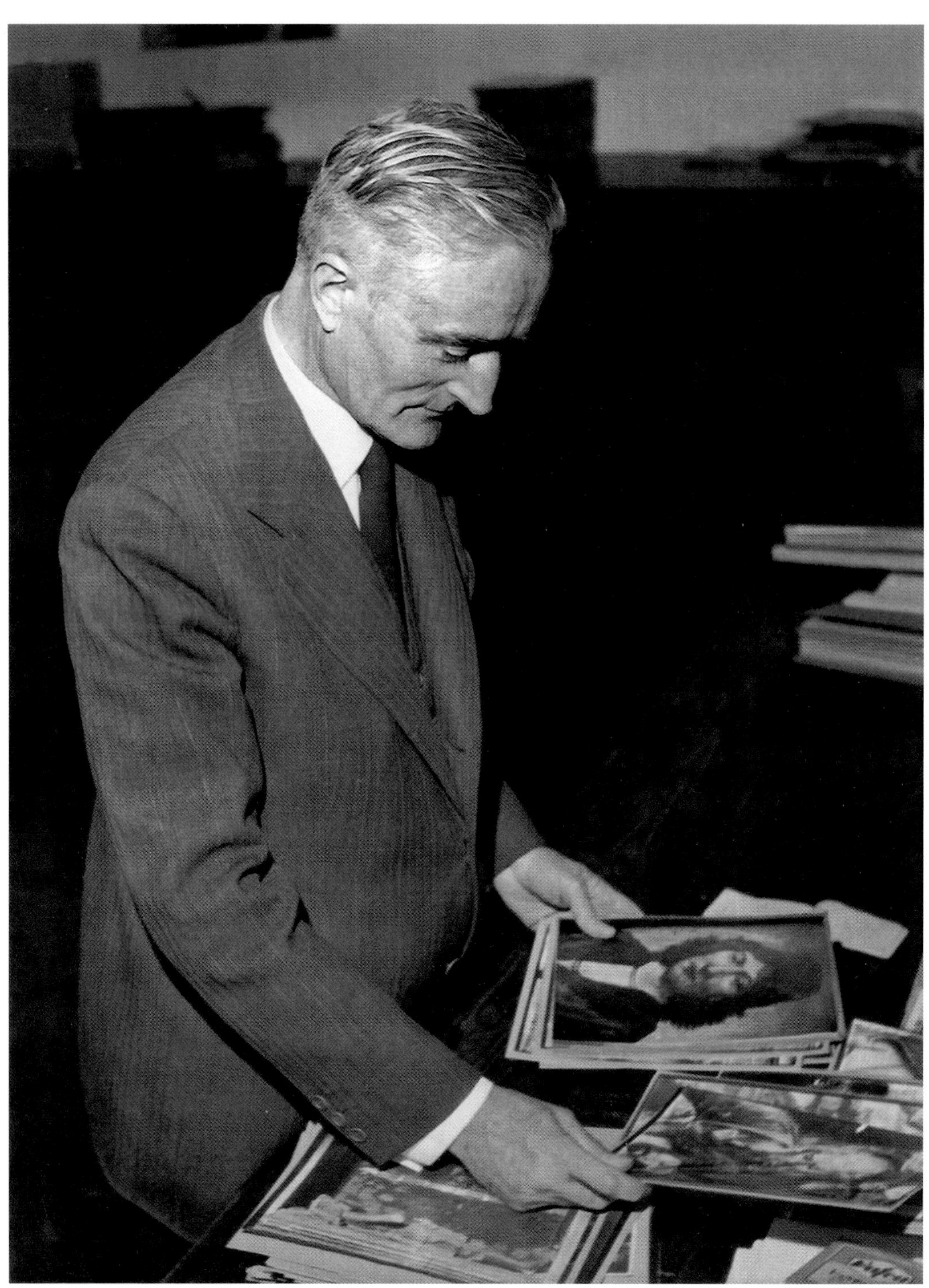

15 Diego Angulo Iñiguez.

Good libraries of art history were at a premium. The University of Madrid did not have an art history library at all; students were compelled to use the Biblioteca Nacional, much to the displeasure of scholars, who needed the collections for their research. The Prado had a library but it was small and contained only minimal space for readers. The best library was at the Instituto Diego Velázquez, which formed part of the Consejo Superior de Investigaciones Científicas, the government-sponsored agency for advanced research. I spent most afternoons working in this collection. And it was here that I again encountered Diego Angulo Iñiguez, Director of the Instituto Diego Velázquez and Spain's leading art historian (pl. 15). He did not remember me from the course he had offered to students of New York University, but I certainly remembered him; he occupied much space in my intellectual world.

By any measure, Angulo was the most influential Spanish art historian of the twentieth century. And by any measure, he was the most productive art historian in Spain if not in all of Europe. As such, it is worth taking some time to examine his extraordinary career.

Angulo was born in 1901 and died in 1986. This long span of life, combined with his precocious start in art history, was certainly one component of his success. Another was the opportunity in 1921–22 to go to Berlin and to experience the influence of the great German medievalist Adolph Goldschmidt (1863–1944), professor at the University of Berlin (pl. 16). This experience is always mentioned in Angulo's biography but warrants further investigation because it was the formative event of his career. Goldschmidt's copious publications are now known mostly to specialists in medieval art. However, as Kathryn Brush has demonstrated, his approach to the field was widely influential.[2] Goldschmidt was professor first at the University of Berlin from 1892–1904; then he moved to the University of Halle, where he taught from 1904–12. He returned to Berlin in 1912, and remained there until the rise of the Nazis. By all accounts, he was a charismatic lecturer and personality and a gifted mentor; he supervised nearly a hundred doctoral dissertations in a wide range of fields.

As a youth, Goldschmidt had taken a keen interest in science and was torn between following a scientific career or one in art history. Art history, of course, won the struggle, but in the end he found a way to reconcile his two passions by adapting some of the procedures of the scientific method to the study of art, producing what Brush terms as scientific connoisseurship. She describes Goldschmidt's method as such:

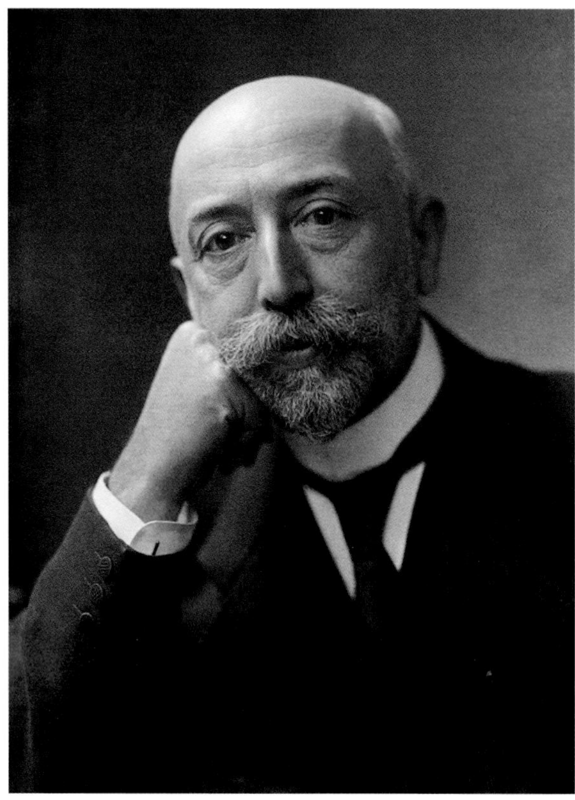

16   Adolph Goldschmidt.

Goldschmidt was among the first to survey the terrain of medieval art and he saw the introduction of intellectually rigorous standards for the analysis and classification of individual works and the establishment of basic data about those works (i.e., place of origin, date, chronology) as being necessary before more comprehensive questions could be asked.[3]

Nowadays this approach, commonly known as formalism, is considered by many art historians to be antiquated and ill-equipped to answer the questions that are now asked about a given work of art. In the 1920s, however, as German art historians struggled to create a space in the university curriculum, it was revolutionary and provided the young Diego Angulo with the concepts he needed to restructure the field of art history in Spain, moving it in the direction of scientific connoisseurship.

28

Angulo's rise to the summit of Spanish art history was meteoric. In 1925, at the age of twenty-four, he was appointed to the chair of Literature and the Arts at the University of Granada. Two years later, he moved to Seville, where he had spent his childhood, and occupied the newly created chair of Hispanic Art. In Seville, he joined the ranks of art historians affiliated with the Laboratorio de Arte, an organization whose very name demonstrates the commitment to a scientific art history. During the Civil War, he formed part of the Servicio de Recuperación del Tesoro Artístico. When the war ended in 1939, Angulo moved from Seville to Madrid, where he was appointed to the chair of History of Modern and Contemporary Art at the University of Madrid, a position he held until his retirement. The coincidence of his promotions with the start of the Franco era might suggest that he collaborated with the regime, which began to "purify" the universities immediately after the war. However, I have not seen a shred of evidence that he was connected to the political powers at any point in his career. At any rate, he was not seen as dangerous by the government and was allowed to continue his work. In 1942, he was elected to the Real Academia de la Historia and served as director from 1976 until he died. His election to the Real Academia de Bellas Artes occurred somewhat belatedly in 1958.

His involvement with the Museo del Prado began in 1923, when he became a member of the team that was charged with producing a catalogue of the collection. However, his close and continuous connection to the Museum dates to 1941, the year he was named Adjunct Curator to the Director and member of the Board of Directors. For a brief time, from 1968 to 1970, he occupied the Director's office, after which he remained involved with the institution as Honorary Trustee.

Closest to Angulo's heart was the Instituto Diego Velázquez. He began there as Secretary in 1940 and was promoted to Director in 1953. As a part of the Consejo Superior de Investigaciones Científicas, the Instituto was supported by governmental funds, and under Angulo's leadership, it became the major center for advanced research. The facilities were excellent, including a good library, especially strong in the often-ephemeral journals produced in the provinces and books published abroad. The final component was a photo archive. The Instituto published the leading journal in Spain, *Archivo Español de Arte*, of which Angulo was the editor-in-chief, the most frequent contributor, and sole referee of submissions to the publication. By controlling the contents of the *Archivo*, Angulo could control the discourse in the field.

Angulo's copious writings are of a piece. He kept an astonishing number of visual images in his memory and had a keen sense of topics that needed to be studied.

In the first part of his career, while at Seville, he became expert in Latin American art of the colonial period. With co-authors Enrique Marco Dorta and Mario Buschiazzo, he produced in 1945–56 a three-volume history of art and architecture in Spain's American territories, which remains one of the major contributions to the field.[4] After he moved to Madrid, he concentrated on Spanish old master drawings, painters of the Renaissance and Baroque, especially in Madrid and Seville, and paintings by non-Spanish artists in Spanish collections. Another talent was his ability to synthesize information. He produced survey texts on Spanish Renaissance and Baroque painting and a general history of art that, I'm told, is still used in art history classes all over Spain. Once in a while he wrote an iconographical study, particularly after a spell at the Warburg Institute in London, but they were marginal to his principal interests.

In keeping with his scientific approach to art history, Angulo habitually divided the history of Spanish painting into categories determined by geographical regions and chronological periods. In 1969, he, together with his favorite pupil and anointed successor, Alfonso Pérez Sánchez, published what they intended to be a complete catalogue of seventeenth-century Spanish painting. The titles of the published volumes (the project was never completed) explain the conceptual basis of this ambitious undertaking: *Toledo, siglo XVII, primera mitad*; *Madrid, primer tercio del siglo XVII*, etc.[5] The painters were discussed in chronological order. When he wrote of individual artists, Angulo used the same template – biography; formation and style; catalogue of works. Rarely did he generalize; never did he contextualize, theorize, synthesize or intellectualize. Attribution, evolution of style (which placed a heavy emphasis on sources of influence), and chronology of works were at the center of his art-historical universe. Strange to say, he mostly avoided the archives. His style of writing could best be characterized as clinical, admirably lucid but somewhat lifeless.

This unvaried pattern of studying the history of painting was intentional. In the first instance, every publication had to meet the criteria of being "scientific and rigorous," two words used frequently by Angulo and his disciples to praise an article or monograph. The meaning of the terms seems to be self-evident, but how they came to be the hallmark of excellence was never explained (although we now know that it was inspired by Germanic art history). Nor were the terms ever precisely defined and they could be therefore quite elastic. My guess is that they were used when they conformed to Angulo's quasi-scientific ideas about the production of art-historical knowledge. Although Angulo certainly looked forward to the day when larger problems would be addressed, there was little point of interpretation until all the facts were known. As one of his disciples reported, he was often heard to say in sotto voce, "Es tanto lo que desconocemos" (There is so much that we don't know). As I understand the statement, it can be read in two ways. One is as an expression of humility, the recognition that despite the historian's best effort to reconstruct the past, there are always gaps in knowledge that, if filled, might lead us to alter or amplify our conclusions. The other interpretation is as a prescription of how we would recognize the end of our quest when we reached it. Although never spoken, the implication was that Angulo knew the answer and would inform us when we had arrived at the final destination and could commence the arduous task of interpretation.

Angulo's method had another important consequence; it detached art from culture. The scientific method as interpreted by Adolph Goldschmidt was founded on observation and classification and was adapted from the processes of understanding and describing the physical world. Having participated at Princeton in the seminars of Kurt Weitzmann, Goldschmidt's leading disciple, I was thoroughly acquainted with what we reverently called the "Method." However, as I came to realize, art, as situated in the wide world of culture, required some sort of speculative structure fabricated from the intangible realm of ideas. Otherwise works of art drifted through time and space without rhyme or reason.

I have mentioned before that Angulo steered clear of the political currents of the day. However, the thought occurs that his methodology was by coincidence well-suited to the Franco period. By draining the content from forms, the discipline became "politically correct." Someone in power, likely to have been the Marqués de Lozoya, was well aware of the need for what might be called a "patriotic" art history. In the preface of the first issue of *Archivo Español de Arte* to appear after the end of the Civil War, Lozoya established these priorities for the journal and the field of art history.

Reparar los daños de la Guerra es la más urgente tarea de los españoles de este momento; reanudar el trabajo interrumpido e infundir en él las altas aspiraciones que están de la médula de la España de Franco.[6]

At this moment, to repair the damages of the war is the most urgent task for Spaniards; to renew the interrupted work and to infuse it with high aspirations which are in the marrow of Franco's Spain.

That the history of art was being politicized is beyond doubt. The evidence is provided in the career of one of the most respected art historians of the post-war period, Enrique Lafuente Ferrari (1898–1985), a contemporary and in a certain sense the rival of Angulo. Lafuente, an art historian of broad culture and wide-ranging interests, in touch with the most recent developments outside Spain, never gained a university appointment and spent his career teaching art history to artists in the Escuela de Bellas Artes de San Fernando. It seems unlikely that Angulo personally blocked Lafuente's appointment, but there were others higher on the political ladder who would have been interested in muffling Lafuente's voice. By the 1950s, Angulo's domination of Spanish art history was secure. Javier Portús has recently described his position and his powers.

> La posición central que (Angulo) ocupaba en el mundo académico y la incansable actividad personal y colectiva que generó han dejado una huella importante en el desarollo de la historia del arte peninsular. Su influencia fue decisiva en varios aspectos. Por un lado, el poder que alcanzó en una España autocrática, con una cultura muy dirigida, y en los centros de actividad histórico-artístico eran escasos y las posibilidades económicos limitadas, fue muy grande, lo que influyó no sólo en la fortuna profesional de sus alumnos, sino en la de muchos colegas de su propia generación. Por otro lado, Angulo abrazó una opción metodologica deter-minada, el posivitismo formalista, y si bien a lo largo de su carrera se mostró abierto a otras posibilidades, lo cierto es que fue un acérrimo defensor de una historia del arte filológica que ha venido dominando la universidad española y otros centros de investigación histórico-artística durante varias décadas. Es un fenómeno que, lejos de reflejar la riqueza de posturas que en realidad había entre los historiadores del arte español de su generación, responde más bien a la muy dispar fortuna profesional que tuvieron.[7]

The central position that Angulo occupied in the academic world and the inde-fatigable personal and political activity that he generated have left an important mark on the development of the history of peninsular art. His influence was decisive in several aspects. On one side is the power that he attained in autocratic Spain, which had a very controlled culture and in which centers of art-historical research were few and far between. Angulo was a staunch defender of a philologi-cal history of art, which even now dominates art history as taught in Spanish universities. This is a phenomenon that determined the success of the professional careers of Spanish art historians.

∿

His disciples, of course, saw it another way. To them, he was a beloved mentor, generous with his knowledge and favor. Allow me to quote a few lines of the necrology written by his pupil and long-time collaborator in the Instituto Velázquez, Elisa Bermejo. She emphasizes his role as teacher and scholar.

> Sin embargo, lo singular en la personalidad de Don Diego (the title of courtesy used by Spanish art historians when addressing or speaking of him) es que su magisterio se extendía más allá de su calidad de profesor universitario. Todos aquellos que se le acercaban para pedirle una información sobre cualquier obra o tema de arte, recibían, con gran cortesía y sencillez, una parte de su profundo saber en el campo artístico. Siempre rerpresentó la imagen ideal que todos tenemos del Maestro en la más alta y entrañable significación de esta mágica palabra.

> Nonetheless, what is singular about the personality of Don Diego was that his teaching extended beyond his position as a university professor. All those who approached him to ask information about any work or subject of art were given, with great courtesy and humility, a part of his deep knowledge in the field of art. He always represented the ideal image that we all have of the "Master" in the highest and most affectionate meaning of this magical word.

As for his humble approach to scholarship, she characterizes it in the following words.

> A pesar de su indiscutible categoría cientifica, acreditado por sus amplíssimos conocimientos, nunca tuvo inconveniente en manifestar sus dudas sobre cualquier cuestión que se le plantase y tanto que los que tuvimos la inapagable suerte de recibir sus continuas enseñanzas, por trabajar cerca de él, como los que le visitaban para consultarle, en más de una ocasion, quizá por vez primera, pudimos escucharle, en más de una ocasion, una de sus frases favoritas: "es tanto lo que desconocemos."[8]

> In spite of his unquestionable qualities as a researcher, validated by his very broad range of knowledge, he did not shy away from showing his doubts. Nor did he sidestep any sort of question that was presented to him and such that those of us who had the undying luck to receive his ongoing teachings, working at his side, as well as those who came to consult with him, on more than one occasion, could hear him utter one of his favorite phrases: "There is so much we don't know."

At first it seems difficult to reconcile such contradictory impressions of the same person. However there are explanations, two of which are certainly sentimental and generational. Bermejo's text was written in 1986, that of Portús, in 2007. Bermejo was obviously influenced by her long-time association with the deceased, whereas for Portús, Angulo belonged to history. In reading what Portús has written, one word seems to leap off the page – autocratic, a personality trait that perhaps best explains how Angulo came to power and managed to hold it for so many decades. Autocratic personalities demand unconditional loyalty and in return reward those who demonstrate it by bestowing, for example, university professorships and museum curatorial appointments on the faithful. (Until 1996, the majority of curators at the Prado were disciples of Angulo, and a few remain at their posts to this very day.) Opponents become the enemy and are marginalized and banished to the provinces. I mentioned before the coincidence between the methods used by the regime to control thought and action and the milder form of these methods used by Angulo to channel art history into his networks of belief. By nature, he was an authoritarian personality and by luck he appeared on stage just when the political and social circumstances made it possible for him to concentrate authority in his chosen field.

My contacts with Angulo were infrequent and unforgettable. The first sustained conversation (that word is not very apt when recalling interactions with Don Diego) occurred in 1974 at a small dinner organized by the publisher of John Elliott's volumes on the letters and memorials of the Conde-Duque de Olivares. Angulo was on the guest list and when I saw him, I greeted him with the customary handshake. We were having drinks on the terrace and making small talk when Angulo steered the conversation to the subject of Murillo. For the next fifteen minutes, he bombarded me with information about Murillo, never pausing to hear what, if anything, I had to say. I was mystified by the mini-lecture until I finally realized that he was warning me off the subject. I had already informed him that I was preparing an exhibition of Murillo's drawings, due to take place at the Princeton University Art Museum in 1976. Angulo had long been writing a book and catalogue raisonné on the painter from Seville, which in the event was published in 1981. In effect, he was telling me that Murillo belonged to him and that I would be well-advised to find something else to work on, particularly as it was clear that he knew much more about the subject than I did. In the next issue of *Archivo Español de Arte* he published an article, "Algunos dibujos de Murillo," in which he attributed a number of drawings that I was planning to bring to light in my exhibition.[9] Had I been a Spaniard, I would have dropped the scheme like a hot potato; in fact I would never have dared to trespass into Angulo's territory. It was well known that he was preparing a monograph on Murillo, that Murillo was his property and thus unavailable for study by any other art historian. For some twenty years, Murillo was placed in cold storage while Angulo prepared his text. Scholars naturally try to avoid working on a subject that another person has in hand, but this consideration is different from putting a "hold" on the study of a given artist. I shrugged my shoulders and continued with my plan. The catalogue elicited a strongly negative review by Angulo, which was published in the pages of the *Archivo* in 1977.[10]

We met again, probably for the last time, a year or two later. I had passed by the Instituto Velázquez to pay my respects to Professor Angulo. He invited me into his office, which was poorly lit and rather shabbily furnished. I remember sitting in a well-worn easy chair, covered by a stiff, dark fabric, the arms of which were soiled by the sweaty palms of countless petitioners. Angulo habitually spoke in a quiet voice, his speech inflected by a southern accent that tended to run words together. I confess that I had a hard time hearing what he had to say. Eventually, it became clear that he was telling me the story of how, through his efforts, he had kept the field of art history alive during the dark days after the Civil War. As a young American, it would be impossible for me to understand what an enormous effort had been required to start the Instituto Velázquez and to keep it running when government funds were so badly lacking. After he finished his speech, we said goodbye and I left in a thoroughly confused state of mind.

Eventually I realized what was going on. In 1978, I published *Images and Ideas in Seventeenth-Century Spanish Painting*. The introductory chapter was a historiographical essay, in which I criticized the positivistic, formalist approach of Angulo and his followers and called for a contextualization of Golden Age painting, via social, economic, and religious history. In and of itself, this idea was not a novelty. A book by Julián Gállego, *Vision et symboles dans la peinture espagnole du Siècle d'Or* (French edition, 1968; Spanish translation, 1972) had already proposed an alternative way of looking at the painting of the period. Gállego had been trained in Paris and was abreast of more up-to-date methods of art-historical inquiry. And I completely missed the importance of Angulo's student year in Berlin and the influence on his thought of the teachings of Adolph Goldschmidt. However, in the discourse on Spanish painting, my essay offered new perspectives and prescriptions for invigorating the field.

My book was controversial in Spain although it was talked about much more than it was written about. Critical book reviews of a type that are common in the

Anglo-American world did not exist at that time; the *tertulia* was the cockpit for criticism, and I had to content myself with the rumor mill to find out if the book was having an impact. However, in 2008 I received the response I was looking for. This is an evaluation of my work written by Professor Bonaventura Bassegoda of the University of Barcelona; it is published as the Foreword to my collected studies of Velázquez. (I confess that I read it every night before I go to sleep . . .) Here is one of my favorite passages.

> One of the elements that best defines Jonathan Brown's intellectual profile is the assurance and confidence which he has, and has always had, in art history as a discipline. It now seems ridiculous, of course, to state this, but those of us who trained at the beginning of the 1970s well remember our discontent at the traditional art history then being practiced in Spain, with its limited form of positivism, and also our uneasiness with the pseudo-theorizing based in sociology or structuralism by which some people sought to redeem the discipline. So at the end of that decade and in the eighties, having access to Brown's researches was one of the ways that we used to resolve our doubts and our questions.[11]

If these words represent an unbiased assessment of my work in the 1970s and 1980s, I can understand why Angulo was trying to throw me off the track, to intimidate and bring me into line with his precepts of art history. He had ways of stifling dissent in Spain, but none was applicable to a scholar whose base of operations was the Institute of Fine Arts in New York City. I had criticized his basic assumptions as no one before had dared or cared to do and I had to be stopped and made to pay. None of the instruments at his disposal or at the disposal of his successor was able to achieve this goal.

It is misleading to tell this story as if it were only a personal rivalry, although inevitably this component has to be taken into account. More accurately, it was a case of conflicting conceptions of the goals of art history. My training at Princeton emphasized criticism of previous and current writings on a work or works of art, the close analysis of primary texts, and the iconographical studies of Erwin Panofsky. The Spanish system prized conformity to the rules of research as established by Angulo and his followers. There was also a fundamental difference in the audience for art history. Historians of art trained in Spain wrote with a Spanish readership in mind. For one thing, books produced in Spain were poorly distributed, if distributed at all. Thus the writings of Spanish art historians were little known. I had to travel to Spain with some frequency just to acquire the latest books.

Perhaps as a consequence of these circumstances, the research produced by Spanish scholars was sometimes overlooked by non-Spanish writers. I often shook my head in amazement when, for example, a foreign art historian would publish an object or a text that had already been unearthed and discussed in Spain. Few if any non-Spanish specialists appeared to know even rudimentary Spanish, although knowledge of Italian should have made the language of Spain accessible to them. In the early modern period, Madrid had been at the center of European politics. Its importance as a capital of art was recognized, and its position as a crossroads of the art trade known to all. The decline of Spain and the persistence of the Black Legend, embodied in General Franco, sent the artistic accomplishments of the Golden Age to the sidelines and the failure of nerve of painters of the later nineteenth century put the final nail in the coffin. As Spain dropped out of its place as a primary world power, and as the negative stereotype embodied in the Black Legend passed from calumny to verity, the understanding of its visual culture suffered accordingly.

The nadir was reached in 1969, when Kenneth Clark published his book, *Civilization. A Personal View.* The book was based on a twelve-part television series, which enjoyed great success. In his later years, Clark had become a sort of ambassador of high culture to the masses. He was dapper in appearance and eloquent in his speech, the perfect incarnation of a cultured English aristocrat. Americans, of course, reveled in Clark's brand of mild, but impregnable snobbery. In the former colonies, the program attracted a wide audience.

However, Clark was no hispanophile. In the preface, he explained why he had omitted Spain in his narrative of the evolution of western civilization. In just a few lines, he manages to recapitulate almost five centuries of anti-Spanish sentiment in England and elsewhere in the Protestant world:

Some of the most offensive omissions were dictated by my title. [He speaks of the book, not about the peerage he was granted as Lord Clark of Saltwood.] If I had been talking about the history of art, it would not have been possible to leave out Spain; but when one asks what Spain has done to enlarge the human mind and pull mankind a few steps up the hill, the answer is less clear. *Don Quixote,* the Great Saints, the Jesuits in South America? Otherwise she has simply remained Spain, and since I wanted each programme to be concerned with the new developments of the European mind, I could not change my ground and talk about a single country.[12]

Reverberations of the Black Legend rattle down through the ages and are echoed in the plummy voice of an English milord.

From my point of view, the Golden Age was a golden opportunity. There was much to be studied and new ideas were needed to do it. Beyond the frontiers of the Iberian Peninsula, there was a teeming bazaar of approaches to art and art history, which only expanded as time went on. Nations like France, Italy, and the Netherlands had discovered cultural politics and were assiduously promoting their artistic achievements to construct a favorable political image. Scientific formalism as practiced in Spain certainly had its uses, but in the complex, competitive world of art and art history as it developed in the 1970s, the limitations became all too apparent.

3

EL GRECO AND RIBERA

THE WORKSHOP AS FACTORY

Since the early years of the Renaissance, indeed since time immemorial, painters have worked in what might loosely be called a corporate manner. It is only recently that art historians have been examining the nuts and bolts of how the artists plied their trade. Following the lead of the economic historian John Michael Montias, who studied the art market of seventeenth-century Holland, the study of the business of art is now in full flight. A recent survey of the market place in seventeenth-century Rome by Patrizia Cavazzini, *Painting as Business in Early Seventeenth Rome* (2008), is a fine example of this genre. Our image of the artist as lone eagle was shaped by the era of Romanticism. The photographic documentation of the working methods of such twentieth-century painters as Picasso and Pollock has spread this image far and wide. With an artist like Andy Warhol, who was a devoted practitioner of collaborative works and multiples and objects that were created without the intervention of the master, the resulting confusion drives the art market crazy and leads to such lunacy as the creation of a Warhol Authentication Committee, now happily and unavoidably extinct.

I do not mean to imply that patrons and collectors of the Renaissance and Baroque were indifferent to what might be called the "master's touch," far from it. However, in the seventeenth century the copy retained value as documentation of a master's work and particularly of his inventions. The evolution of European art is unthinkable without the agency of the painted copy and the reproductive print. Eventually, however, the copy lost prestige and became relatively worthless as compared to the original. In practice, copies existed in two forms – the authorized copy, produced by an assistant of the master, sometimes with the minimal intervention of the head of the shop, and the unauthorized copy, made by imitators and forgers.

Painting was a mercantile activity and not only a display of individual talent. The best painters were able to find patrons and protectors. However, a sizable retail market existed, in which individual paintings were sold "off the peg" to customers, usually from the artist's studio (pl. 17). This retail market offered a spectrum of images, from cheap devotional works to more expensive versions of well-known paintings produced by well-known artists. The recent "rediscovery" of the copy of Leonardo's *Mona Lisa* in the basement of the Museo del Prado would be a timely example of the latter. In this chapter, I hope to show how two elite painters devised strategies to capitalize on their reputations by framing marketing tactics based on the copy as a major component of their production. My examples are El Greco and Jusepe de Ribera.

It is difficult to think of two painters who have less in common than El Greco and Ribera. El Greco's career was mostly confined to the late sixteenth and early seventeenth century. His artistic trajectory is unusual, indeed unique. He was born in Crete in 1541 and started as a practitioner of the post-Byzantine manner and then emigrated to Venice in 1567, where he acquired the rudiments of Italian painting. Next he went to Rome, where he resided from 1570–76. By the time he moved to Spain, he was a mannerist tried and true. From 1577 until his death in 1614, he lived in Toledo, where he became the city's premier painter.

The itinerary of Ribera took him in the opposite direction; he traveled from west to east. He was born in 1588 in Játiva, a town near Valencia, and went to Italy perhaps in 1610, spending time in Parma (1610–11) and Rome (1612–16) before moving south to Naples in 1616. He remained in Naples, then a territory of the Spanish monarchy, for the rest of his life. Naples was governed by a viceroy, chosen from the ranks of the Spanish nobility and clergy. Ribera's manner of painting is usually described as "naturalism" and is considered to have been powerfully influenced by Caravaggio. Rather quickly, he became the leading painter in Naples. As already noted, it would be difficult to find a more antipodal pair of painters than El Greco

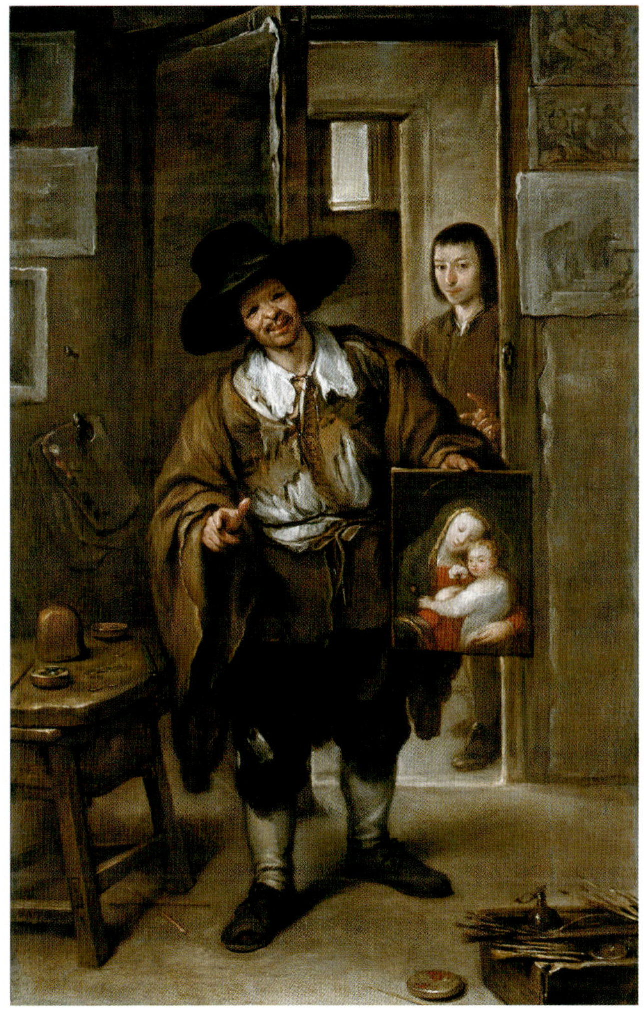

17   José Antolínez, *Picture Dealer*, Munich, Alte Pinakothek.

and Ribera. However, despite the chasm that separates these two powerful artists, there are commonalities in how they organized their production.

Although counter-intuitive, I will discuss the painters in reverse chronological order, first Ribera, then El Greco. This ahistorical decision is prompted strictly by autographical factors of the most mundane sort – my interest and study of Ribera preceded my work on El Greco by a dozen years. In 1973, I organized an exhibition, "The Prints and Drawings of Jusepe de Ribera."[1] The subject of Ribera's drawings was then entering a heightened state of interest, thanks to the work of Michael Mahoney and Walter Vitzthum. They had opened the way to a fresh understanding of Ribera as draftsman.

Ribera's small corpus of etchings, on the other hand, had not been systematically catalogued, although the prints were usually listed in monographs on the artist. My decision to study these fine but somewhat secondary works requires explanation. Ribera's interest in exploring the medium of etching was short-lived. All but one of the eighteen (I now accept as authentic numbers seventeen and eighteen of the catalogue) were done between about 1618 and 1630. Ribera picked up his etching needle only one more time – in 1648.

Then as now, Ribera's etchings were rare. I came to know them through my friendship with the artist Leonard Baskin (1922–2000), who was Professor of Art at Smith College, located in Northampton, Massachusetts, about a half an hour distant from my parents' house. It was they who introduced me to Baskin, a well-known sculptor and graphic artist.

Baskin's artistic career coincided with the rise of Abstract Expressionism; he was a champion of figurative art. As abstract painting was winning the day, Baskin stubbornly resisted the "dehumanization of art" and continued to believe that the human body was the optimum subject for understanding the nature of man. In some ways he was a *pintor sabio* who had inadvertently wandered into the later twentieth century. His principal interest was the creation of figurative statues in wood and bronze. He was also an accomplished draftsman and printmaker, with a deep knowledge of the history of European graphic art. He paid homage to his favorite draftsmen by making imaginary portraits of admired forerunners and colleagues, from the Renaissance to the present. Another facet of his activity was the printed book; he established the Gehenna Press, which brought a high degree of craftsmanship to this genre.

The intellectual support of his various endeavors was provided by an extensive collection of rare illustrated books and prints and drawings by the old masters. These were installed in a separate space within his house, a sort of Morgan Library in miniature. It was from one of the innumerable boxes in which he stored his collection of prints and drawings that he extracted the etchings by Ribera for me to look at. He carefully explained Ribera's technique, which was quite conventional. Ribera was a delicate etcher, who worked mostly with a needle on a copper plate. The results were subtle, silky impressions, which were subject to the rapid wearing of the lines as the etched plate was printed.

Thus fired by Baskin's tutelage, which also taught me a lot about how to look at works of art, I packed my bag and hit the road to visit the major printrooms in the United States, England, and western Europe. I believe that my Ribera catalogue has held up as well as can be expected. Nowadays, with the huge expansion of art historians and curators, ideas and theories go in and out of fashion with dizzying speed, but catalogues raisonées have retained their usefulness. Having done my bit for Ribera, I moved on to other subjects, as will be discussed in due course. However, I kept abreast of developments in Ribera studies, which in the last few years have taken a dramatic turn. I refer to Gianni Papi's book of 2007, *Ribera a Roma*, which was the basis of the important show organized by the Prado in 2011, "El joven Ribera."[2] In brief, Papi argues that the unknown artist called the Master of the Judgment of Solomon is in fact the young Ribera. Fortunately the Prado was able to purchase in 2001 an important work from Ribera's Roman period, the *Resurrection of Lazarus*. From that insight, it has been possible to identify several more paintings from this stage of Ribera's development and to situate him in a place of honor among the followers of Caravaggio.

These events started me thinking again about Ribera and in particular about the thorny question of workshop practice. In 2008, the Neapolitan scholar Nicola Spinosa published the third edition of his catalogue of Ribera which, among other things, provides a useful compendium of illustrations of all the works he attributes to the artist.[3] Leafing through the book, I noticed, not for the first time, that many of Ribera's compositions were repeated and that he had signed his paintings with unusual frequency. However, he rarely signed the works produced before 1624, the earliest being the *Virgin and Child with St. Bruno* (Weimar, Schlossmuseum, Kunstsammlungen), about the same time as he started to date his etchings. For this occasion, Ribera designed a new signature, which he used thereafter. This signature is characterized by the sweeping letter "J" (pl. 18). In other words, Ribera created a logo to ensure that he would be identified as author of the painting. From the mid-1640s until his death in 1651, Ribera wrote his signature and the date on nearly ninety percent of his canvases. As I looked at the illustrations in Spinosa's monograph, I noticed other characteristics of Ribera's

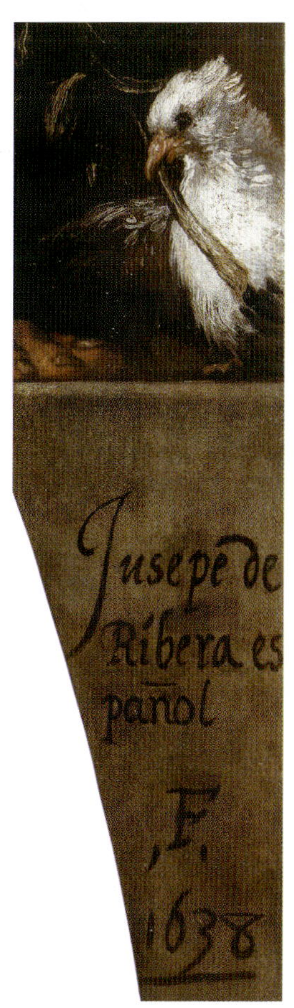

18   Jusepe de Ribera, *Noah*, signature, Naples, San Martino.

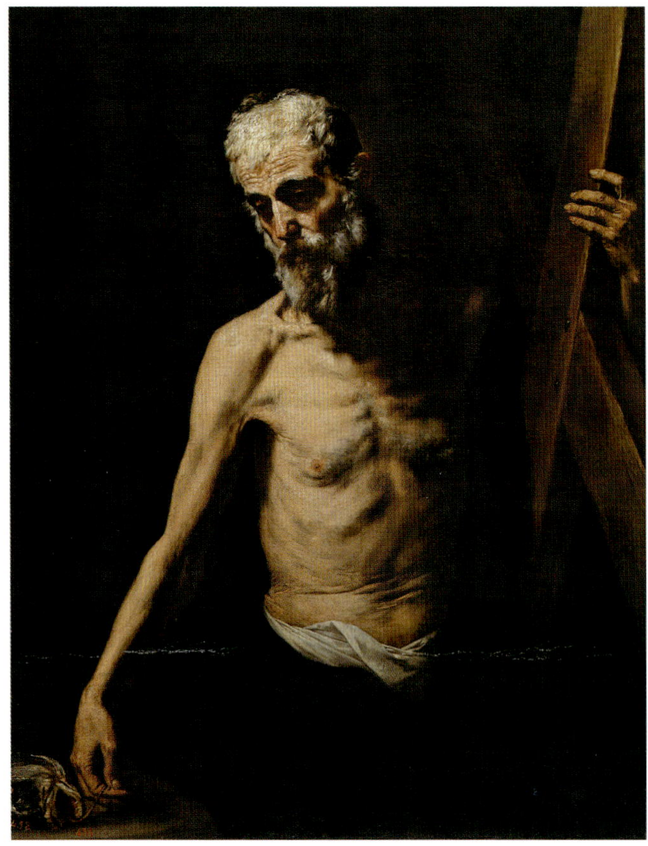

19   Jusepe de Ribera, *St. Andrew*, Madrid, Museo del Prado.

production. Essentially, he relied on just a few compositional formulas. In general, his paintings do not evince much depth; most of the activity occurs on the front plane. The most popular type of subject is the strongly illuminated full-length or half-length figure – a saint, a philosopher – set against a black background (pl. 19). The next is what I call the "splayed-figure" composition, based on a twisting pose of a scantily clad male figure which dominates the foreground and is typically deployed in scenes of martyrdom and torture (pl. 20). Another format is the figure or figures set against a partial, distant landscape (pl. 21). A final hallmark was the use of thick impastos. The reason behind this approach is obvious; Ribera was a market-driven painter who depended for his livelihood on devotional works. His formulas were ideal for creating models that could easily be reproduced by members of his

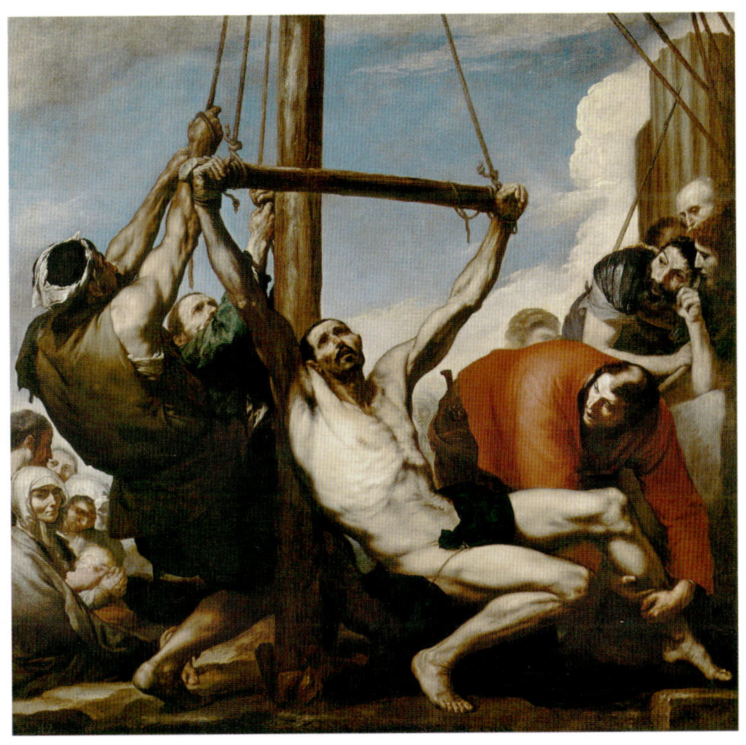

20   Jusepe de Ribera, *Martyrdom of St. Philip*, Madrid, Museo del Prado.

21   Jusepe de Ribera, *Dream of Jacob*, Madrid, Museo del Prado.

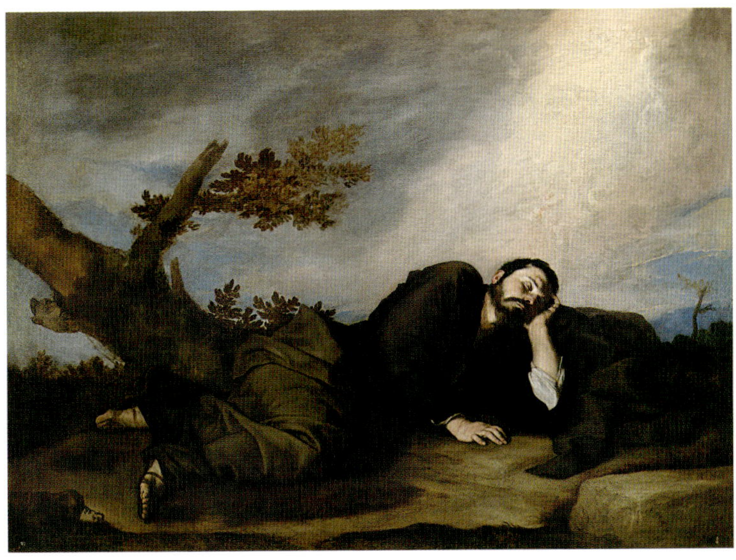

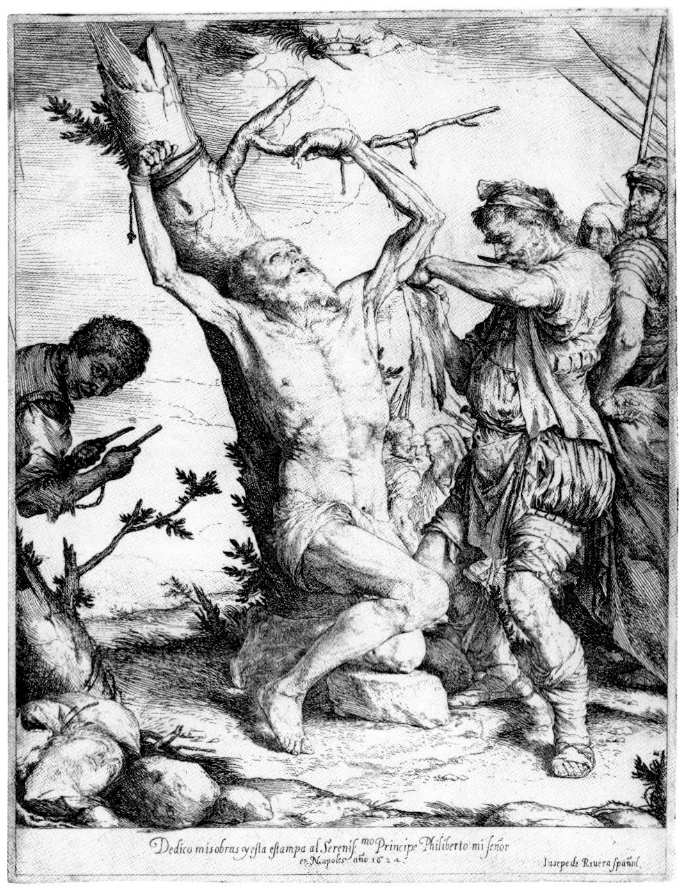

22   Jusepe de Ribera, *Martyrdom of St. Bartholomew*, etching, Berlin, Kupferstichkabinett.

shop. Major, multi-painting commissions were relatively few in Naples, which made Ribera dependent on a survival strategy that made the most of his recognized talents. It is puzzling that Ribera did not begin to sign his paintings until the early 1620s – the earliest signed work is *St. Jerome* (Toronto, Art Gallery of Ontario), datable to his Roman period. Then there is a gap until 1624 (*Virgin and Child with St. Bruno*, Weimar, Kunstsammelungen). The earliest dated print was done in 1621, the first version of *St. Jerome Hearing the Trumpet of the Last Judgment*. A group of varied subjects was followed by the great print of 1624, the *Martyrdom of St. Bartholomew* (pl. 22), which is dedicated to Prince Philibert of Savoy and signed

"Iusepe de Rivera Spañol." Four years later, he signed the *Drunken Silenus* with a longer signature – "Joseph a Ribera Hisp.o Valenti.o/Setaben.f. Partenope/1628" (José de Ribera, Spanish, Valencian (of) Játiva, made in Naples). If these observations are accurate, then the question naturally arises, why in the early years of the 1620s did Ribera adopt the practice of signing and sometimes dating his paintings?

With no evidence to guide us, we can only speculate on the reasons for this modus operandi, or business model. Perhaps the results explain the cause. Ribera was seeking to increase his market share. This would explain the references to his connection to his native land. His principal clientele was comprised of Spaniards, and in particular the viceroys. However, these officials came and went with some frequency (eleven occupied the office during Ribera's life) and stayed at their post for differing lengths of time. Not all had an interest in the art of painting. There was no opportunity to forge a lasting connection between patron and painter, as exemplified by Philip IV and Velázquez. Next in the line of customers were Neapolitans, for whom the identification of Ribera as a Spaniard was irrelevant, but who recognized his quality and eagerly sought examples of his work. To maintain solvency, he invented a "brand," as we would say nowadays, a distinctive type of painting that would be readily identified as made by his hand and guaranteed as authentic by his signature. The practice of this formula made Ribera a wealthy man. A proof of his financial status are the houses he bought in 1619 and 1641. If the prices of houses are a reliable measure of the wealth of the owners (and who would doubt that proposition?), Ribera's forays into the real estate market of Naples may prove useful. The first was located in the heart of the artists' district in the Strada de S. Spirito. Ribera paid 1,900 ducats for it. In 1641, he upgraded and moved to the suburbs in the fashionable area of the Borgo di Chiaia, where he bought a small villa with a garden for 3,100 ducats (financed with a mortgage).

Given the relative paucity of large commissions that came his way (his work for the Carthusians of San Martino, begun in 1638, would be the acme), Ribera depended on increasing the production of small and medium-sized devotional paintings, which comprise the majority of his output. To meet the demand, Ribera recruited a workshop. Bernardo De Dominici, the main source of information on Neapolitan painters of the seventeenth century, mentions several members of the shop, with laconic appraisals of their talents.[4] Giovanni Dó (Játiva; 1604–c. 1656) is one and is described as "such a true imitator, that his copies were taken for originals . . . especially some half-figures of philosophers and of St. Jerome, which in the handling of colors and in modeling of the impasto, the two were as one" (*Vite de'*

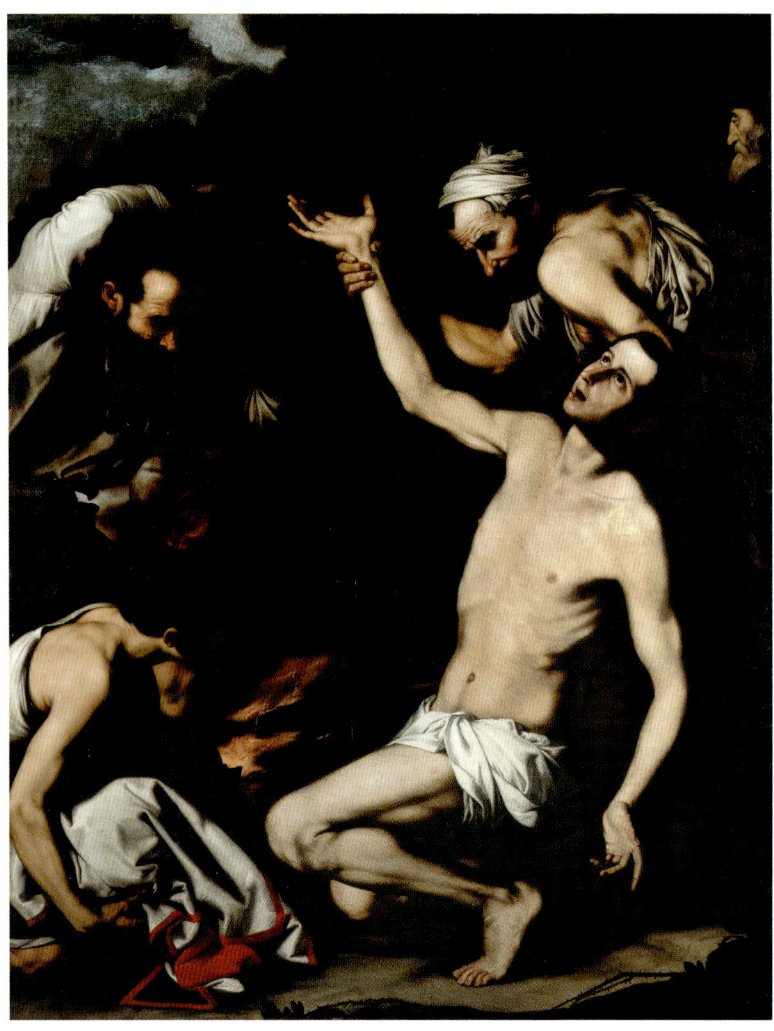

23   Jusepe de Ribera and Giovanni Dó, *Martyrdom of St. Lawrence*, Granada, Cathedral.

pittori, p. 37). Dó was born in Játiva, the same town as Ribera, and showed up in Naples in 1621. If Ribera was in contact with his family (he had a brother, Juan, with whom he traveled to Italy and was also a painter) he could have been informed that a native of his home town was leaving for Italy. Thus, Dó would have had entry into Ribera's workshop. A fascinating testimony to the collaboration between Ribera and Dó is the version of the *Martyrdom of St. Lawrence* (pl. 23) in a side chapel of

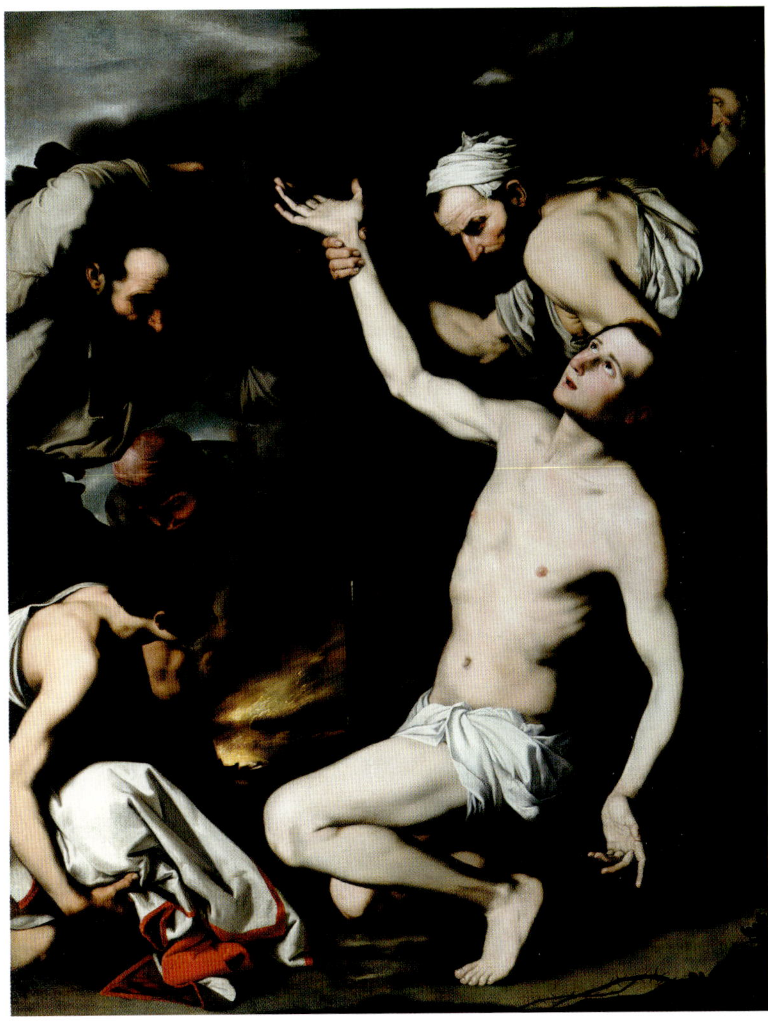

24   Attributed to Jusepe de Ribera, *Martyrdom of St. Lawrence*, Dresden, Staatliche Kunstsammlungen.

the Cathedral of Granada. The painting replicates a composition that Ribera used on other occasions (pl. 24).

Another associate was Errico Fiamingo, a rather generic name applied to painters from the Lowlands, who is now believed to be two separate painters, both of whom were connected to Ribera. Somewhat better known is Bartolomeo Passante, who specialized in the export markets. About him De Domenici remarks: "He is so similar to the works of Ribera that you have to be well-practiced in their manner if you want to recognize it." The list goes on to include the Fracanzano brothers, Cesare and Francesco, and is topped by Luca Giordano. Giordano's father, Antonio, was a plodder and is mentioned only because an anecdote sheds some light on one of the ways the workshop functioned. "Antonio did nothing but copy some saints painted by the master, and specifically St. Anthony, some of which were retouched by Ribera, such was their insufficiency."

The analogy of Ribera's workshop to a factory is not entirely frivolous. This practice would explain the multiple versions of many compositions. The danger occurred when a painting executed by the workshop was signed by Ribera, with his logo-like signature. Ribera's habit of turning a signature into a logo made it tempting to sign workshop pieces as originals and for imitators to forge the signature as well as to purloin the composition.

Ribera's compositional formulas became a two-edged sword. They made his paintings into a fashionable item for collectors and consumers and promoted an increase in demand, which was sometimes met by copyists. His distinctive logo unintentionally facilitated their task, just as it complicates the lives of dealers, collectors, and art historians today.

The universe of canvases purportedly signed by Ribera is vast and expanding. Here I can offer only a selection of works in order to exemplify the problem. The martyrdom of St. Bartholomew was one of Ribera's most famous subjects and was spread far and wide by the print of 1624. This version in the Nationalmuseum, Stockholm, bears the signature "Jusepe de Ribera español/F.A. 1644" (pl. 25). The balance of opinion tilts toward an attribution to the workshop.

Another example would be *St. Peter in Meditation* (Glasgow, Corporation Art Gallery), which uses the long form of Ribera's signature – "Joseph a Ribera Hisp,/ Valent.F. Partenope/ 1628." I depend on Spinosa's opinion, since it has been many years since I saw the original. As he points out, the date is incompatible with the style. This painting is also useful for another purpose; it demonstrates the popularity of Ribera's compositions and the copies they inspired. Spinosa lists eleven, of which two are inscribed "JR." A version of the *Adoration of the Shepherds* (Aachen, Suerdmont Museum) wins the medal for the longest inscription on a work of dubious authenticity: "Jusepe de Ribera Hispanus/ Accademicus romanus/Faciebat Partenope/ 1629."

These paintings and the innumerable unsigned copies and versions raise questions which cannot now be answered, the most important of which is how Ribera's

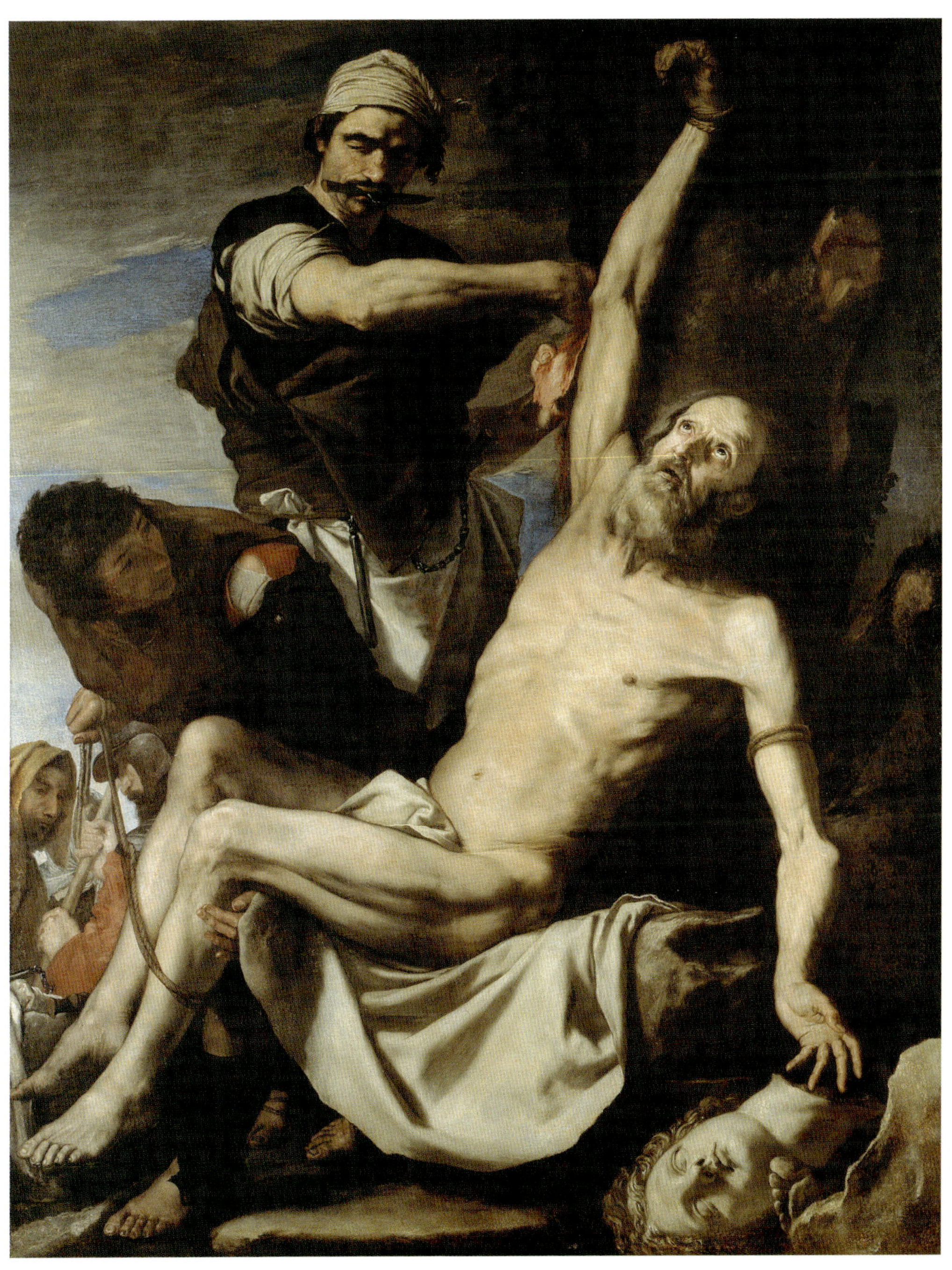

25 Workshop of Jusepe de Ribera, *Martyrdom of St. Bartholomew*, Stockholm, Nationalmuseum.

workshop was organized and the role Ribera played in the process. If the anecdote concerning the participation of Antonio Giordano is to be trusted, then Ribera kept close watch on the product. As already mentioned, the names of several assistants are known, but how they functioned in the manufacturing process remains a mystery. I suspect that the number was not fixed and rose and fell with demand. In any event, it could be argued that, given the distinctive compositional formulas that underlie his works, Ribera created a "look," as they say in the world of fashion today, that responded to the needs and tastes of the moment. "Lo riberesco," or the paintings that can be related to compositions by Ribera, is a phenomenon that we disparage at the cost of understanding how he became the leading painter of Naples and how he cultivated the market for his work at the court of Spain. In addition to the limpid clarity of his compositions, Ribera's paintings demand no specialized knowledge of classical or Christian texts; the subjects are self-evident. It is beyond the scope of this book to examine fully the role played by repetitions in creating a reputation; suffice to say that in a way, the copies, taken as a whole, magnified his prestige and enhanced his financial status. Further examples include *St. Andrew* in Brussels, Musées Royaux, which inspired a version now in the Prado, another in Dresden as well as four others; and *St. Humphrey* in St. Petersburg, signed and dated 1637, is the prototype of versions in Munich and Dublin, which are signed but not dated, as well as at least three more. To borrow again from the world of high fashion, the process can be described rather irreverently as: Look, Logo, Knock-off. With this thought in mind, let us now to turn to El Greco, whose modus operandi is not too different from that of Ribera.

Putting aside the consideration of specific problems, I want to return to the big picture and begin with the assertion that El Greco is the most complex painter of his epoch and one of the most complex ever to touch brush to canvas. At the root of the problem is the phenomenon of nationalism, an invention, as we know, of the nineteenth century. Having lived and worked in three different places and cultures – Greek, Italian, Spanish – El Greco has been claimed as a national cultural hero by each. The Spanish claim has led to the most serious misunderstanding of his art. El Greco was discovered in the late nineteenth century, when his singularity begged for an explanation. This was provided by Manuel Cossío, the author of the first monographic study, published in 1908.[5] Cossío knitted together two circumstances to explain El Greco's unique and occasionally bizarre art. Noticing, as others had done, that El Greco did not hit his stride until his move to Toledo in the early part of 1576, Cossío drew the conclusion that the special spiritual atmosphere of

Toledo served to stimulate El Greco's imagination. In his quest for a rational explanation of El Greco's sudden transformation, Cossio lighted upon the presence in the city just before the arrival of El Greco, of two of the most important mystical writers, St. Teresa of Avila and St. John of the Cross. This was a powerful idea, uniting a great, intense painter with the unforgettable emotional writings of the "out-of-body" experiences of these two visionaries. Among other factors, this imaginary union of painter and mystics had the virtue of all simplistic explanations – it reduced a complex subject to a neat, memorable, and seemingly rational formula. Such was the power of the idea that it is still prevalent today, despite the recent, concerted efforts to re-frame El Greco's art and career along other, more prosaic lines.

The re-interpretation of El Greco that has transpired in the last thirty years provides a more accurate, if less theatrical, vision of the artist. The turning point was the publication in 1981 of an annotated copy of 1555 of Vitruvius's treatise on architecture, discovered by Fernando Marías and Agustin Bustamante, who convincingly identified the author of the marginal notes as El Greco.[6] Despite the fragmentary nature of the marginalia, they showed El Greco's deep engagement with current Italian art theory. This discovery had been preceded by an article of 1967 by Xavier de Salas, who by chance had acquired a copy of the 1555 edition of Vasari's *Lives*, which recorded in the margins El Greco's opinions on some of the painters of the day. At the same time, Richard Kagan and I were examining El Greco's interactions with his Toledan clientele, the first results of which were published in the exhibition catalogue of 1982.[7] Our findings and interpretations, which aimed primarily at deconstructing the supposed links between the artist and the mystics and invigorating the somewhat dormant study of the artist, identified El Greco's "support group" as a small number of learned friends, many of whom were officials of the town and church. El Greco emerged from these writings and documents, some of which had been known for nearly a hundred years, as an irascible, stubborn, arrogant, and opinionated man, and a poor manager of his finances, flaws which were mitigated by a brilliant and profoundly original mind. As Kagan demonstrated, the artist was also unusually litigious; almost all his major commissions ended in disputes and sometimes in litigation, although he never won a case. El Greco had a high opinion of himself, which clearly was not shared by those who had hired him to deliver an altarpiece by a set time, only to find at the end that the work was undervalued. (Artists' compensation in Spain was inherently conflictive. Each side – painter and patron – hired their own expert to determine the price. The painter's expert aimed high, the one of the patron aimed low. Given the unequal power of the social system, the painters usually compromised or capitulated.) By dint of these character traits, El Greco alienated potential clients and had to scramble to sustain an apparently quasi-aristocratic lifestyle as a merchant-painter, specializing in devotional paintings and copies of his own works.

Since 1982, there has been intensive publication on El Greco, including a full-scale biography by Marías (1997), the papers of the symposia organized by Nicos Hadjinicolau and the unfinished catalogue raisonné by José Alvarez Lopera, whose premature and unexpected death in 2008 prevented him from completing his monumental and exhaustive work, two volumes of which were published in 2005 and 2007.[8]

Given El Greco's prickly personality, he could not depend on a fixed position with fixed emoluments. To stay solvent he organized a workshop, with a floating population. Some recent attempts have sought to reconstruct the activities of these assistants. As in the case of Ribera, I believe that this effort complements the major altarpieces as a way to deepen our understanding of the artist's personality and performance.

There are some clues as to how the workshop functioned. From September 1585 to around 1590, and again from 1604 to his death, the artist rented a spacious palace of the marquis of Villena, an ideal site to house a flourishing workshop. For major commissions of altarpieces, the artist assembled a team of painters, sculptors, gilders, and carpenters. In this respect, El Greco was following standard procedures for the fabrication of these monumental works (Toledo, Santo Domingo el Antiguo). Unfortunately, there were stretches of time between these major undertakings, time when El Greco had to resort to the retail trade to keep his household financially afloat. As the years went by, he fell deeper and deeper into debt and had to rely on the kindness of friends, just to survive. This fact alone may have caused him to ramp up the number of paintings produced by the workshop. To obtain a rough idea of the extent of this trade, we can turn to Wethey's monograph, where 460 paintings are classified as "school works, copies and wrong attributions."[9] The point is not so much whether Wethey's count is accurate; rather it is the sheer size of the operation, even if we omit a number of works. El Greco, far from being an isolated genius, was the most popular Spanish painter of his day.

There is one eyewitness to the workshop in practice, the painter Francisco Pacheco, who in 1611 visited the artist's dwelling. As he writes in his treatise, published in 1649: "In 1611, Dominico (*sic*) Greco showed me something which exceeds imagination — the originals of everything that he had painted in his lifetime, painted in oil on canvases smaller than a *cuadra*, that were shown to me at his orders by his son."[10] As Fernando Marías has pointed out, the word "original" as used by Pacheco can be interpreted in more than one way.[11] First would be to consider these pieces as *modelli*, or preparatory sketches. Another would be to think of them as *ricordi*, or copies made after the finished work. Some might have served both purposes. And finally they also might have functioned as a sample case for potential clients. Marías directs our attention to El Greco's death inventory of 1614, where forty-six small-scale works are recorded, mostly of subjects known to us from large versions. In the 1621 inventory, compiled by Jorge Manuel, the number had risen to ninety, some of which the painter's son may have done. The purpose of these small works is demonstrated by the *Expolio* and its descendants. The original, of course, was executed in 1577–79 for the sacristy of the Toledo cathedral, where it remains (pl. 26). Connected to the altarpiece are two small versions, one in Upton House (pl. 27), the other in the Barnes Foundation, Philadelphia (pl. 28). Both are considered as authentic, although their relationship to the altarpiece is not clear; that is to say, whether they are *modelli* or *ricordi*. For our purposes, the question need not be answered at this time. More to the point is how the composition is recycled in versions in Munich (Alte Pinacoteca), in the Prado, and in Toledo (Museo de Santa Cruz), none of which is considered as authentic.

This story can be told over and again. For instance, El Greco frequently painted images of St. Francis, including one known as *St. Francis and Brother Leo Meditating on Death*. The best version is in the National Gallery of Canada (pl. 29), which is signed but not dated (it appears to have been done in about 1600–05). The Prado owns one, also signed but not dated. The canvas in the Colegio del Patriarca, Valencia, is neither signed nor dated and has been attributed to the workshop. A third version in the Barnes Foundation, Philadelphia, is signed only (pl. 30). In addition, twelve more versions have been recorded. This manner of operation exposes the huge gap between El Greco's illusions and reality. He aspired to a social and intellectual status but was consistently undermined by his need for money. His success as a painter of devotional subjects forced him to rely on individual consumers looking to acquire an example of a fashionable artist, whereas he dreamed of large commissions that would offer the opportunity to display his spectacular, high-strung style.

As with Ribera, El Greco used experienced painters as his assistants. The name of the Italian Francesco Preboste appears in many El Greco documents, acting as a

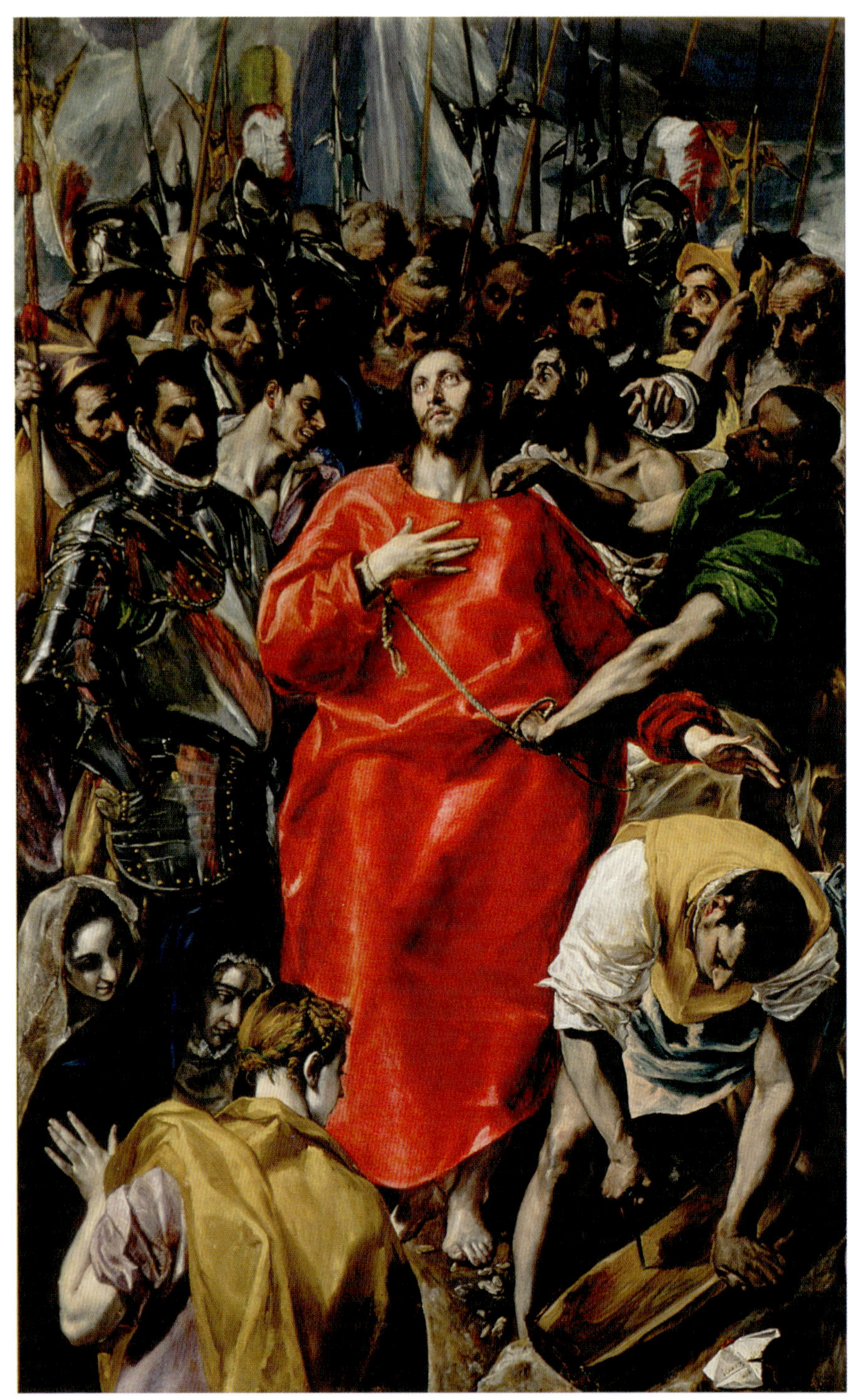

26   El Greco, *Disrobing of Christ*, Toledo, Cathedral, Sacristy.

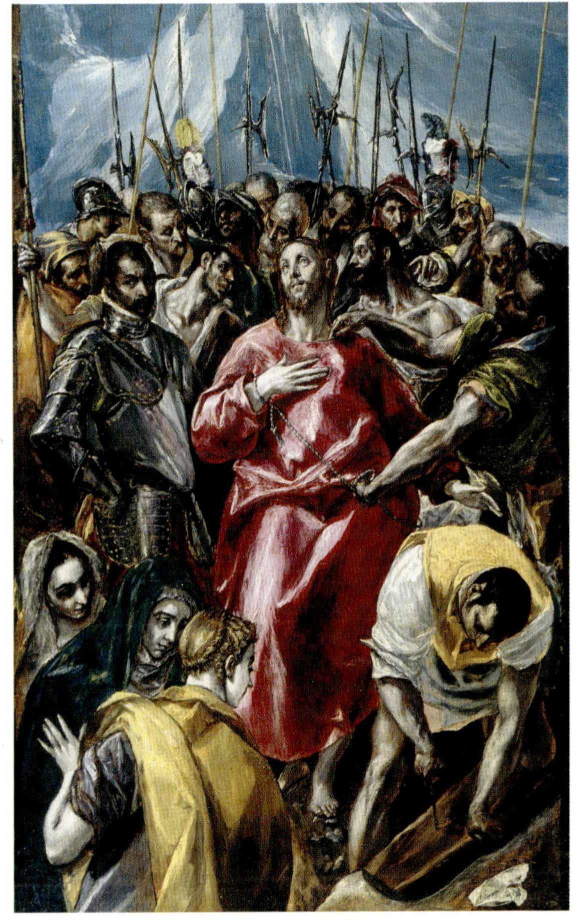

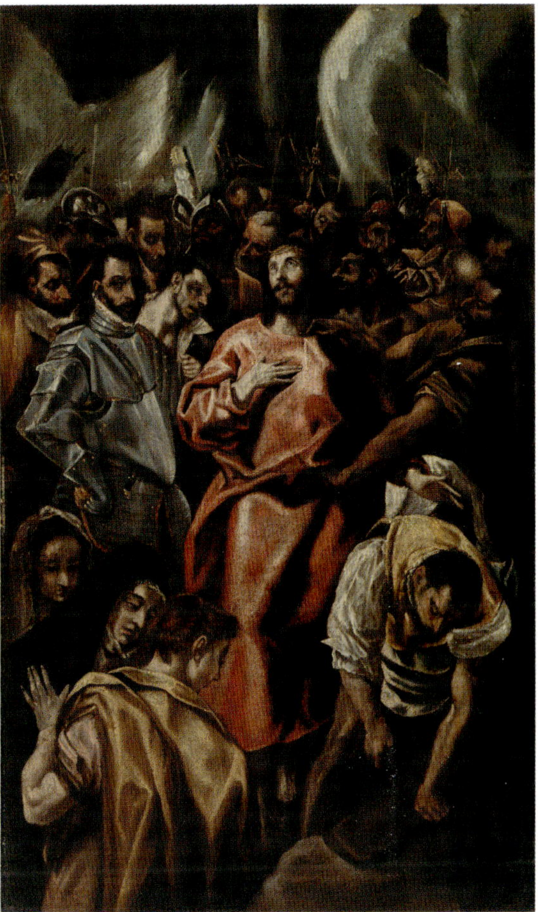

27   El Greco, *Disrobing of Christ*, Upton House, Warwickshire.

28   El Greco, *Disrobing of Christ*, Philadelphia, Barnes Foundation.

painter and business agent. Luis Tristán participated in the workshop from 1603–07. After a trip to Italy, he returned to Toledo, where he had a successful if abbreviated career. The best-known member of the shop was El Greco's son, Jorge Manuel (1578–1631), who was also his father's collaborator and closest follower.

Given the enormous popularity of the artist and consequent demand for his work, El Greco did as Ribera was to do some years later – he created a logo, which was his signature written in Greek in an elegant hand, to avoid "diluting the brand" (pl. 31) and to complicate the tasks of imitators, who had no direct link to the master

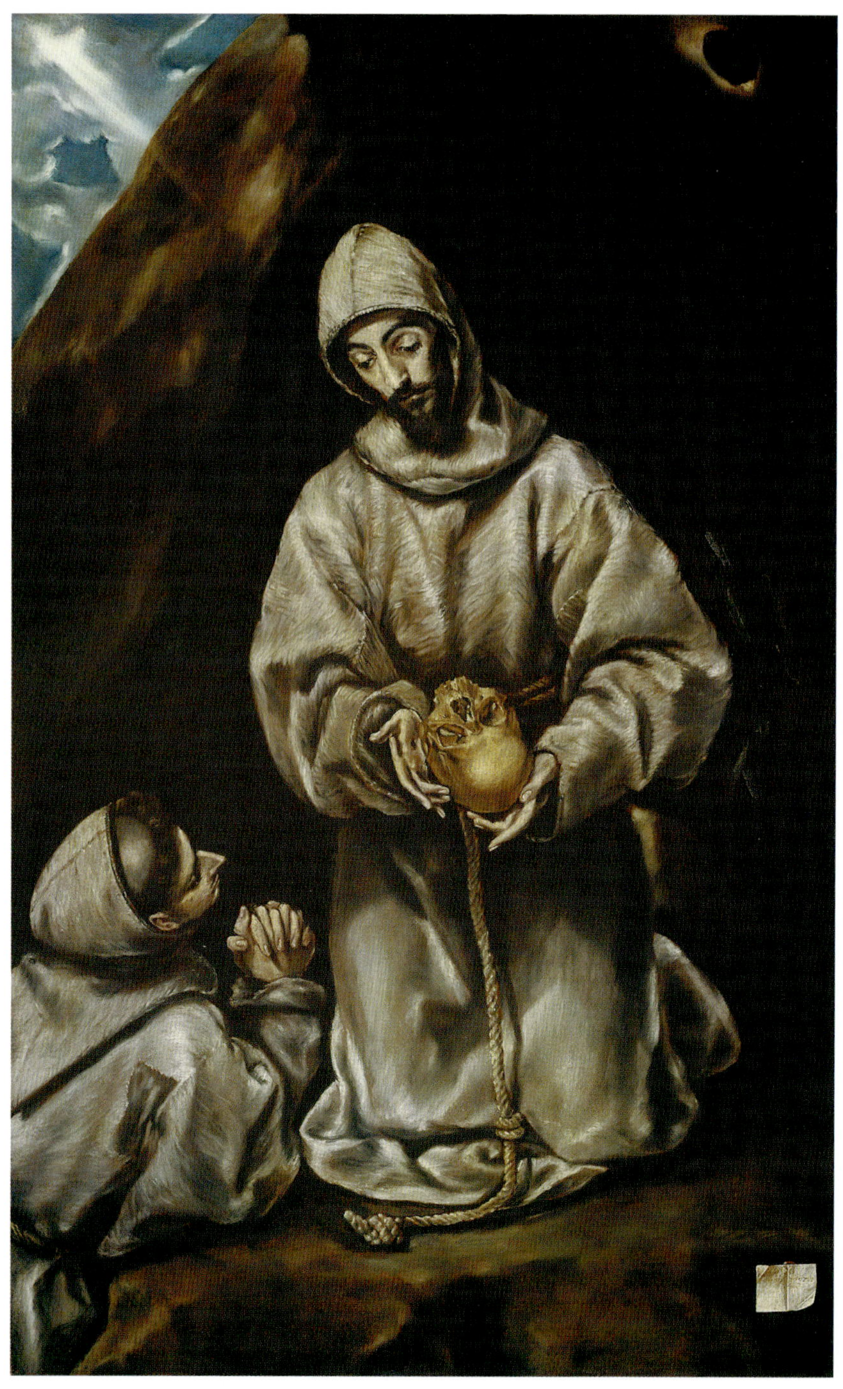

29   El Greco, *St. Francis and Brother Leo Meditating*, Ottawa, National Gallery of Canada.

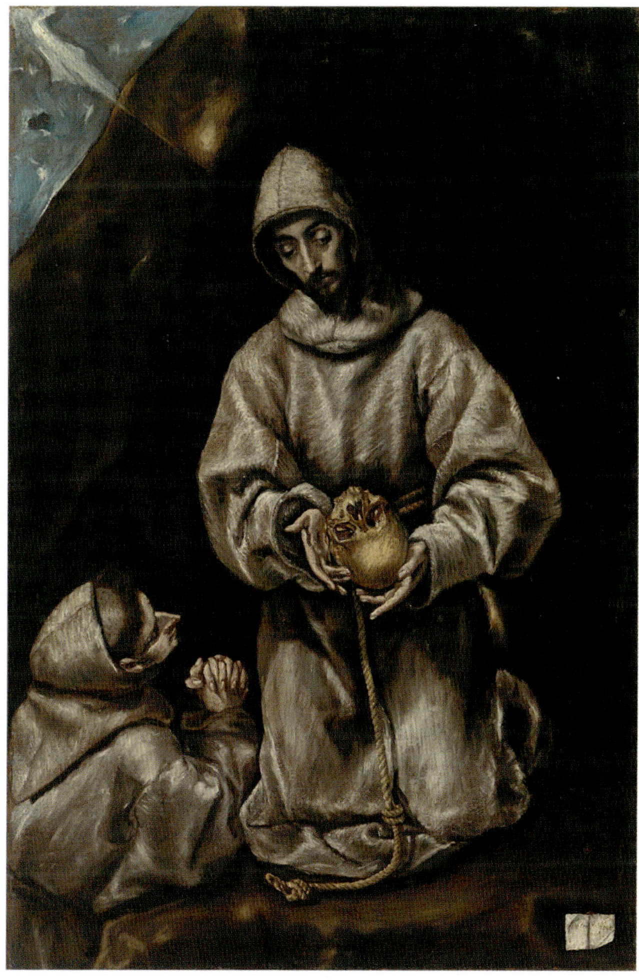

30 Workshop of El Greco, *St. Francis and Brother Leo Meditating*, Philadelphia, Barnes Foundation.

and his workshop. We will probably never be certain precisely how the workshop functioned because it seems not to have had set procedure. This factor always makes the acquisition of an El Greco a risky transaction. The rise of importance of Jorge Manuel after 1607, when he became a partner in the family business, produces yet another layer of complication. He was an able imitator of his father's idiosyncratic style, and the attributions of certain works have fluttered back and forth between the two of them (pl. 32).

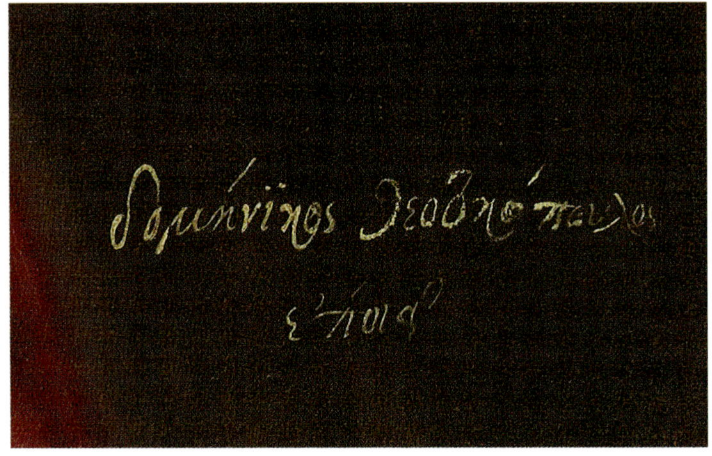

31 Signature of El Greco from *St. Jerome*, New York, Frick Collection.

There was a chasm between El Greco's ambitions and reality. His success as a devotional painter forced him to cater to the retail end of the market while he aspired to be a *pintor sabio*, working for the delight of a select few. The workshops of Ribera and El Greco, both modeled on Venetian practices of the late fifteenth to mid-sixteenth century, remind us that even the best artists had to earn a living in a profession that, with few exceptions, was poorly rewarded. Here the comparison with Ribera stops in its tracks. Ribera was a successful practitioner of an established style; El Greco invented his own manner of painting which is inimitable and highly personal but which nonetheless seems to have appealed to a wide range of *toledanos* with a few spare *reales* in their pockets.

As these two examples demonstrate, the problem of a painter's signature is vastly more complicated than it might seem to be. El Greco and Ribera apparently devised a distinctive signature to identify and protect the brand. However, this practice could have the opposite effect. The needs of the moment, or more likely, a change in the painter's aspirations and financial expectations, could require the head of a workshop to become a manufacturer of pictures. Thus, as we see in the case of Ribera and Antonio Giordano, the master might come along as an assistant was completing a picture and add the touches necessary to meet the standards of quality expected of an autograph work. And always lurking in the background were the unlicensed practitioners, also known as imitators and forgers. But let us stay within the four walls of the workshop. How do we detect collaborations and, no less important,

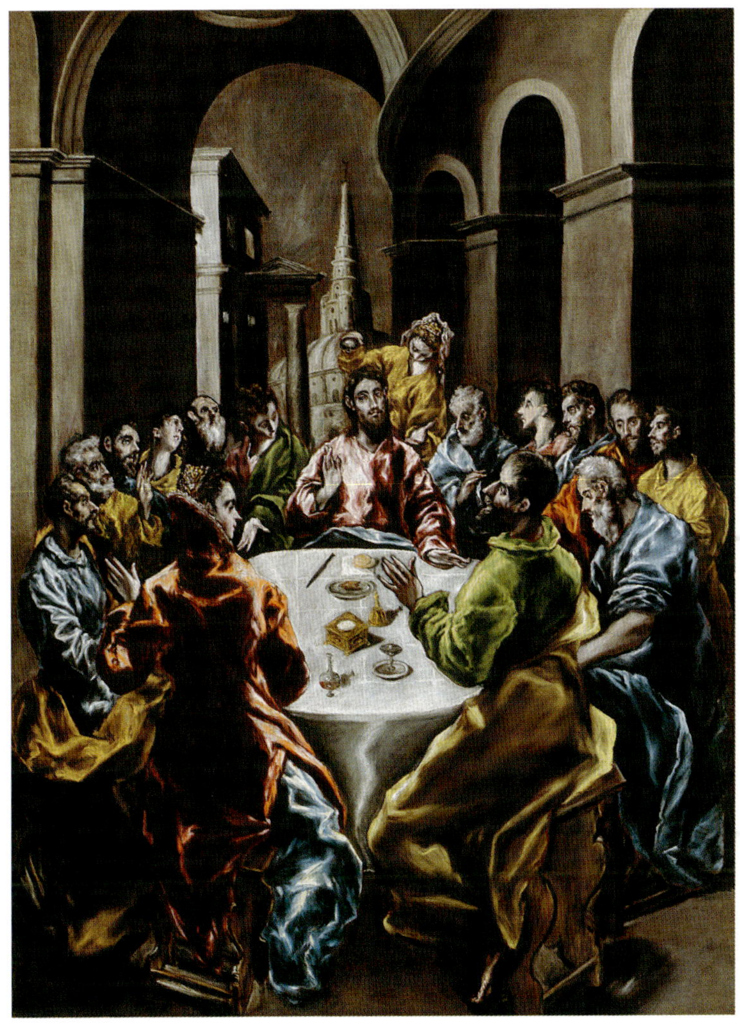

32 Jorge Manuel Theotocópoli, *Christ in the House of Simon*, Chicago, Art Institute.

how can we identify the persons who would buy a work in the knowledge that it was not fully authentic? Part of the answer can be found in death inventories of El Greco's clients, although the number is small in comparison to the putative output of El Greco, Inc.

Here we enter the world of speculation. In brief, I would suggest that clients were purchasing a Catholic image, not merely a painting. That is to say, the acquisition was intended to have a devotional function which was more important than the demonstration of artistry. A secondary consideration involved fashion, or in other words, style. Ribera and El Greco, as they settled in their new-found homes in Naples and Toledo, brought something exciting to the local artistic scene and thus altered the parameters of expectation among the local clientele.

A final observation is in order. It is not my intention to undermine the validity of a signature as the basis for a confirmed attribution, but only to suggest that the word "autograph" is used today with a confidence that is not warranted by the realities of the time in which the works were produced.

4

ART AT THE COURT OF
THE SPANISH HABSBURGS

It would be difficult to say with confidence when the subject of art at the courts of Europe began to attract the interest of historians. Certainly the social historian Norbert Elias was instrumental in laying the ground for what has become known as court culture, in which art plays a large if not always predominant role. The publication of *The Civilizing Process* in 1969 made an impact on historians of many stripes. The concept is now so ample as to include almost every type of social, political, musical, literary, and material expression which might be rallied to build and project the image of a powerful and virtuous prince.

In the English-speaking world, one of the important promoters of the study of court art was Roy Strong, who, in the early 1970s, began a period of frenzied activity devoted to the English court during the reigns of Elizabeth I and James I. Other landmark works are Michael Levey's *Painting at Court* of 1971 and the anthology, *The Courts of Europe*, edited by A. G. Dickens in 1977, which includes a ground-breaking essay on the court of Philip IV by John Elliott. To these I would add Martin Warnke's *The Court Artist* (German edition 1985; English edition, 1993). Of course the individual components of court art – painters, sculptors, architects, musicians, playwrights, decorative artisans – had all been examined under their

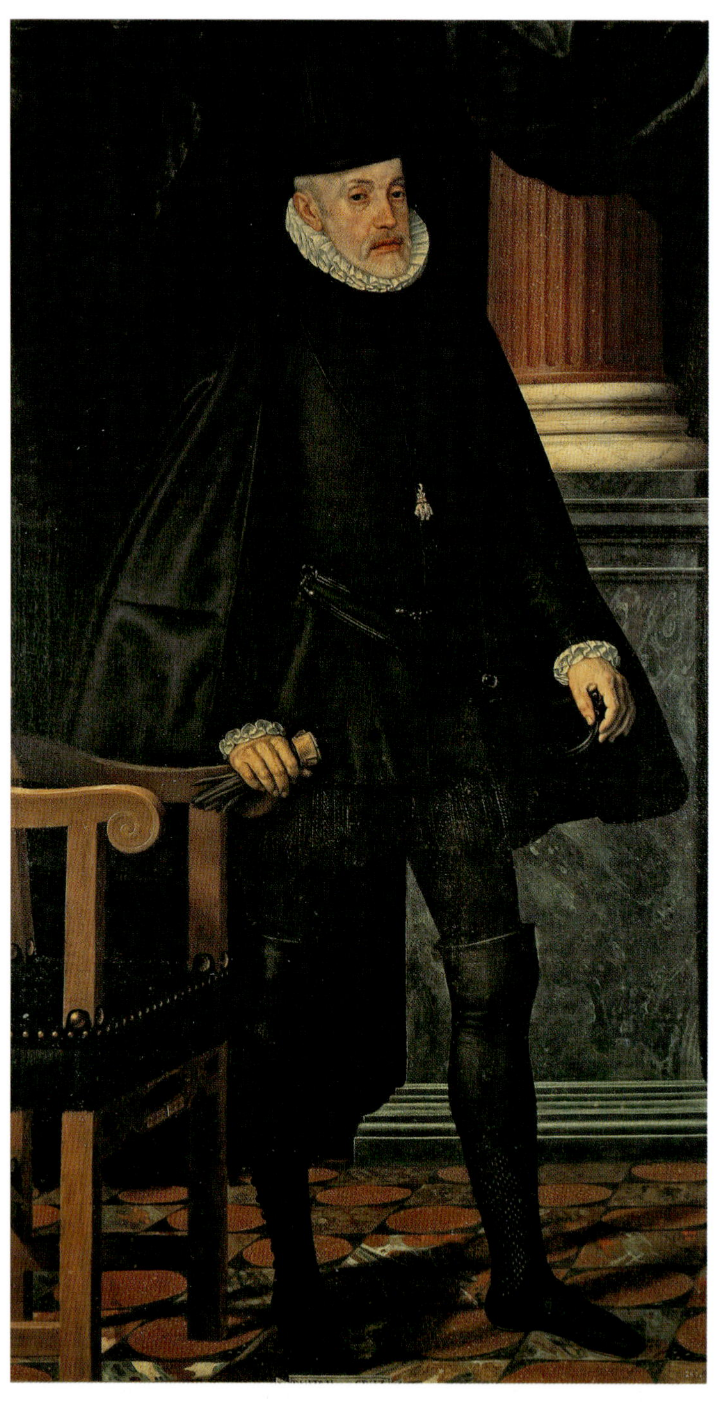

33   Juan Pantoja de la Cruz, *Philip II in Old Age*, Madrid, El Escorial, Patrimonio Nacional.

individual rubrics. The study of court art offered a big tent under which they all could seek shelter.

My way into the court of Spain was opened by Velázquez and specifically *Las Meninas*, which I interpreted in a courtly context. I will return to this subject in the next chapter. What truly awakened my interest was a short study I was commissioned to write on Philip II as a collector and patron of painting.[1] The occasion was the four-hundredth anniversary of the completion, in 1583, of the construction of El Escorial. I went to the library to read what had been written about his collecting, which turned out to be precious little. As I made my way through the bibliography on this component of El Escorial, it became apparent that the importance of the pictorial decoration was far greater than anyone had imagined. Nevertheless, I realized that both parts of the enterprise – architecture and painting – were linked.

As far as I could see, there were a number of possible explanations for the neglect of the subject. As always, the powerfully negative image of the patron, Philip II, headed the list. Hugh Trevor-Roper cites a particularly nasty characterization by the nineteenth-century English traveler Richard Ford, whose comments were inspired by a portrait of Philip II by Juan Pantoja de la Cruz (pl. 33): "The portrait is full of identity and individuality; here we see him in the flesh and spirit, lowering from his den, with a Medusa head that petrifies; his wan, dejected look is marked with the melancholy taint of his grandmother (Juana la Loca); observe his big, gray eyes, cold as frozen drops of morning dew; note the cadaverous chilliness, which even the pencil of Titian could not warm. The grave seems to give up its dead, and the suspicious scared bigot walks out the frame into his own library."[2]

Philip II had chosen to build the monument to his dynasty not in the political center of the monarchy, but in an isolated, somewhat remote location. El Escorial (pl. 34) was a day's trip from Madrid, not very far by the standards of the period, but far enough to discourage the king's subjects from making a pilgrimage unless they were prepared to spend the night. Imagine if the Escorial were located in the center of Madrid, on the site now occupied by the unfinished Palacio de Oriente; it would be as famous today as the Palais du Louvre. However, Philip had no interest in addressing his subjects. He was concerned with pleasing the Holy Trinity and the Blessed Virgin Mary. Hardly less important was his vow to find a suitable place to entomb the remains of his father, Emperor Charles V, and the future rulers of Spain.

Following the Spanish Civil War, Philip II's image took a further turn for the worse. He was appropriated by Francisco Franco. It is little known that the only

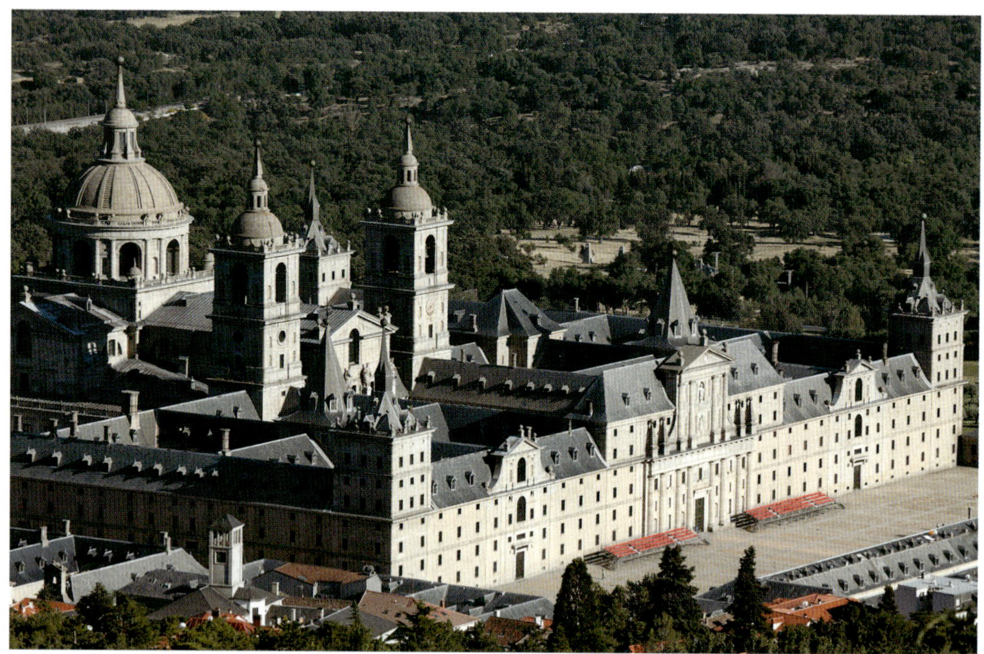

34   View of El Escorial, from north.

evidence we have of Franco as a man of letters is an essay published under his name on the Hall of Battles of El Escorial. Franco used the occasion to align himself with the Habsburgs and their creed of the state as the guardian of the true Christian faith. As reward for their devotion, the kings of Spain and their consorts would rise from the grave on Judgment Day and take their place among the saints and martyrs. The expected reward is depicted in Titian's *Gloria* (Prado) and El Greco's *Burial of the Count of Orgaz* (Santo Tomé Toledo). Although Franco was not quite audacious enough to order that his remains be buried in El Escorial, he nevertheless made his presence felt with the construction of the vapid Valle de los Caídos, just down the road from Philip II's imposing building.

Yet another obstacle was placed in the way of scholars, and especially art historians. The former crown properties had been nationalized and placed under the control of the Patrimonio Nacional. For eighteen years, ending in 1981, the CEO (*gerente*) was the conservative Fernando Fuertes de Villavicencio, who seemed to live in constant dread that something – anything – could harm the buildings and collections placed in his care. This attitude, which continued well past his tenure, made it difficult to have access to the *sitios reales* and the palace archives. Visitors to the former crown properties were handed over to guided tours and led along the same route. Perhaps fifty percent of the buildings and collections were hidden from view. Never seen were the collections of ecclesiastical vestments, of prints and drawings, of decorative arts, of rare books and manuscripts; access to these objects could be obtained only through a letter from the ambassador of your home country, testifying to your good faith. The fabulous holdings of tapestries and arms and armor did see the light of day, although not always under favorable conditions. I remember how the famous and fragile fifteenth-century tapestries, known as Los Paños de Oro (pl. 35) were put to use as adornment of a temporary altar erected in the Lonja in front of the monastery. The occasion was the celebration, in 1988, of the feast day of St. Lawrence (August 10th). Around 10 a.m., the tapestries were folded into quarters and transported on the backs of laborers, who then draped them on the dais, from which Mass would be celebrated later in the day. There they remained, exposed to the blazing sunlight of the Castilian summer until the conclusion of the service, which took place just before sunset. If the Paños were frying in the mid-day sun, great paintings, like Titian's *Martyrdom of St. Lawrence*, were lost in the shadows, in this instance, kept under lock and key in the Provisional Chapel.

Recently, the operations of the Patrimonio have been transformed and the buildings and collections are open to the public as never before. In this connection, I wish to recognize the tenure of Alvaro de Fernández-Villaverde, marquis of Santa Cruz, as President, and Professor Rosario Díez del Corral, the Asesora Cultural, as being exceptionally fruitful. Another milestone is Fernando Checa's *Felipe II: Mecenas de las artes*, 1992, which provided the first comprehensive overview of Philip's accomplishments in the realm of the visual arts.[3] A culmination was reached in 1995–2000 when the government of José María Aznar sponsored an extensive program of exhibitions and publications dedicated to Charles V and Philip II. As a result of these efforts and many, many more, El Escorial has received its due as one of the great monarchical buildings of the sixteenth century, and Philip II, as one of the great patrons of all time.

This is not the place to enter into an analysis of the Escorial. It will suffice to repeat that the basic function is to serve as a funerary monument dedicated to the dynasty of the Spanish Habsburgs as defenders of the true Christian faith. In form and function alike, the building is quite original. Indeed, even the length of time required to construct the fabric is noteworthy – 1563–83. (The decoration and furnishing consumed another twenty years.)

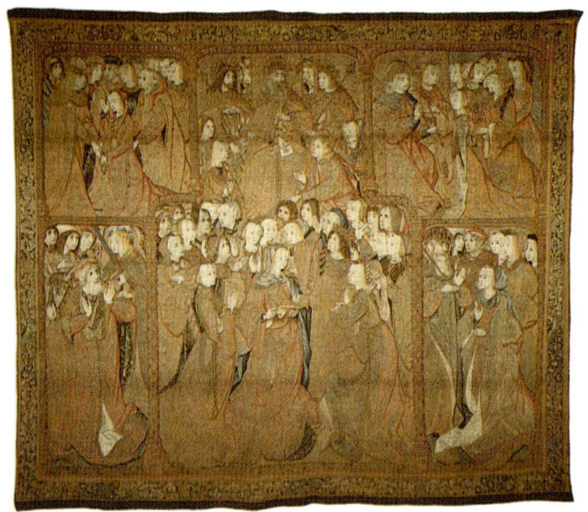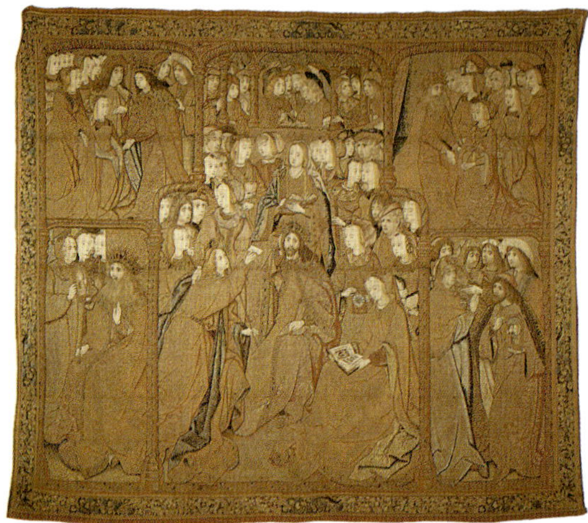

35 "Los Paños de Oro" tapestry panels, Madrid, Patrimonio Nacional.

The Escorial can be seen from another angle, as a demonstration of the role played by the European court as a transmitter and transformer of artistic modes. Over the last twenty years, there has been an increasing interest in cross-cultural exchanges. I will delve into this question in my discussion of painting in New Spain. Here I want to focus on the powerful impact of Philip II's patronage of Italian painters and how his aesthetic choices re-oriented the course of the practice of painting in Castile. By modifying these ideas to fit the existing systems of belief, Spanish painters formulated a local style.

Philip II was a firm partisan of the superiority of Italian art, which he had encountered during his two voyages to northern Italy en route to the Netherlands. From the first years of his reign, he favored Italian painters or Spaniards who had lived in Italy. His first appointment was Gaspar Becerra, who returned to Spain in 1557.[4] Becerra had been a member of the workshop of Giorgio Vasari and was fully conversant with Vasari's mannerist style. In 1562, he was recruited as a royal painter and created decorations in fresco and stucco at the Alcázar and El Pardo. Philip II, impatient to complete his mammoth project at El Escorial, decided to turn to Italians to paint the fresco cycles. These commissions are one of the largest enterprises of their kind in the sixteenth century, surpassed only by the decoration of the Vatican. There is another, purely practical reason for the choice – Italians were skilled fresco painters whereas there were hardly any to be found in Spain.

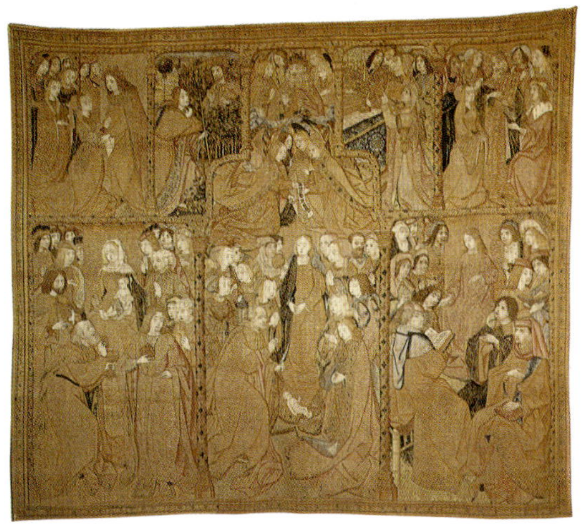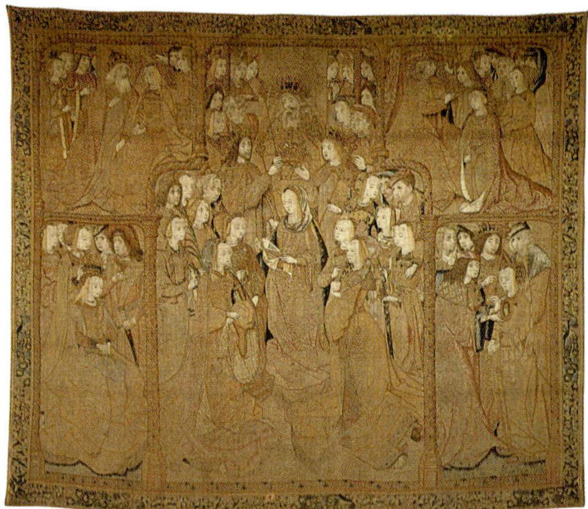

The fresco painters can be divided into two categories; one comprised decorative specialists, mostly from Genoa, who were assigned to paint such spaces as the sacristy of the Basilica, the chapter rooms, and the Hall of Battles. The other and more important coterie consisted of some of the leading Italian painters – Luca Cambiaso, who came to the site in October 31, 1585; Federico Zuccaro, who arrived in 1585; and Pellegrino Tibaldi, who was on the scene in 1586. Cambiaso executed the *Gloria* over the monk's Choir and Tibaldi was in charge of the fresco decorations for the cloister and the Library. Zuccaro was brought to the Escorial to paint the pictures for the major altar. His trial pieces did not win the king's favor and Zuccaro was dismissed in 1586. The one Spanish painter who earned the king's approval was Juan Fernández de Navarrete, who had lived in Rome for several years.[5] He moved to Madrid in 1565 and was soon appointed as royal painter. His premature death in 1579 was a blow to the king, who had counted on him to play a big role in the decoration of the Basilica.

The story of the decoration is long and complex and is best told at another time. I am taking this opportunity to exemplify the court as a major agent in the transmission of Italian artistic ideas and techniques to Spain. Philip's decision to ignore the local talent and use imported labor was not novel. François I had already blazed the trail by luring Italians to his court, including no less a figure than Leonardo da Vinci. Rudolph II is another example of how a single-minded ruler possessed the power to alter the course of painting in his court and domains. In this way, Italian art crossed frontiers; we must imagine a constant ebb and flow of artists and artisans from Italy to almost every part of Europe if we wish to understand how the art of painting developed in the late sixteenth century. I am hardly the first art historian to make this observation. However, I do want to emphasize these dynamic examples of "La peinture sans frontières."

The reverberations of Philip's choices echo through the succeeding decades, as the leading painters of the young generation in Castile were now competent to produce up-to-date interpretations of the Italians summoned to Spain by Philip II.[6] Some of these artists, who would be the principal royal painters of the reign of Philip III, were the offspring or relations of Italians who had decided to remain in Castile. Their names are fairly well known and include among them Vicente Carducho, younger brother of Bartolomé and tenacious rival of Diego Velázquez at of the court of Philip IV.

A drastically abbreviated summary of the transformation of painting in Castile initiated by the patronage of Philip II is useful at this point and can be exemplified by an interpretation of the Annunciation by painters of three generations. Juan Correa de Vivar (1510–1566) represents painting in Castile around the middle years of the century; he executed this work in Toledo in 1559, a year after Philip's ascent as king of Castile. Correa's understanding of Italian painting is partial, noticeable in the scale and treatment of the figures and the composition, which still have a whiff of the Flemish painting that dominated in the first half of the century (pl. 36). Federico Zuccaro's version, executed in 1586 and placed in the Basilica (pl. 37) demonstrates mastery of the canons of central Italian painting toward the end of the sixteenth century. One of Zuccaro's assistants, Bartolomé Carducho (c. 1560–1609), eventually became a royal painter to Philip III (1598–1621). In his dual role of artist and importer of paintings from his native Florence, Carducho was to become the conduit for Florentine art to Madrid. After 1600, the impact of re-formulated Florentine painting became the norm in Castile. This power was magnified by familial relationships. Bartolomé's younger brother, Vicente (c. 1576–1638), was to emerge as the most important painter at the Spanish court until the arrival of Velázquez in 1623. Eugenio Cajés (1574–1634), the son of Patrizio Caxesci (Cajés), may be little known today, but he became another beneficiary of the clan initiated by Federico Zuccaro. In a version of the Annunciation by Vicente Carducho (pl. 38), dated 1616, the infiltration of Tuscan painting in Castile is fully accomplished. The latter would prevail until 1638, when Carducho died and Velázquez took charge of painting at court.

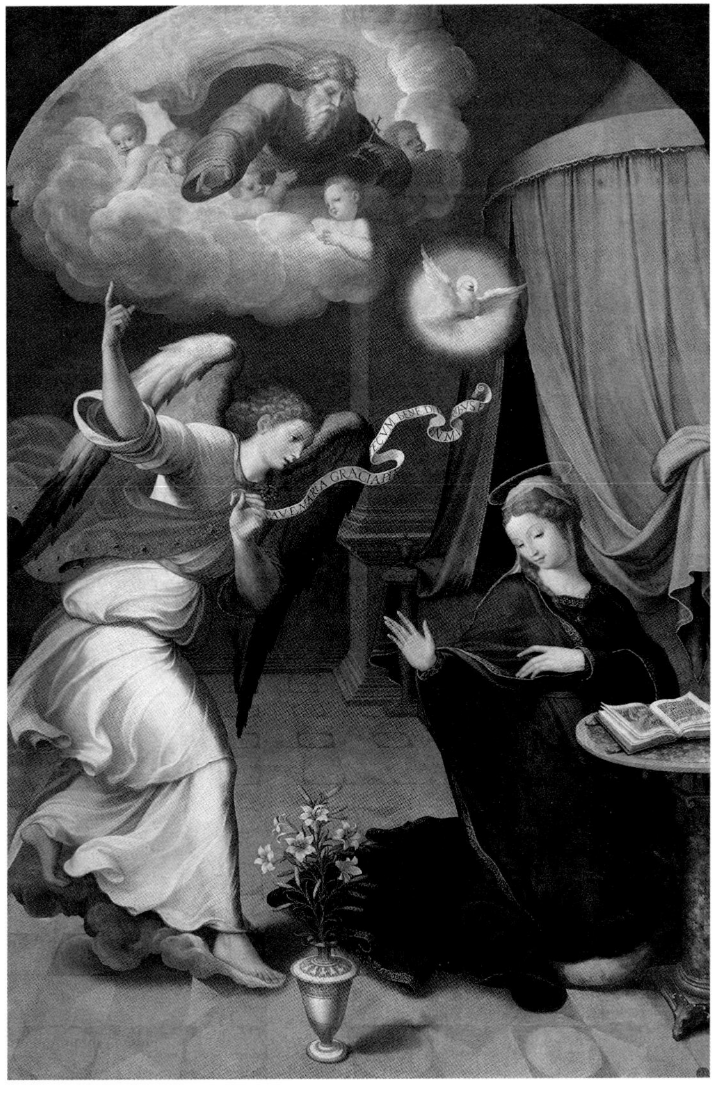

36   Juan Correa de Vivar, *Annunciation*, Madrid, Museo del Prado.

The oil paintings installed in other spaces of the Escorial were heterogeneous, although the majority were sent from Flanders and Italy. About a thousand were brought from Madrid; the highlights are paintings by Titian, Veronese, Tintoretto, Bosch, van der Weyden, and Patinir. By the time of his death in 1598, Philip possessed the largest and finest collection of paintings to be found anywhere. Between

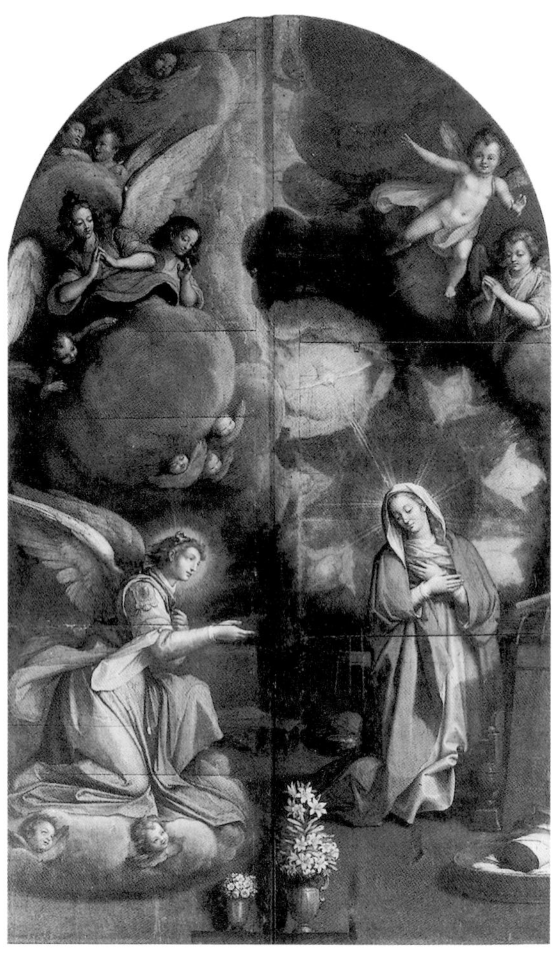

37   Federico Zuccaro, *Annunciation*, Madrid, El Escorial, Basilica.

the collections housed in El Escorial, the Alcázar of Madrid, and the Palacio de El Pardo, there was a virtual encyclopedia of Flemish and north Italian painting of the fifteenth and sixteenth centuries available to Spanish painters of the early seventeenth century.

The architecture of the Escorial combines Flemish and Italianate sources in an original way. It evinces a highly restrained, virtually unadorned Italian Renaissance classicism, which is surprisingly mixed with the slate roof and towers commonly used in the Netherlands. This unprecedented combination is a reflection of the

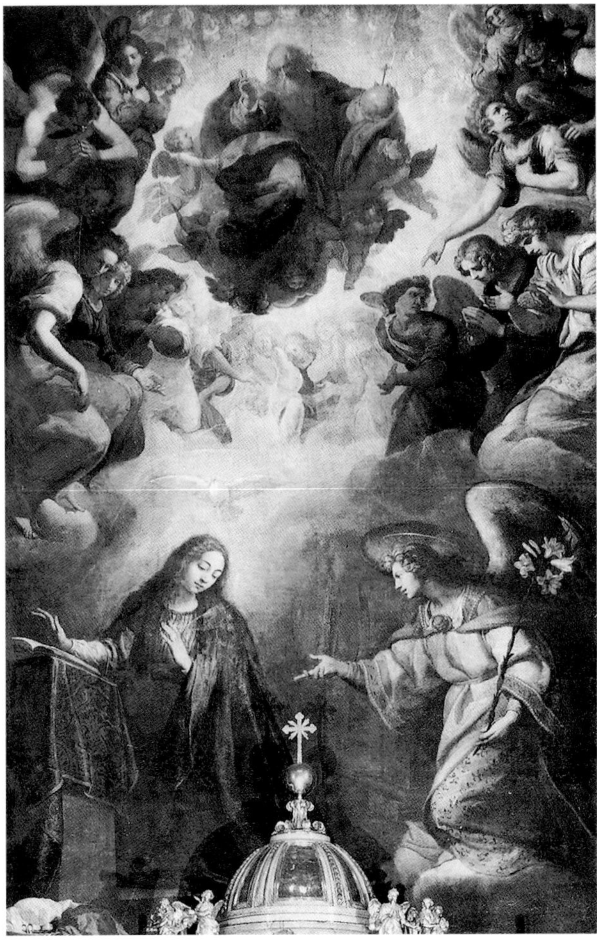

38 Vicente Carducho, *Annunciation*, Madrid, Convento de
la Encarnación.

crown's territorial dominions in Italy (Naples and Lombardy) and the Netherlands. Although the style had no ancestors, it had many descendants in Castile, where it became a signature of the patronage of the Spanish Habsburg monarchy. The best-known example, although construction was not commenced until after the king's death, is the Plaza Mayor, Madrid, which has been subject to several modifications through the centuries.

To return to my point of departure, a major conduit for the flow of artistic goods was the court of Spain during the two centuries of rule by the Habsburg dynasty.

How is it possible then that, as late as 1976, there was very little written about the patronage and collecting of Emperor Charles V, not to mention his close relatives in Flanders and Austria – Margaret of Austria, Mary of Hungary, and Rudolph II being the cream of the crop? Only one scholar had the insight to see that the Habsburgs were by far the greatest patrons and collectors of the sixteenth and seventeenth centuries – greater by far than the Medici, the Gonzaga, the Este, the Sforza, the Farnese, and a long list of papal collectors and patrons, including Julius II and Paul III. This was Hugh Trevor-Roper, who in 1976 published a series of lectures with the title *Princes and Artists. Patronage and Ideology at Four Habsburg Courts, 1517–1633.*[7] His choices are Charles V, Philip II, Rudolph II, and the Archdukes Albert and Isabella, governors of the Spanish Netherlands. I would take exception to the inclusion of Charles V, who played on the international stage and was in Spain on only three occasions. In addition, Charles was not known as a serious collector, although he was an outstanding patron. In seeking common ground between these other great artistic figures, Trevor-Roper, a historian, put it this way: "Among these competing courts of Europe, I have chosen the Habsburg courts partly because the rulers of the house of Habsburg showed the most continuous interest in the arts, partly because the changing pattern of patronage in their several and successive courts illustrates vividly, as I believe, the distinct phases of the great ideological crisis of the time [by which he means the wars of religion]."[8]

There were of course three other Spanish Habsburgs who ruled in the seventeenth century – Philip III, Philip IV, and Charles II. They never aroused much interest among historians of Italian, French, English, German, or even Spanish art. Little was known about these three monarchs, leading people to the assumption that there was little to be known at all. These are the tropes that were used to define the successors to Philip II. Philip III was ineffectual and left the conduct of state policy to the upstart nobleman, the duke of Lerma. Philip IV was misguided into political and financial disasters by the powerful favorite, the count-duke of Olivares, and presided over the decline of Spain. Charles II, the last of the line, was mentally deficient. On top of this, the rulers had to grapple with the legacy of Philip II. His style of court culture continued to influence his successors. This style was like no other and was determined in the later years of the reign by strict observance of the rituals of the faith. Philip seldom appeared in public; he sponsored no pageants or processions, no masques or dances, no theatrical representations. He prayed, he confessed, and he governed. His taste in clothing was almost Jesuitical. In sum, his was a court without visible splendor, the very antithesis of the courts

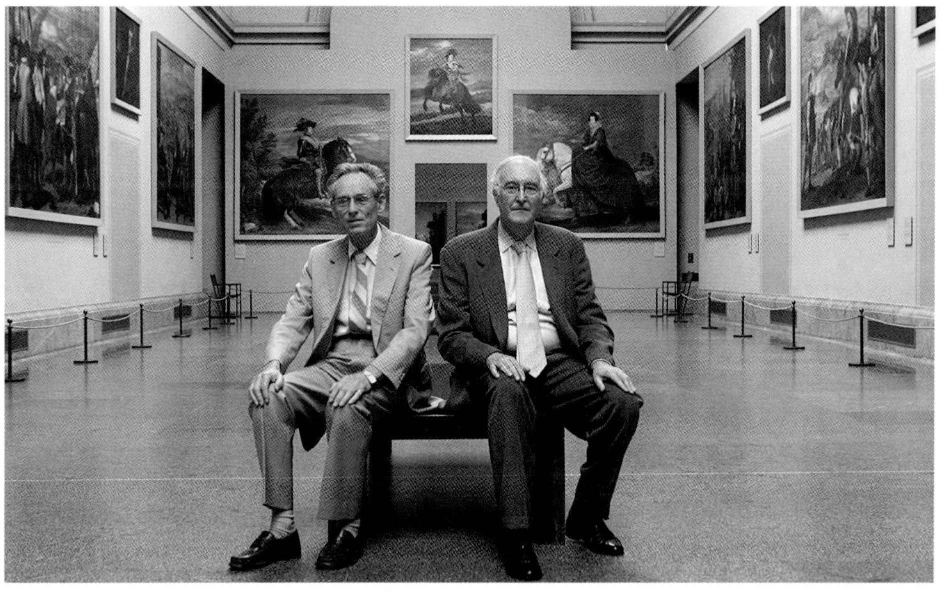

39   John Elliott and Jonathan Brown in temporary exhibition (Museo Nacional del Prado) of
Hall of Realms, 2005.

of England, France, and Italy. His successors could not have hoped, or wanted, to
emulate these practices.

We now know, of course, a great deal about the courts of "los Habsburgos
menores." As I said before, I found my way through the gloomy magnificence of
the Alcázar during the reign of Philip IV in search of Velázquez. It would be quite
a while before I caught up with him, and then it was only with the assistance of
the pre-eminent historian of early modern Spain, Sir John Elliott (pl. 39).

The year was 1973, when John left the University of London to take up his
appointment as Professor of History at the Institute for Advanced Study in Princeton.
He arrived just as I had resigned my professorship at Princeton to accept the directorship of the Institute of Fine Arts. As I remember, we first met at a lecture I gave
at Princeton on *Las Meninas* as a sort of valedictory to the department which had
served as my professional home for thirteen years. John came forward and introduced
himself at the conclusion of the lecture (which was much transformed when I
published it in 1978). We agreed to meet and discovered that we had much in
common, especially a passionate interest in the reign of Philip IV and a desire to
re-integrate the history of Spain into the history of Europe. In the course of one

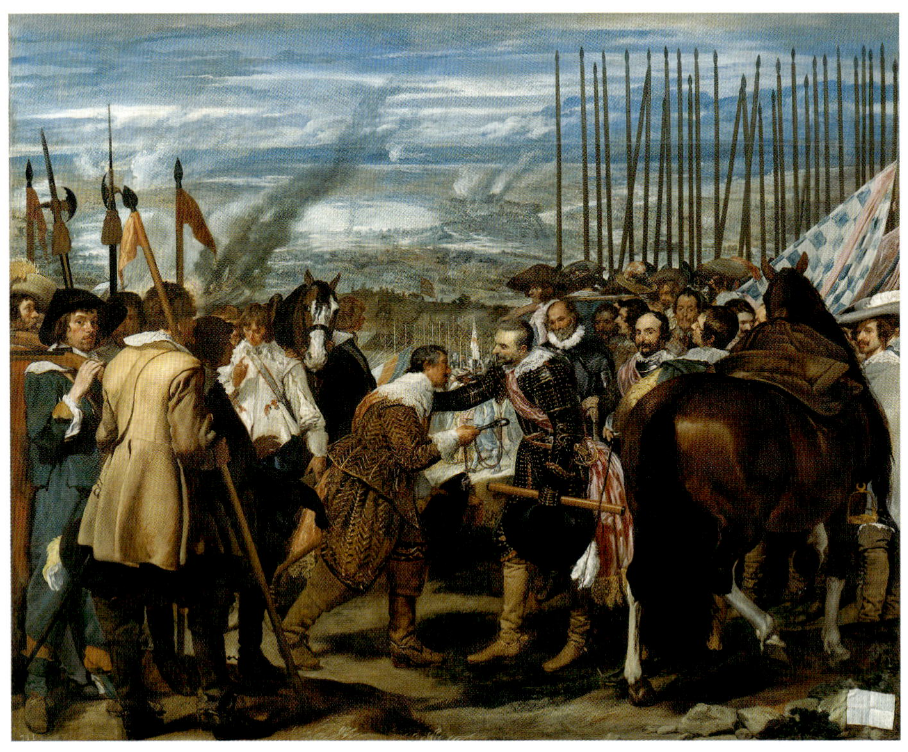

40   Diego Velázquez, *Surrender of Breda*, Madrid, Museo del Prado.

of our chats, we talked about a recent series edited by Hugh Honour and John Fleming entitled "Art in Context," thinking to write on the *Surrender of Breda* (pl. 40), which would combine John's long-term research on the count-duke of Olivares with mine on Velázquez. The more we looked at the project, the more we could see that any attempt to understand the painting had to take into account the site for which it was executed, the Hall of Realms of the Palace of the Buen Retiro. It was not long before we recognized that we would have to include the palace and the gardens to really round out the project. This was a fine idea, except that the palace had largely vanished, having collapsed under the weight of the hasty, shoddy original construction and British cannon fire during the Peninsular War (known in Spain as the War of Independence). The importance of the Retiro had been recognized by the great German Hispanist Carl Justi in his classic book *Velázquez and His Century*, published in Bonn in 1888. His account is the first serious attempt to reconstruct the history of the palace and its uses. Otherwise, the palace paid the price of its almost-total destruction; most of the subsequent research was based on the fact that Velázquez was a major contributor to the pictorial decoration. The time had come to build our castle in the sky.[9]

During the summers of 1975–77, we researched in the Archivo del Palacio Real; the Archivo Municipal, Madrid; the Archivo Histórico de Protocolos, Madrid; the Archivo Nacional; and the Archivo General de Simancas. Fortunately, the twisting route through Protocolos had been illuminated by María Luisa Caturla, the independent scholar who often laid claim to her discoveries by writing her name in blue pencil at the top of the document – thus spake "Caturla."

In the summer of 1978, I left my post as Director of the Institute of Fine Arts and accepted a one-year appointment as a Visiting Fellow at the Institute for Advanced Study. One circumstance that favored the collaboration is that we had kept our house in Princeton, located a mere five minutes from the Institute and the house of Oonah and John Elliott. Another was that, by arrangement, our offices were side by side in the West Building of the Institute. I have often been asked how our collaboration was accomplished, a question that is deceptively easy to answer. Propinquity was essential; e-mail had not yet been invented and it would have been very difficult to complete the work were we not neighbors at home and at work. We were fortunate in that our prose styles were similar – lucid, concise, and supple, if I may be allowed to say so. We were bent on writing a book that could be read with profit and pleasure by anyone, specialist or not, with an interest in later European history. Such differences as existed between our writing styles were smoothed over by the constant reading and correcting of each other's text, which imparts stylistic unity to the book. This method requires a sturdy but flexible ego and a willingness to accept criticism. And, of course, the pace of writing had to be fast because the deadline was determined by the expiration of my fellowship in June and the return to full-time teaching in New York. Mental stamina therefore became a very important pre-requisite.

As the research progressed, our ambitions expanded. What had started as a short monograph on the *Surrender of Breda* morphed into a reconstruction of the palace and inevitably an examination of the patron, Olivares, who was squeezed between the costs of fighting wars in France and Germany while simultaneously spending large sums of money on a pleasure-palace that would be used only a few weeks per year. The count-duke was removed from his favored position at court in 1643, but not before he had struck gold, the gold of the Golden Age. Among the small army of first-class artists and artisans who worked at the Buen Retiro were the giant figures of Velázquez and Pedro Calderón de la Barca. We attempted to write a detailed study of patronage in action, a total history, as we called it, and to test the possibilities of a full-scale collaboration between a political historian and an art historian.[10]

This account is somewhat misleading in that it might suggest that we each dumped our knowledge into a mixing bowl and flipped the switch. From my point of view, this was certainly not the case. As I was soon to discover, Spanish history was known to me in a superficial way. I always had worked from the image to the text, which unavoidably left big gaps in my historical knowledge.[11] I also discovered that, by relying mostly on published histories of Golden-Age Spain, I accepted received knowledge as authentic knowledge. While searching for new information on his subject, the count-duke of Olivares and his impact on the domestic and foreign affairs of the Spanish monarchy, John had mined the archives of Spain and other European countries.[12] This hard-won knowledge imparts an authority and depth to his writings, which I greatly admire, and it was crucial to the writing of our book. To cite one example of the reach of his studies: he kept in his office, on a shelf just behind his desk, a green metal box that contained index cards. It turned out that, in his almost illegible scrawl, he was compiling biographical information on just about every person at the Spanish court who was mentioned in the documents. Whenever I came across mention of one of these people, I could get immediate, unpublished information simply by knocking on the door of John's office. Our collaboration, the first of several, has left me somewhat skeptical of art-historical writings that begin with a chapter on the "historical background." History and art history may overlap a certain points, but their goals and working methods are by no means identical. Although we judge our attempt to be a success, we do admit that the planets have to be aligned for those wishing to undertake such a venture.

The Retiro brought the Spanish court into line with court cultures in other parts of Europe; it was a stage for plays, machine plays (*comedias de tramoyas*), mock aquatic battles, battles between wild animals, and other pleasurable pastimes. As a projection of the power and glory of the monarch, the palace seems to have been almost as effective as Olivares had desired. Several foreign ambassadors and travelers commented on it. As they observed, the Retiro had a personality unlike that of any other European court. The huge size of the palace and grounds was itself astonishing. Equally amazing, if not perplexing, was the architecture, which was modeled on the Escorial, a building that no one associates with pleasures of the senses.

Fortunately, all agreed that the austerity of the Retiro's exterior was balanced by the lavish decoration of the interior. None of the furnishings and decorative elements has survived, but a goodly number of the paintings are in the Museo del Prado, although many are relegated to storage for lack of space. (There are enough excellent paintings in the basement to start "Prado II", which would not suffer in comparison to Prado I – the museum we know today.) The pictorial decoration was singular in that many paintings were made to form part of a series. We focused on these ensembles, which were not unpublished but certainly were under-studied. One example is the Landscape Gallery, a series of twenty-four landscapes in a horizontal format and another twenty-four or so in a vertical format, all executed by northern painters resident in Rome, including Claude Lorrain and Nicolas Poussin. Another consisted of scenes from Roman imperial life, the work of painters residing in Naples, such as Domenichino and Giovanni Lanfranco. (The latest word on these innovative series is to be found in the catalogues of two exhibitions, organized by Andrés de Ubeda, the Prado's curator of eighteenth-century Italian painting – *Paintings for the Planet King: Philip IV and the Buen Retiro Palace* (2005), and *Roma. Naturaleza e ideal. Paisajes 1600–1650* (2011).[13]

Perhaps the best-known component of the Retiro is the one that interested us too – the Hall of Realms, the major gallery of state, completed in 1635 (pl. 41). As early as 1911–12, the Hall of Realms had been reconstituted by Elías Tormo, one of the founding fathers of modern art history in Spain. The decoration consists of twelve battle scenes depicting Spanish victories won during the reign of Philip IV, ten scenes from the life of Hercules by Zurbarán, and five equestrian portraits of Philip III, Margarita de Austria, Philip IV, Isabel de Borbón, and the heir to the crown, Baltasar Carlos. Three of the portraits of rulers are by Velázquez and assistants (pl. 42). In its totality, the Hall of Realms is one of the most important political statements made in an artistic medium during the course of the seventeenth century. By a stroke of luck, all but one of the paintings is extant and they are kept in the Museo del Prado. Even more extraordinary, despite the near total destruction of the Retiro Palace, the Hall of Realms remains standing, embedded in what was originally the north quarter of the Palace. The building is also known by its traditional name, the Museo del Ejército (The Army Museum), and was founded in 1841 and subsequently expanded to its present form. It was obvious to us that the Hall of Realms should be restored to life, not only for its unique artistic and cultural value but also as a reminder of the immense creativity of the Golden Age of Spain.

We started to lobby for the re-creation soon after the publication of the first edition of *A Palace for a King* in 1980. Like petitioners to Philip's bureaucracy, we were kept waiting and waiting and waiting. Then in 1996, when the conservative party won the

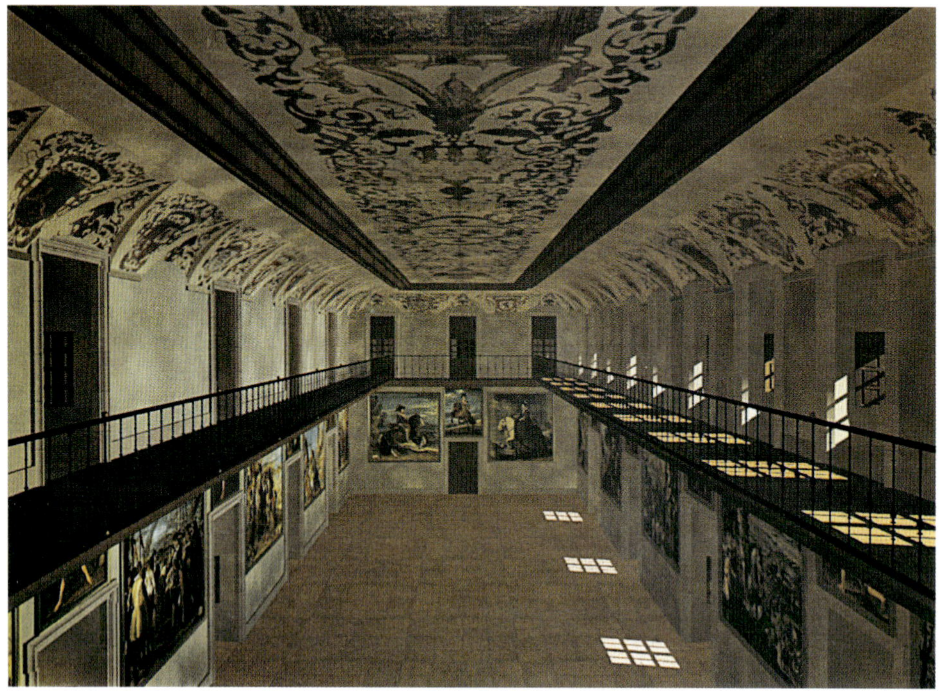

41   Carmen Blasco, reconstruction of Hall of Realms, Madrid, Museo del Prado.

elections, there was considerable interest in the highest echelons of the government to bring the Hall of Realms back to life (pl. 43). Obstacles remained and they were by no means insignificant. As mentioned, the building had long served as the Museo del Ejército and the installation consisted in large measure of trinkets and trophies of war, all presided over by a large-scale equestrian portrait of General Franco. The government, headed by José María Aznar, took the decision to move the collections to Toledo and to provide a structure built for the purpose of an army museum. This decision was controversial, to say the least, but the plan was accomplished.

Once the gallery spaces were released, the first phase of this ambitious project was finished. Next, preliminary discussions commenced, involving the incorporation of the site into the jurisdiction of the Prado and the reconditioning of the Hall of Realms (which is only one small portion of the usable space; the rest would be available for the display of the permanent collection). Then on March 11, 2004, the terrorists struck and the socialists suddenly found themselves in power. As might be expected they had scant interest in the Hall of Realms; the Centro de Arte Reina

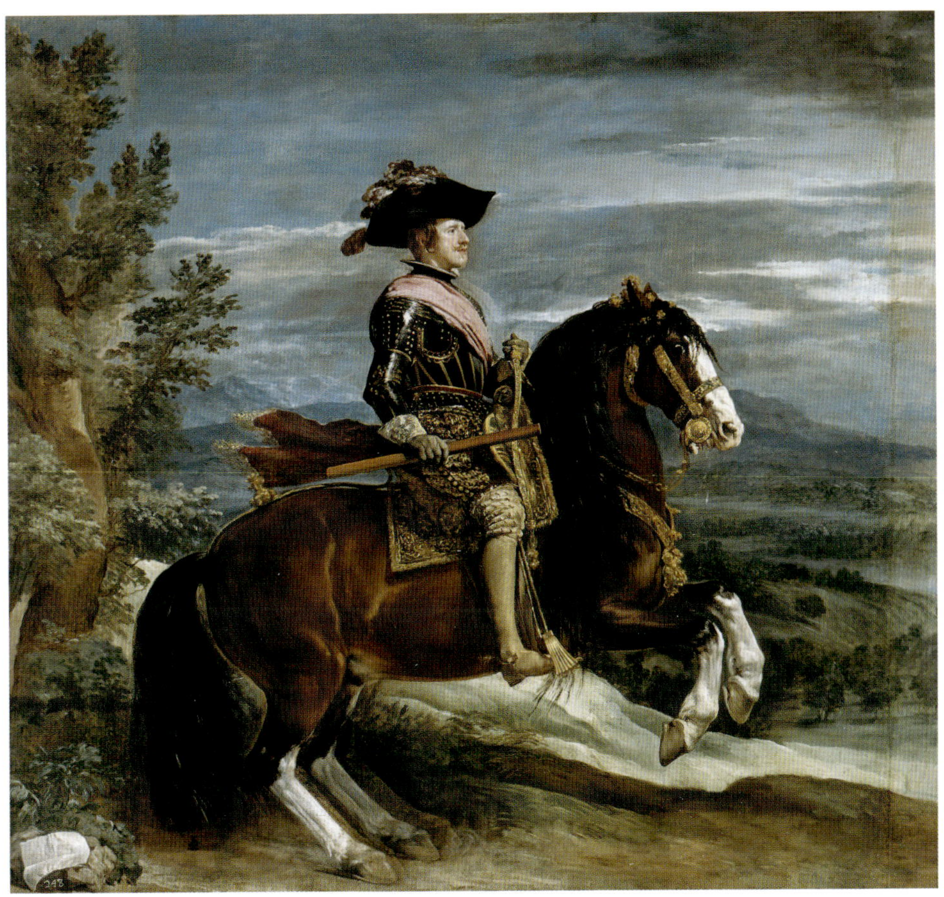

42 Diego Velázquez, *Philip IV on Horseback*, Madrid, Museo del Prado.

Sofía was nearer their heart. Obviously now is not the moment to contemplate state-sponsored plans for costly cultural ventures. As far as I know, the former Army Museum is currently occupied by staff of the Prado. We continue firmly to believe that the re-creation of the Hall of Realms would be unique as an artistic showcase, a tourist attraction, and, above all, a living reminder of Spain's cultural achievements during its Golden Age.

If at times Philip IV seems like a remote spectator to the construction of the Retiro, he was in reality taking great interest, particularly in the assemblage of some eight-hundred paintings that had been acquired almost overnight. Most were by living artists, making the Retiro the first museum of contemporary art. (This

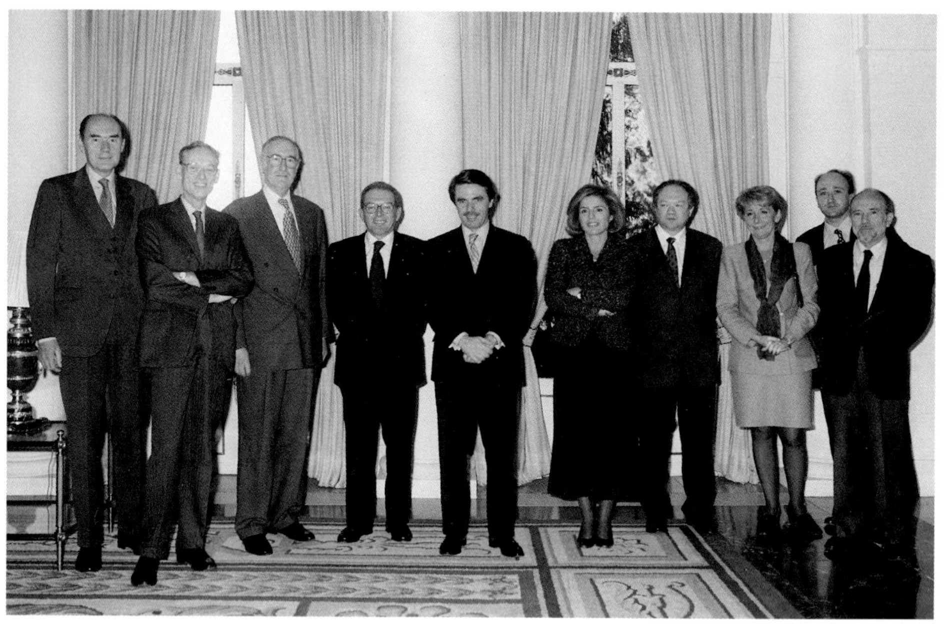

43   From left to right: Marqués de Tavarón, John Elliott, Jonathan Brown, Eduardo Serra, José María de Aznar, Ana Botella de Aznar, Fernando Checa, Esperanza Aguirre, Miguel Angel Cortés, Antonio Fernández Ordoñez.

observation should not be taken too literally.) By the time of the king's death in 1665, he possessed the largest and best collection in the world. This is the hallmark of the culture of his court. His interest in fine painting, specifically Venetian painting of the sixteenth century, was intensified by the visit of Peter Paul Rubens to Madrid in 1628–29. Rubens set up his easel and created painting after painting, thus becoming a source of inspiration and rivalry to Velázquez. No less important, Rubens made the ideal of painter-courtier a living reality, which could only have enflamed Velázquez's desire to elevate his social standing.

Philip's passion for paintings and the history of his acquisitions were not well-understood until as recently as thirty years ago, although many pieces were scattered about here and there. I could not find any detailed study of Philip IV's love of art. I believe that an article I published in 1987 was the first attempt to take the measure of this great collector.[14] The primary sources of information on the royal collection are the death inventories of the monarchs. The first to see the light of day was the partial inventory of Philip IV, not started until 1686. This document was published

in two installments by Yves Bottineau in 1956 and 1958.[15] They are carefully annotated and, to my mind, mark the start of the resurrection of Philip's place in the
history of European collecting. Almost certainly, my passionate interest in the history
of collecting has a genetic component, that is to say, the influence of my parents'
collection stayed with me over the ensuing three decades. Eventually I formed the
idea of creating a study center for the subject, which I presented to the Frick Art
Reference Library. Anne Poulet, Director of The Frick Collection, supported the
concept which, under the inspired leadership of Inge Reist, has become a major
force in the development of this growing field.

Bottineau's articles regrettably were published in the *Bulletin Hispanique*, a vener-
able journal dedicated primarily to studies of literature and history but not much
read by historians of art. Another drawback was that they did not appear in successive
numbers of the *Bulletin*. Scholars of course knew Bottineau's work, but there was
no context in which to insert the information except insofar as it provided data on
a famous painter, such as Titian, Rubens, or Velázquez. Velázquez, in his capacity as
Aposentador Mayor de Palacio (Chamberlain), provided my key to Philip IV as
collector. From around 1645, the painter devoted increasing amounts of time to
acting as "curator" of the royal collection, designing the re-installation in consulta-
tion with the monarch. Following in his footsteps and using the inventory as a guide,
it was eventually possible to recreate major zones of the Alcázar and almost the
totality of the spaces in El Escorial. (Steven N. Orso and Bonaventura Bassegoda
have written fundamental texts on the installations of these sites.[16]) At the end of
this imaginary visit, the quantity and quality of the collection were obvious.

Philip's decision to enlarge and upgrade his collection was witnessed by the English
ambassador, Sir Arthur Hopton, in a letter to Sir Francis Cottington, dated August
5, 1638. Hopton's observation that noblemen were beginning to imitate the king's
interest in fine painting must be treated with some caution, because Spanish aristo-
crats had been collecting art since the early sixteenth century. Philip II, as already
noted, was a world-class collector, inspiring members of his court to follow his lead.
Nevertheless, something new was indeed happening at the court of Philip IV.

Bottineau's labors began to bear fruit in the late 1980s. In 1985, Miguel Morán
and Fernando Checa published the first overview of collecting in Spain.[17] I continued to pursue the subject in rather a piecemeal way, always with Velázquez at the
center. However, two of my students, Orso and Marcus Burke, wrote dissertations,
later published, on aspects of collecting at Philip's court. In 1986, Orso produced a
monograph, based on his dissertation, on the decoration of certain galleries of the

Alcázar, while Burke was set a near-impossible task – the investigation of so-called private collections (non-royal). It is a measure of my ignorance in particular and the state of the field in general that I encouraged him to undertake such an immense subject. We knew the pictures were out there; Vicente Carducho in his book *Dialogos de la pintura* (1633) mentions quite a few collectors by name, but the wealth of their collections exceeded all expectations. Burke defended his dissertation in 1986 and some years later pooled his archival researches with those of Peter Cherry to produce what has been called the "Bible of seventeenth-century art collecting in Spain" – *Collections of Paintings in Madrid, 1601–1755*, published in 1997, in two volumes, with an exhaustive index.[18] It is now almost impossible to keep track of new publications on collecting at the Spanish court, and I shall not mention any for fear of omitting not just one name but several. I will make an exception only for writings on Luis de Haro, the successor to Olivares as the favorite of Philip IV.

Burke was the first to shine light on Haro. While working in the Archivo de la Casa de Alba in Madrid, he discovered a bundle of documents concerning Haro's participation in the most celebrated sale of the seventeenth century – the Commonwealth Sale of the collection of Charles I of England, which began in 1649 and ended in 1653. In his dissertation, Burke published a few of these documents translated into English but I was curious to see the originals and others that might be related. What I found was amazing – sequences of documents concerning the Spanish participation in the Sale. Haro's agent in London was the ambassador, Alonso de Cárdenas. The documents contain the exchanges of letters (a few already published) and detailed accounts of the transactions between Cárdenas and the representatives of the Commonwealth.

English art historians had come to regard Charles's collection as the greatest of the epoch, and the dispersal as an enduring national tragedy. The Spanish were known to have participated, but it was Cardinal Mazarin who was believed to have been the leading protagonist. This belief was mistaken. As the Alba documents show, the most energetic buyer was Cárdenas, using funds supplied by Haro. The minister presented many of the best pictures to the king. He was a distinguished collector in his own right and kept a goodly number for himself, such as Correggio's *Education of Cupid*, now in the National Gallery in London. (Much of Haro's collection was merged with that of his son Gaspar, marquis of Eliche and was put up for sale in 1689 to settle his estate. The full extent of the Haro collection and much new information about the dispersal is found in the recent monograph by Letitia de Frutos.)[19] As a champion of Philip, I knew that Charles was over-rated and really

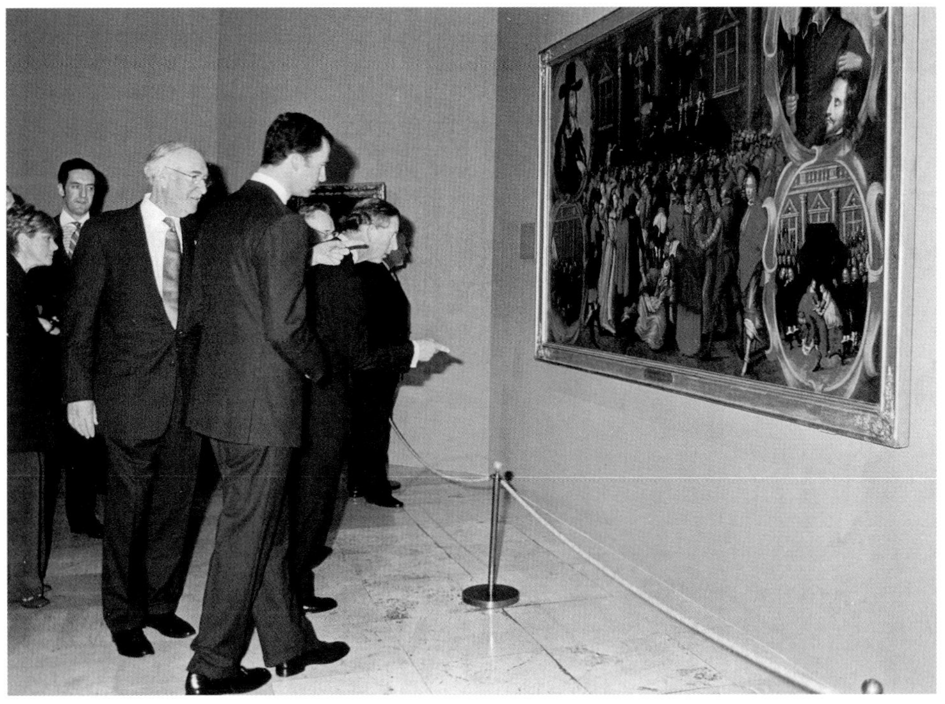

44 Jonathan Brown, Felipe, Príncipe de Asturias, Charles, Prince of Wales, and John Elliott opening "The Sale of the Century," Winter, 2002.

did not come close to Philip IV in the quest to assemble a collection of fine paint-ings. I tried to redress the imbalance in a series of lectures at the National Gallery of Art, Washington (known as the Andrew W. Mellon Lectures), which was published in 1995 under the title of *Kings and Connoisseurs: Collecting Art in Seventeenth-century Europe*.[20] (I wish very much that I had thought to use the title I invented for the Spanish edition – *El triunfo de la pintura* – which is the main point of the book.) Seven years later, I joined forces again with John Elliott to organize an exhibition at the Museo del Prado, "The Sale of the Century," which amplifies considerably my account of the Sale (pl. 44).[21]

Despite the fact that the history of court culture in Habsburg Spain is better known today than it was forty years ago, there are still gaps. Unfortunately, time has not been gentle with the buildings constructed for the use of the monarchs. Except for El Escorial, there are only a few significant structures that survive from the period of the Spanish Habsburgs and, as noted, none has preserved the original decoration. The Alcázar of Madrid, principal seat of the monarchy, was a medieval palace, large but not grand; in any event, it was nearly destroyed in a fire of 1734. Much of the Buen Retiro simply fell apart, but the Hall of Realms is there to be rescued. Once restored, as I have said, this splendid array would pay fitting tribute to Philip IV and the Golden Age which he did so much to foster. This is the reason that John Elliott and I have been lobbying for its restoration for over thirty years. The Torre de la Parada, originally decorated with paintings by Rubens, Velázquez, and many Northern artists of lesser renown, no longer exists. The houses and gardens built by noblemen that once lined the western side of the Paseo del Prado have been replaced by modern structures of differing quality.

The Spanish Habsburgs presented a stern face to the world, as befitted the defenders of the faith. It was only upon entering the royal sites that the extraordinary material and artistic wealth of the crown was revealed. In the major staterooms, to which few had access, a visitor could see the collection of masterpieces that define the court culture of Spain. Inagurated by Philip II and then given a decisive turn to the pictorial arts by Philip IV, this court culture survived until 1700, when the dynasty died out. Fortunately, one important part of the Habsburg legacy has survived, to the delight and instruction of succeeding generations of art lovers. I refer, of course, to the galleries of the Prado, which display masterpieces of sixteenth-century Venetian painting, especially by Titian; the largest collection of seventeenth-century Flemish painting, featuring some ninety paintings by Rubens; and most of Velázquez's major pictures. (A host of works by Goya later enriched the collection.) No wonder that the Prado is considered by many as the greatest museum of European painting in the world.

5

VELÁZQUEZ

MASTER AND MASTERPIECES

If I were asked to name the greatest painters of the seventeenth century, my immediate response would be Caravaggio, Rubens, Rembrandt, Poussin, and Velázquez. Admittedly it is difficult to find the common threads that bind them. There is a certain logic that unites Caravaggio, Rembrandt, and Velázquez. All were painters who broke ranks with the classical tradition and, to a greater or lesser extent, used nature — that is to say, unmediated nature — as a source of inspiration. Poussin, of course, is a defining figure in the classical tradition, while Rubens dominated the mainstream of western painting, infusing almost every pictorial tradition then in existence with intellect and energy.

In most ways, however, these painters differ one from another. This is no surprise; the hallmarks of their genius are originality, individuality, and imagination. From the perspective of the art historian, there is an important difference that may not be perceptible to outsiders. This is the nature of the evidence for reconstructing their biographies which includes such matters as how one lives his life, the choices that he makes, the people he encounters, his thoughts about his engagement with the traditions of his art — all these considerations need to be taken into account as part of an artist's creative process. Although we are taught

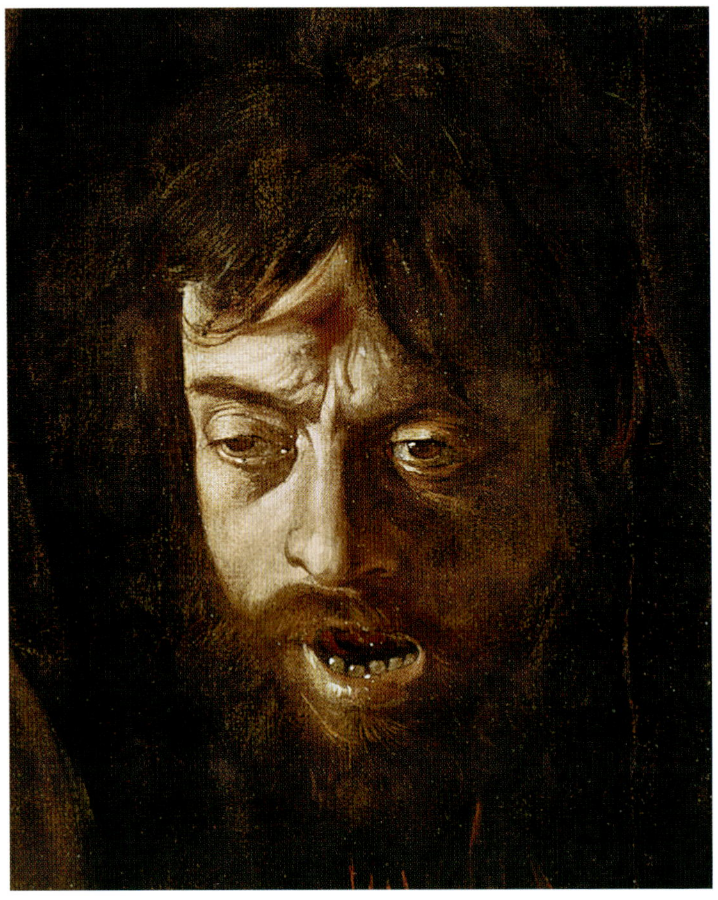

45 Caravaggio, *David and Goliath*, detail showing the head of Goliath, Rome, Galleria Borghese.

to acknowledge that even the primary sources are open to interpretation, there is still an undeniable satisfaction in hearing from the artists themselves and from their contemporaries, who observed their participation in the world of art and culture. It is worth a few lines to review the sources upon which we base our understanding of these painters.

Caravaggio, of course, did not write a word to explain the intention of his art (pl. 45) Nonetheless, the documentation of his life and the testimony of eyewitnesses are complete enough to allow us to analyze his artistic goals and reconstruct the course of his life in some detail. In our day, Caravaggio has achieved celebrity

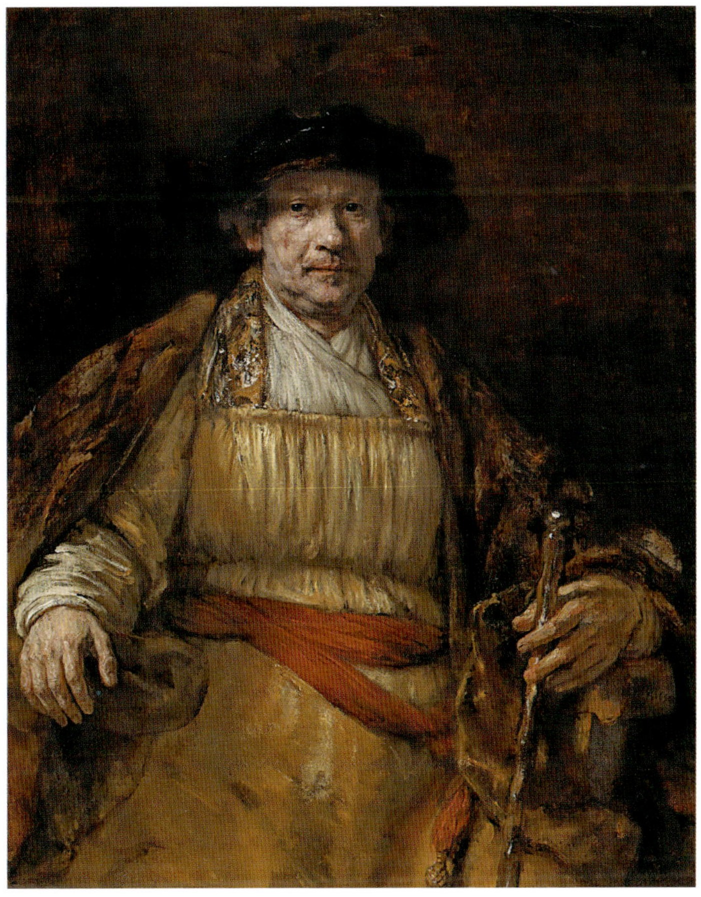

46 Rembrandt, *Self-Portrait*, New York, Frick Collection.

status – his life is melodramatic, marked by aggressive behavior to the point of murder, sexual license, daring pictorial innovation, and a grim, premature death. Hardly a year goes by without a book or exhibition dedicated to some part or aspect of his short career.

From the point of view of historiography, the life and art of Rembrandt are comparable to Caravaggio (pl. 46). Although the Dutch master left behind no written evidence of his artistic goals, his life is extensively documented and his basic premises are well-understood. As a famous painter, his activities were observed and recorded by those among whom he lived. His final years, filled with loss and sadness, can be

47   Rubens, *Self-Portrait*, Vienna, Kunsthistorisches Museum.

said to provide a prototype of the great artist rising above a sea of troubles to create great works, journeys into the soul which were revealed to those who saw his works.

Rubens's life and art might be called super-documented (pl. 47). His network of friends, patrons, and admirers was spread throughout Europe, and he maintained contact by letter-writing. His letters, which number around 250, permit us to enter both his private and public worlds and to understand some of the motives for creating art as he did.

The sources for the reconstruction of the life, art, and artistic thought of Nicolas Poussin are abundant (pl. 48). From the texts of his letters, particularly with his

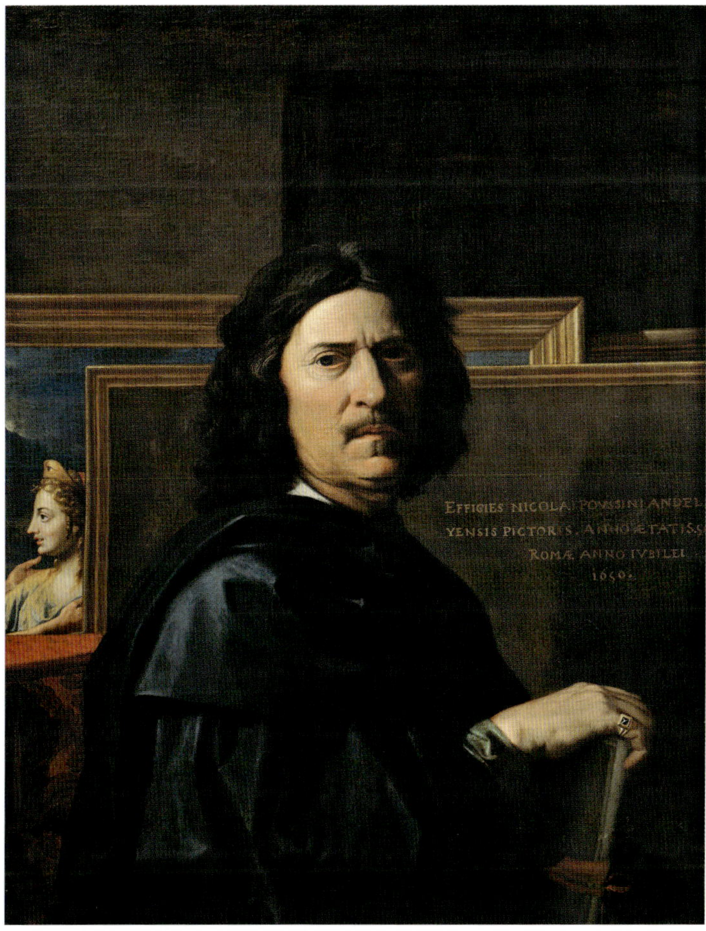

48   Poussin, *Self-Portrait*, Paris, Louvre.

French correspondent, Roland Fréart, sieur de Chantelou; his association with a circle of scholars of antiquity, notably Cassiano dal Pozzo; and from the early biography by Giovanni Bellori (1672), there are many windows that open on to Poussin's life and his views about the art of which he was a great master.

Velázquez in certain ways is a case apart (pl. 49). Caravaggio, Rembrandt, Rubens, and Poussin were already famous in their day. Velázquez was little known outside the court in Madrid. Fortunately, substantial documentation exists concerning some of his activities, particularly after his return from Italy in 1630. In an invaluable project, Ángel Aterido and his associates published nearly 450 documents pertaining

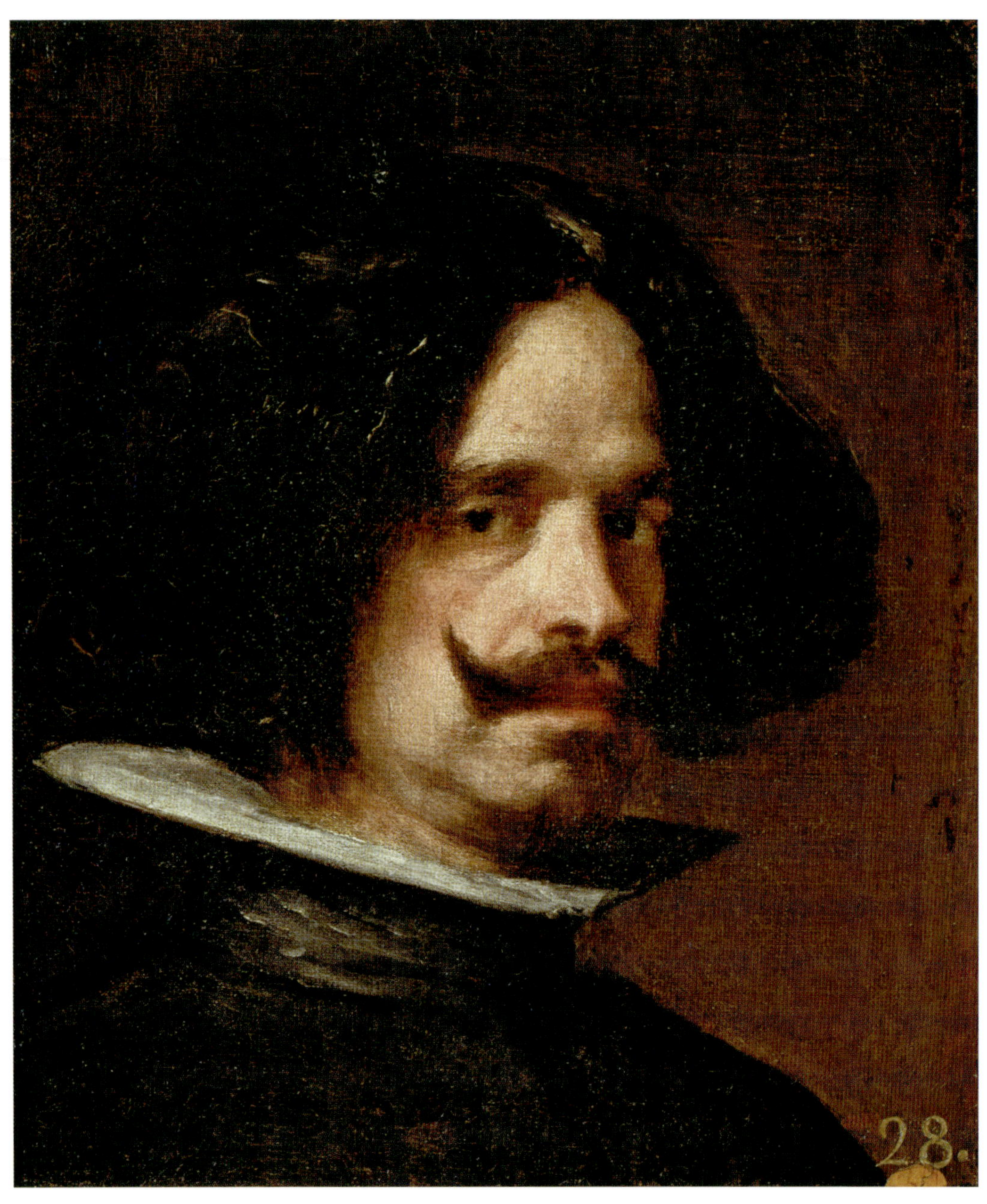

49   Diego Velázquez, *Self-Portrait*, Valencia, Museo de Bellas Artes.

to the painter and his immediate family.[1] While it is true that the majority of these documents were generated by his duties and responsibilities at the court of Philip IV, they can, like pieces in a mosaic, be fitted together with contemporary sources to compose an approximate portrait of the life and art of this tight-lipped subject. Furthermore, it is possible to tease a few hints from the sources about Velázquez as a person, which may help to enlarge our understanding of his art.

The earliest full-scale biography of Velázquez was written by Antonio Palomino. This text, which forms the third section of the book *Museo pictórico y escala óptica (1715–24)*, put the artist on the cultural map of Europe.[2] The title is *El Parnaso español pintoresco laureado* and it was published in 1724, almost sixty-eight years after Velázquez's death. Palomino, who was himself a painter at court, was able to garner information from the younger contemporaries of Velázquez who were residing in Madrid in 1678, the year that he arrived from his native Córdoba.[3] However, Palomino had a specific goal in mind when he set to write the biography, which was to offer up Velázquez as a paradigm of the nobility of painting. As a result, Palomino's text is part biography and part hagiography. And by no means does it trespass the boundaries of the inner world of the artist. Palomino's biography has stood the test of time, and the details he provides may be considered as accurate unless proved otherwise.

Needless to say, there are no writings by Velázquez himself on any but the most mundane matters. The financial rewards of his position at court, working for a wealthy, admiring patron, liberated Velázquez from the uncertainties of the public marketplace. An unintended consequence of royal patronage was to shelter his creations in the palaces of the monarch of Spain. He truly was little known outside Madrid until the early nineteenth century, although his genius was recognized by influential Spanish writers and painters (Francisco de Goya was one of his earlier Spanish *aficionados*). The turning point in his critical reception outside Spain was the opening of the Prado in 1819, which finally allowed outsiders to take full measure of his genius. However it was not until the later years of the nineteenth century that the archives were more systematically combed for documentation.

For information about his early years in Seville (1599–1623), the primary source is the treatise by Francisco Pacheco, Velázquez's teacher and father-in-law, titled *Arte de la pintura* (1649).[4] On reading the text, one can deduce that Velázquez was a child prodigy and an independent, even rebellious, young artist. His early paintings defy the idealizing canon of his master, who admired Michelangelo above all other artists (pl. 50). Pacheco forgives his star pupil for straying from this path and turning to

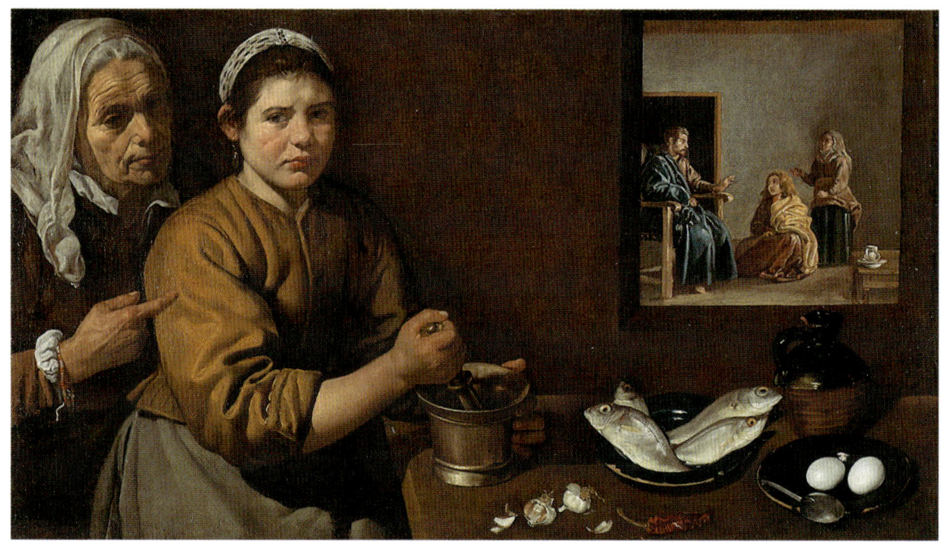

50　Diego Velázquez, *Christ in House of Mary and Martha*, London, National Gallery.

nature as his source of inspiration. In his personal life, however, Velázquez was conventional. In 1618, he married Pacheco's daughter Juana and, with one known exception, was a faithful husband. (The documented instance of infidelity involved an encounter with a woman in Rome, during his second sojourn in Italy, 1649–50. From this union was born a son, Antonio, who is never heard of again.)

His social ambitions are well known and derived from Pacheco's tutelage in the nobility of painting. His struggle to attain the status of nobleman in a social milieu that often treated artists as workmen can be traced back to the late fifteenth century writings of the humanist Alberti. Velázquez was what might be called a patient opportunist. He made his plans well in advance and carefully accumulated the social capital he would need to secure his knighthood in the order of Santiago in 1659, which took almost thirty years to achieve.[5]

We can be certain that when Velázquez was appointed *pintor real* in 1623, he met with stiff resistance from the court painters then in place, notably Vicente Carducho, who knew an upstart when he saw one and was furious that this provincial painter, while ignoring the principles of high art, rose effortlessly to the top of the table among the royal painters. The simmering rivalry came to the boil in the famous competition of 1627, which pitted Velázquez against the veteran royal painters Vicente Carducho, Eugenio Cajés, and Angelo Nardi – all of Italian origin or descent and all appointed during the government of the duke of Lerma. Velázquez owed his summons to court to Lerma's successor, the count-duke of Olivares, who came to power in 1621. Among Olivares's goals was cleansing the court of Lerma's "creatures." Velázquez's version of the *Expulsion of the Moriscos from Spain by Philip III* (lost), the theme of the competition, was declared the winner. This competition is a rare event in the history of Spanish painting; as far as I know, nothing comparable occurred until the reign of Charles III when, in 1781–84, the royal painters, including Goya, executed altarpieces for San Francisco el Grande, Madrid. (I am not counting the annual competitions held at the Real Academia de San Fernando.) From this point, Velázquez was not to be stopped. He was an "overnight" sensation, who had spent years preparing for his eventual triumph.

This steely determination could at times turn into arrogance. A good example is his "signature" on the *Surrender of Breda*, which formed part of an ensemble of twelve battle paintings used to decorate the Hall of Realms of the Buen Retiro. Following a well-established custom, Velázquez included a sheet of paper, known as a *cartellino*, on which a painter would normally inscribe his signature (pl. 51). However, the paper in the *Surrender of Breda* is blank. Two of the battle paintings for the same commission executed by his longtime rival, Vicente Carducho, are ostentatiously fitted with lengthy Latin inscriptions, including the painter's name (pl. 52). As far as Veláquez was concerned, he was certain that any well-informed aficionado would

(*left*) 51   Diego Velázquez, *Surrender of Breda*, detail of the *cartellino*, Madrid, Museo del Prado.

(*right*) 52   Vicente Carducho, *Relief of Constance*, detail of inscription and signature, Madrid, Museo del Prado.

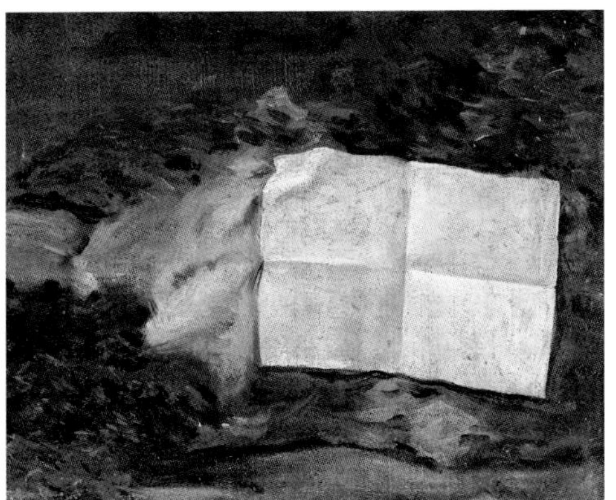

recognize that only he could have painted the *Surrender of Breda*; therefore no textual identification was necessary. Carducho had been trumped again!

In much the same vein is Velázquez's habit of not finishing commissioned paintings, even when they originated from the king. This habit was attributed at the time to what was known as his *flema*, a word that carries the connotation of slowness with a hint of laziness. We know that Velázquez was capable of finishing a work in as few as three days. Documents inform us that the *Portrait of Philip IV at Fraga* (Frick Collection) was completed in that span of time.[6] For some reason, Philip IV was willing to tolerate this behavior. With an inexplicable sense of resignation, the monarch wrote to a correspondent on June 3, 1653, that he still could not send the portraits, presumably of members of the royal family, which were to be made by Velázquez. The portraits had not been completed, and the king believed there was no solution but to wait. These are his words: "Los retratos procuraré que vayan presto, aunque no me atrevo a poner punto fijo, porque Velázquez me a engañado mil veces."[7] (I will endeavor that the portraits go soon, although I don't dare set a fixed point because Velázquez has deceived me a thousand times.) In the context of court artists of the period, these words defy credibility – a royal painter who did not comply with the orders of his patron, the most powerful ruler in the world, who in turn was resigned to wait until his servant could find time to carry out his orders. Is it the headstrong painter or the faint-hearted monarch who was responsible for this strange state of affairs?

If Velázquez was socially ambitious, he also aspired to material rewards. Taking into account his salaries and grants (*mercedes*), Velázquez became wealthy. Following his death in August 1660, the contents of his rooms in the Prince's Quarters (*cuarto del Príncipe*) were inventoried by two court officials, who included the painter's son-in-law and chief assistant, Juan Bautista Martínez del Mazo.[8] The trappings are those of a man of means. Scholars have paid attention to the paintings assembled by Velázquez, which included those he had painted and those by other identifiable artists, without much thought about the household furnishings and clothing. It must be remembered that in the seventeenth century, elaborate gowns and fine Turkish carpets were more costly than paintings. The pieces of decorative art in the Velázquez residence were abundant and often made of precious and semi-precious materials like gemstones and rare minerals. It is impossible to imagine the opulence without reading the inventory. It contained a total of 538 objects (not counting the books), many of utilitarian purpose, to be sure, but many calculated to produce the appearance of luxury and status.

In sum, Velázquez threaded his way through the intricacies of court life as he pursued the goal of re-inventing himself as a gentleman artist. From modest beginnings in Seville, he had ascended to noble rank, to a conspicuous place at court, and to a style of life that befitted a member of the upper class. Given his social and financial ambitions, it is perhaps understandable that he coolly reached the conclusion that his time was better spent in attending to the king's person than to painting His Majesty's portrait. This is one of the explanations for the decline in his production after 1640. The art of painting could take Velázquez only so far in his quest for wealth and glory and, in the circumstances, might even be an obstacle to achieving these goals.

The "private" Velázquez was very private indeed. In the absence of personal writings, the intimate side of his personality and his interactions with family and friends remains unknown. A hint of life at home is found in Mazo's *Family Portrait* (pl. 53). There are many unanswered questions about this fascinating work but this is not the place to attempt to answer them. Instead, let us posit that the portrait represents the family of Velázquez, which in a certain sense it is. Mazo had married Velázquez's daughter, Francisca. This is not the home of a typical painter, few of whom could dwell in such spacious surroundings. In the background, a painter is working on a large portrait. With our refined knowledge of Velázquez, we can recognize that, in all likelihood, the painting being executed in the background is a version of the *Portrait of Infanta Margarita* (Prado), a portrait now attributed by most specialists to Mazo. Could it be that this painting is a domesticated version of *Las Meninas*? The family is well-bred and well-fed. It has sufficient wealth to maintain a comfortable style of life. And less there be any doubt about the elevated status of the artist, he has placed his coat of arms in the upper left. This view of Mazo's home is as close as we can come to recreating an image of Velázquez's domestic life.

Moving outward from family to friends, he certainly was on good terms with colleagues at the court. One name that seems to fit the description is Lázaro Díaz del Valle, a musician and author of a short and fragmented biography of Velázquez. Díaz del Valle's interactions with Velázquez have been studied recently, but I believe it would repay the effort to attempt to expand our knowledge of other members of this cohort.

Outside the confines of the court, Velázquez mingled with writers, poets, and playwrights, replicating to some extent the activities of the group of literati that had been fostered by Pacheco in Seville. The interactions of this circle of friends in

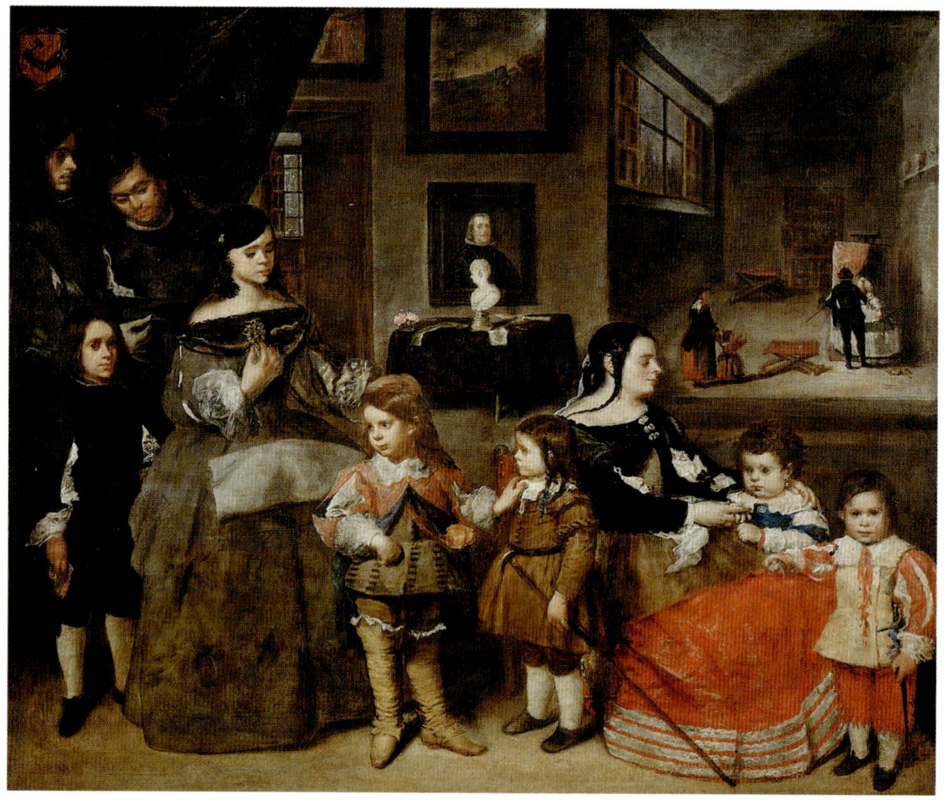

53 Juan Bautista Martínez del Mazo, *Family Portrait*, Vienna, Kunsthistorisches Museum.

Madrid have been brought to light by Javier Portús in a series of writings over the last two decades.[9] Previous to Portús's investigations, I had doubted that Velázquez took many cues from the world of literature but now I am persuaded to believe that the painter and writers were tilling the same cultural soil. Just as the literature of the time was open to different levels of interpretation, so too was the painting. Poets in Madrid celebrated Velázquez's rising star, although it must be said that often-times they used their talents to promote the fame and glory of the protagonist of a given portrait, usually Philip IV. Writers were also active in advancing the cause of painting as a liberal art.

Perhaps the best-known supporter of Velázquez's art and the art of painting in general was Francisco de Quevedo (a copy of Velázquez's portrait of Quevedo is in London, at the Wellington Museum). In his collection of poems, *Silvas*, perhaps written in 1629 but not published until 1670, he offers this prescient appraisal of Velázquez's innovative technique, offered here in a translation by Laura Bass.

Y por ti el gran Velázquez ha podido,
Diestro, quanto ingenioso,
Ansí animar lo hermoso
Ansí dar a lo mórbido sentido
Con las manchas distantes,
Que son verdad en él, no semejantes,
Si los afectos pinta:
Y, de la tabla leve
Huye bulto la tinta, desmentido
De la mano el relieve.

(Through you, the great Velázquez – skillful as he is inventive – can bring beauty to life and confer feeling to flesh with his distant blots. When he paints, the result is not likeness but actual truth, and color jumps out from the picture's thin surface as if a sculpture in three dimensions, its relief belied only by the hand that tries to touch it.)[10]

The poem continues in this vein for several more lines. Naturally the thought occurs that Quevedo, at the time still in favor with the count-duke of Olivares, was hewing to the party line. Olivares had arranged for Velázquez's appointment at court and had a stake in his success. Nevertheless, the poem and the portrait indicate that these two famous figures of the Golden Age, one a subtle poet, the other a subtle painter, had conversed. As indicated by these few observations on Velázquez's private life, which I have extracted from circumstantial evidence, there remain large gaps to fill if we are to achieve a well-informed view of the man who confidently stands in front of the easel in *Las Meninas*.

Of course there is the evidence provided by his paintings which, while not explicitly self-revealing, still has much to tell us about the personality and artistic thought of our enigmatic artist. However, before examining this source of information, we have to confront the problem of authenticity, and here we enter a world of pain. There is a core of some 110 undisputed canvases, the majority of which are in the Prado and come from the royal collection. Additions to the canon are notoriously difficult to make, now more than ever as the values have soared and the supply has plummeted. There is no shortage of pretenders – I receive at least two inquiries per month about paintings that I call, in the parlance of our times, Velázquez "wannabes." I rarely respond to these communications. The owners are convinced that they have struck it rich. Usually they have done some cursory research which, in their eyes, puts the attribution to Velázquez beyond all reasonable doubt. They gather supporting evidence about provenance, cite the bibliography if one exists, pay for the analysis of conservation and technical data, and produce the positive opinions of specialists written as long as fifty years ago, although some are of more recent vintage. The element lacking in their pictures is the distinctive technique found in authentic works, and owners and dealers do not tend to respond with equanimity if I deliver a negative verdict. They have already mined the expected gold and spent it to buy a Ferrari, a seaside villa on the French Riviera, and to pay the exorbitant tuition fees at Harvard for their sons and daughters.

I have written before about the perils and pitfalls of the game of making attributions.[11] For one thing, they are intrusive and consume a lot of time that I would prefer to dedicate to my own research projects. Perhaps the biggest reason for ignoring these inquiries is that I do not wish to surrender the liberty to change

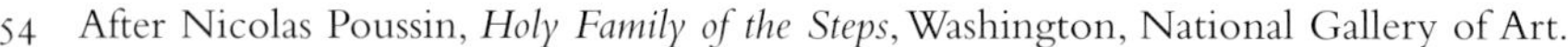

54   After Nicolas Poussin, *Holy Family of the Steps*, Washington, National Gallery of Art.

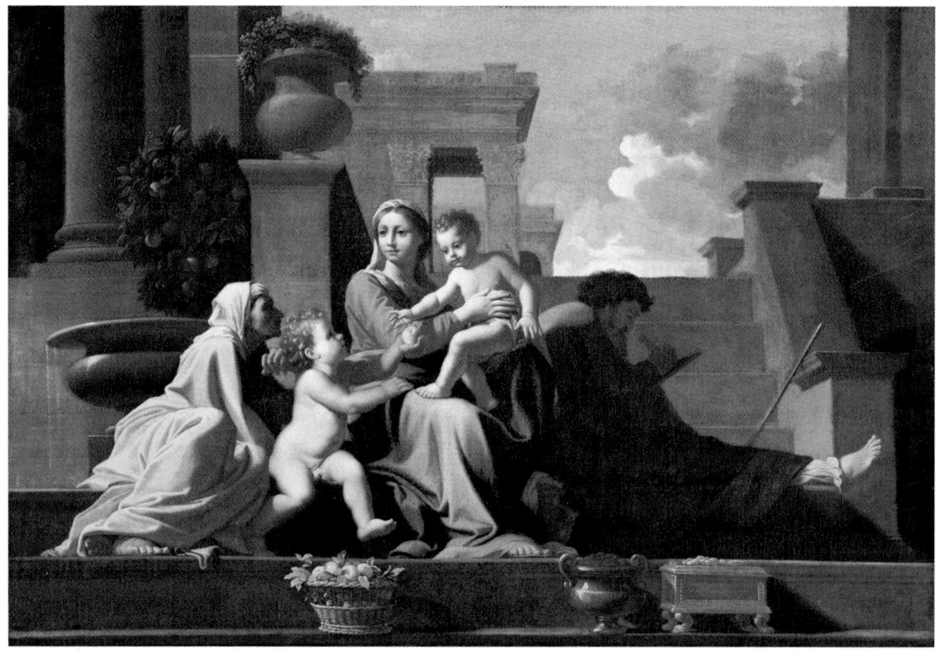

my mind because of market factors or other extraneous circumstances. To illustrate the point, let me shift the focus from Velázquez to his French contemporary Nicolas Poussin. His painting known as the *Holy Family of the Steps* was considered a prize holding of the National Gallery of Art, Washington (pl. 54). In 1981, a better and little-known version of the composition appeared, which had been hidden away in a French private collection (pl. 55). Specialists in the art of Poussin unanimously have endorsed the opinion that the painting in Washington is a replica by a skilled copyist. Suppose for a moment that the Washington version had been owned by a collector and that you, as a recognized authority on Poussin, had advised him to purchase it. The value has now descended from the millions to the thousands, perhaps to a sum that is even less than the collector had paid. Who is responsible for the decline in value? There are a number of scenarios, in none of which I would care to be a principal actor.

This is how the story ends. The original was acquired by the Cleveland Museum of Art; the National Gallery of Art took its medicine. The media descended like packrats on the story, and eventually it was established that the painting had been

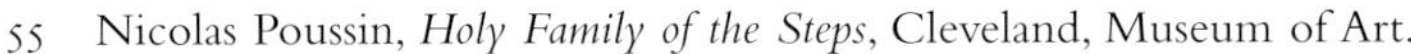

55   Nicolas Poussin, *Holy Family of the Steps*, Cleveland, Museum of Art.

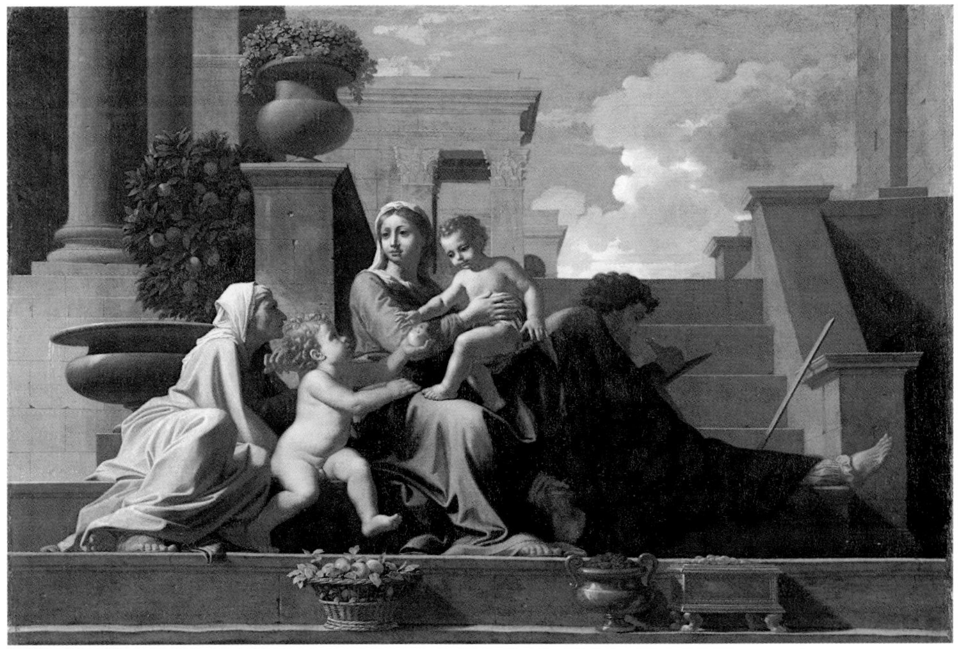

smuggled out of France in a ship's container used to transport household furnishings. The vessel set sail from Le Havre with clearance from the French customs. This story connects to observations I made in chapter three, concerning workshop practice. To say yes or no to an attribution is not cut-and-dry. Many paintings exist in a netherland of uncertainty, the attributions doubted or questioned by reputable scholars. I once proposed that attributions come with a warning label – connoisseurship is an art, not a science. As far as I know, no one has adopted this suggestion.

There is another factor to be taken into account that is never mentioned in the discussion of attributions – personal rivalry between specialists. Rivalry, I am convinced, is part of the human genome. The story starts with Cain and Abel and continues to this day. Almost every month brings a tale of one dispute or another about what may or may not turn out to be an important work of art, be it the Getty Kouros or an early sculpture by Michelangelo. Rivalry exposes emotions that are usually repressed, and from personal experience I can say that contests about attributions can quickly devolve into struggles for power and authority. For example, while I believe I know a lot about Velázquez, I am aware that I am not infallible, and that sometimes we have to take a wrong turn to find the true path.

In 1999, as the four-hundredth anniversary of Velázquez's birth approached, the attributions started to increase (pl. 56). One of these is a *Virgin of the Immaculate Conception*, which had been acquired at auction by a French dealer in 1990 for a sizable sum of money, with a tentative attribution to Velázquez (pl. 57). He had the picture restored and examined by conservation technicians and put it on the market for several times what he had paid. (I can't recall the price, but it was in the vicinity of 10–20 million dollars.) I was asked by the dealer to fly to Paris to offer my opinion. I told him that I found the attribution to be acceptable as an early work by Velázquez. Alfonso Pérez Sánchez, my longtime rival, vehemently disagreed and attributed the painting to the early period of Alonso Cano, who had been in the workshop of Francisco Pacheco at the same time as Velázquez. He advised Pierre Rosenberg, then Director of the Louvre, not to pursue the acquisition (the Louvre does not possess a single authentic work by the master) and then proceeded to argue his negative opinion in three separate publications. The subtext is that Pérez Sánchez was attempting to assert his authority as a Velázquez expert and to diminish my claim to expertise at the same time. His opinion carried the day; the painting was offered at Sotheby's in 1994 and did not make the reserve. Then it disappeared from view until 2009, when the dealer again put it up for sale. I was amazed to learn that the work had been acquired by the Fundación

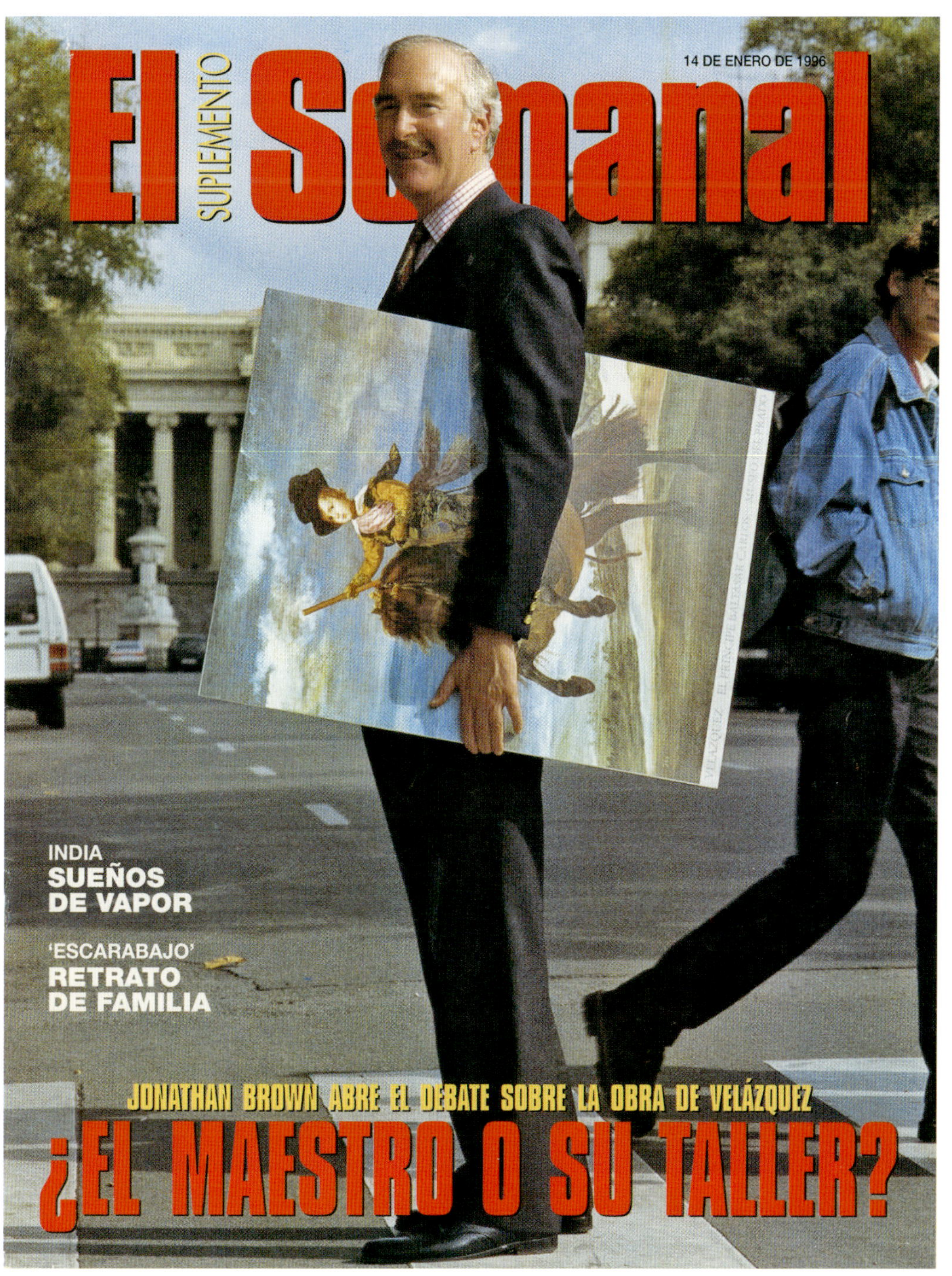

56   *El Semanal*, January 14, 1996. Jonathan Brown opens the debate on the work of Velázquez.

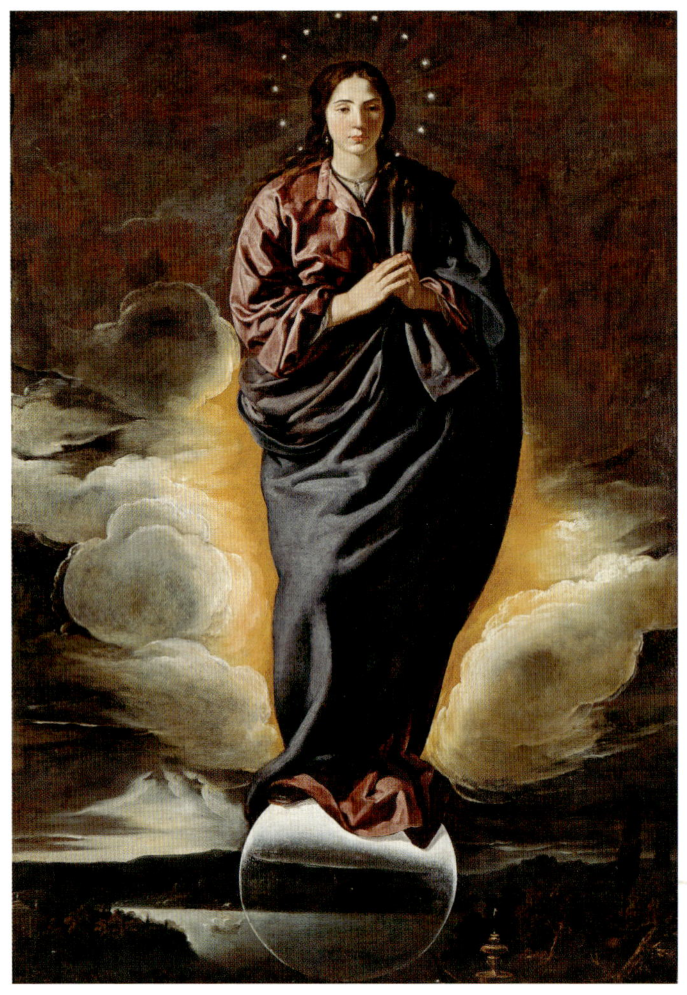

57   Diego Velázquez, *Virgin of Immaculate Conception*, Seville, Fundacíon Focus-Abengoa.

Focus-Abengoa for its collection in the Hospital de los Venerables in Seville. Their artistic advisor was Dr. Pérez Sánchez. I waited to see how the Foundation would handle the attribution. Would they support their advisor's opinion or try to find some way around this delicate conflict? Without fanfare, the supposed intervention by Cano was erased and the painting is now accepted by one and all as an important early work by Velázquez. Until the end of his days, Alfonso held firm to his attribution to Alonso Cano.

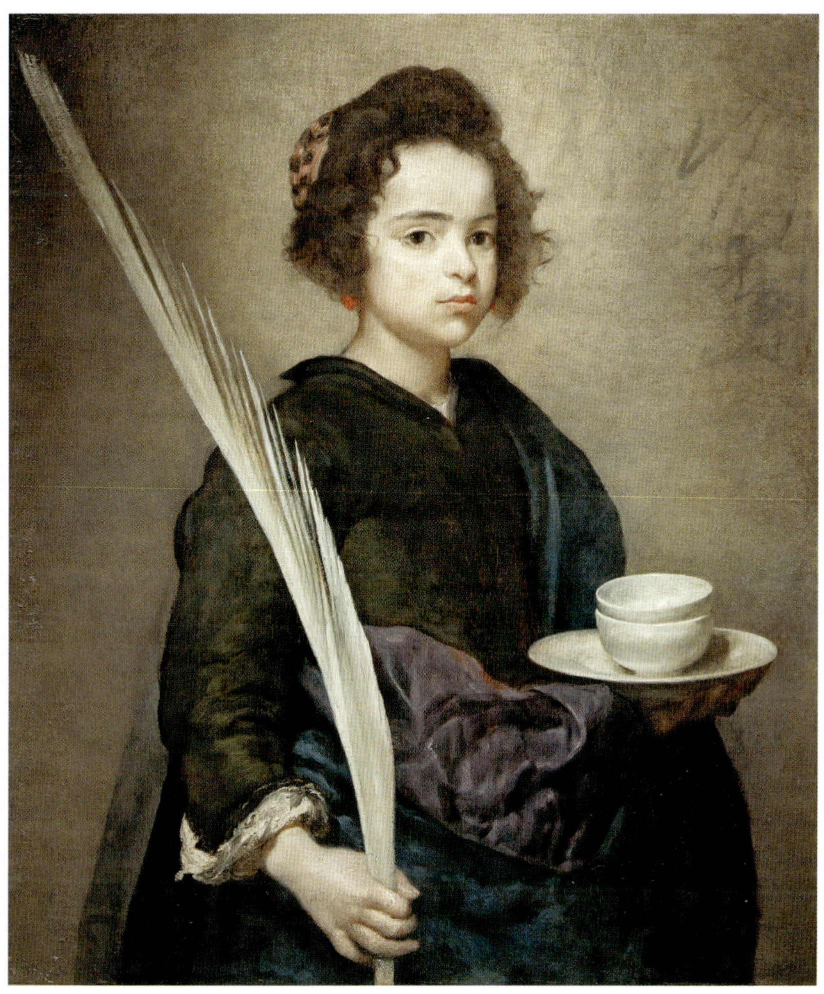

58   Diego Velázquez, *Santa Rufina*, Seville, Fundación Focus-Abengoa.

Next in line was an image said to depict Santa Rufina (pl. 58) and attributed to Velázquez; it was sold at auction and acquired by Fundación Focus-Abengoa in 2007. Pérez Sánchez had a lot riding on the attribution, not least because Santa Rufina is a patron of Seville, so a painting of her by Diego Velázquez would have a more potent cultural combination in that part of the woods than could hardly be imagined. I had expressed my doubts about the attribution and certainly was concerned about the condition, which could only be called "fair." (A local art historian with a sense of humor dubbed it "Santa Ruina.") Alfonso rallied his troops and in the spring of 2008 an exhibition of comparable paintings, borrowed from the Prado, took place to fortify the attribution.[12] The catalogue is in the form of a hundred-page book, with studies by Alfonso, Benito Navarrete, Peter Cherry, and Carmen Garrido, the head of the Scientific Section of the Prado. In a way, this counter-attack was flattering; my opinion was certainly being taken seriously. However, ultimately I swallowed hard and accepted that the evidence was against me. There are bound to be paintings that one dislikes but nevertheless accepts as authentic.

One further point needs to be made – not all paintings by Velázquez are of equal importance. In fact, it is not difficult to separate the major works from the secondary. All the paintings that have been accepted as authentic in recent times are obviously minor; they add little to the store of knowledge and understanding of this great painter. The dispute over the authenticity of *Santa Rufina* was magnified because of external circumstances; if authentic, it is a minor painting. Frankly I doubt that we will ever see a major work by Velázquez come onto the market, unless the duke of Westminster decides to sell his *Riding Lesson of Baltasar Carlos*. However, we have as many great pictures as needed to confirm the place of Velázquez in the firmament of western painting and *Las Meninas* as one of the brightest stars (pl. 59).

I have devoted a great deal of thought to studying this enigmatic painting and have read the numerous interpretations that have been published. I feel in my bones that I may be suffering from the early stages of LMFS – "*Las Meninas* Fatigue Syndrome." I hasten to add that I am not referring to the painting, but to the writing about it. Part of the responsibility must be apportioned to Michel Foucault, whose musings on *Las Meninas* sent numerous writers baying like a pack of hounds after a wily fox. I doubt that Foucault ever expected the reaction engendered by his essay. More dispiriting were the interpretations of his clever followers, each cannier than his/her predecessor.

The line of interpretation followed by empirical art historians was not much more helpful. All suffered from the same deficiency, which was to grab hold of some detail or feature in the painting which would open the door to a definitive interpretation. But first, some of the ambiguities had to be clarified, whatever the cost to credibility. What is Velázquez painting on the large canvas in front of him? Where are the king and queen standing? What is the significance of the pictures on the rear wall? What are the purpose and function of the mirror and its relationship, if any, to reality? Would emblems answer our questions or should we rely on geometry

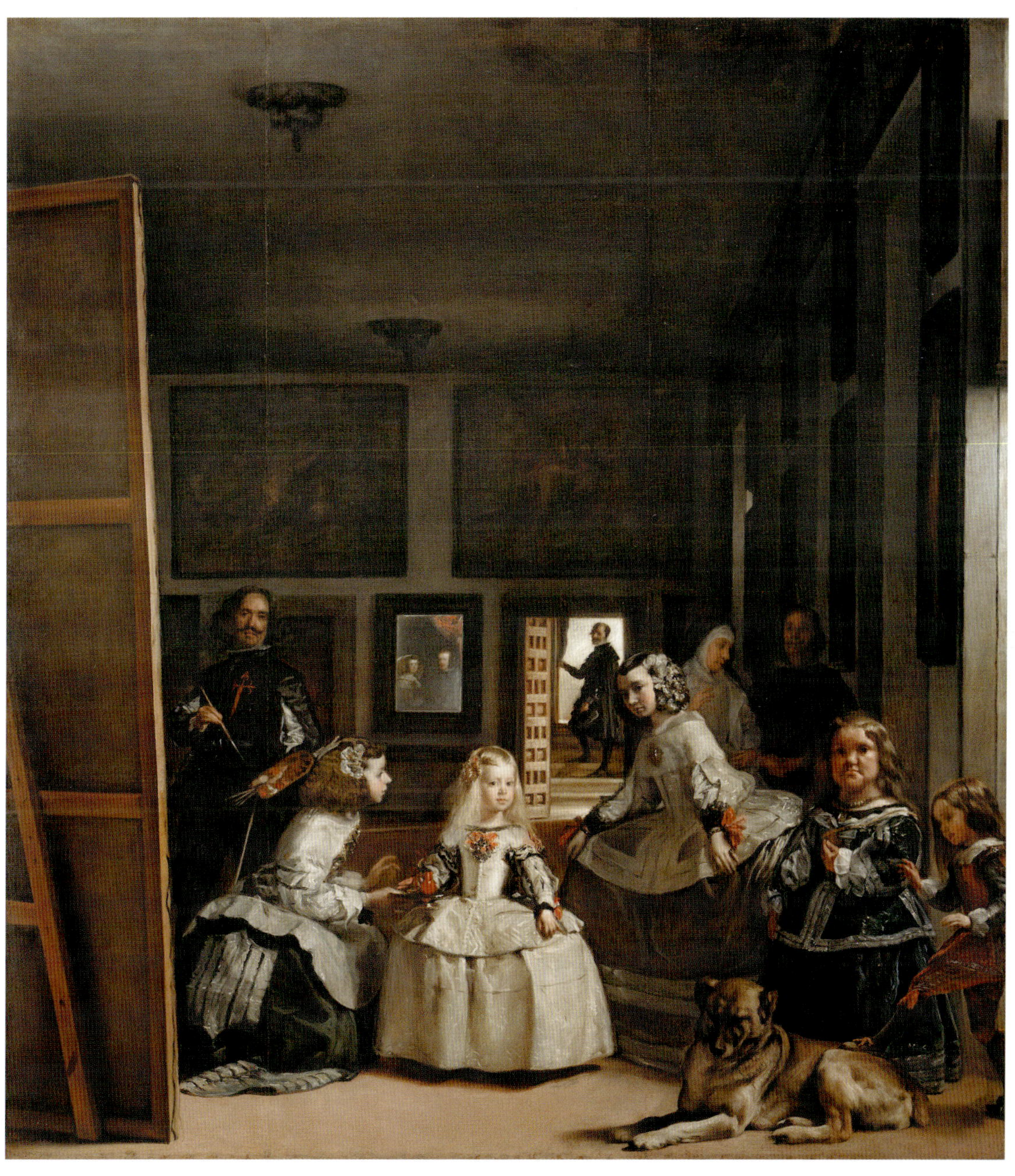

59   Diego Velázquez, *Las Meninas*, Madrid, Museo del Prado.

and the rules of perspective? In desperation, I am almost tempted to give it all up, but the painting's undeniable magnetism draws me in yet again.

One day I was driving in Princeton with the radio tuned to the public station. An interview with a pop singer was in progress; I never caught his name. However, I almost ran off the road when I heard this exchange. The interviewer asked the musician to explain the intention of a song he had written, to which he equivocally replied, "Different people take away different things from it." He had delivered the last word on *Las Meninas*, and many other masterpieces of art, visual and otherwise. (The mixture of grandeur and ambiguity of which masterpieces are contrived is indeed intoxicating.) The multiplicity and variety of interpretations cannot be analyzed here. Instead I want to focus on how the people of Velázquez's epoch – the so-called first audience – understood this enigmatic painting and on its pictorial qualities instead of its textuality.

We know a certain number of facts, thanks to the biography of Antonio Palomino, who furnishes the names of most of those in the tableau. The setting is identified as a specific set of rooms in the royal palace (Alcázar). He dates the painting very late in the painter's life, stating that it was done after he had been accepted as a Knight of Santiago. This event occurred on November 29, 1659. Velázquez died on August 6, 1660. However, most writers believe that the work was executed c. 1656, on the assumption that the infanta, who was born on July 12, 1651, appears to be six years old. (Velázquez painted a portrait of the infanta in which she does appear to be seven or eight years old. It is in the Kunsthistorisches Museum, Vienna.) Nonetheless, the date of 1656 presents an insurmountable obstacle because the painter is depicted wearing the Cross of Santiago before he was elected to this highly prestigious knightly order. Within the social context of the Spanish court, this was simply impossible. Perhaps this is why Palomino invented the anecdote that, after the painter's death, and at the orders of Philip IV, the Cross was added to the self-portrait. Yet there is no evidence on the surface of the canvas to confirm that this event ever occurred, nor does the technical examination find any trace of two layers of paint. The execution of the Cross is entirely consistent with the rest of the canvas and displays the same subtle brushwork. As a consequence, the date of supposed execution can be set aside and confidently placed between November 28, 1659, and April 1, 1660, when Velázquez left to accompany the king to Irún on the French border.

If we accept that Velázquez created the work after his admission to the Order of Santiago, it may be understood as a token of gratitude offered to a monarch whose patronage had affirmed for all time the nobility of the artist and artistic enterprise.

Philip had made it possible for Velázquez to attain wealth, honor, and fame, and had made extraordinary efforts to secure membership for his painter in the knightly order, despite the fact that he failed to satisfy all the criteria set forth in the Regla (rule of the Order).

My premise is that *Las Meninas* is purely a product of the painter's imagination. Fact is turned into fiction. Accordingly, the infanta's figure could be as large or as small as met the needs of the composition. *Las Meninas* was the artist's way of saying, "Thank you, Your Majesty." All the components could have been seen in the palace – the result is what might be called a "manipulated interpretation" of the reality of life in the Alcázar. Velázquez desired to create the greatest painting that the connoisseur-king had ever laid his eyes on. The king evidently understood the gesture and installed the canvas in his private office in the summer quarters (*pieza del despacho en el cuarto bajo de verano*).

This approach leaves a very small window for the execution – four months, in all, at the time when Velázquez was burdened with the complicated arrangements for the royal journey to the French border to sign the Peace of the Pyrenees with the king of France. The feat of painting this large canvas in a short period is a prime example of what is known in Italian art theory as *sprezzatura* – the seemingly effortless conquest of the difficult. As we have seen, Velázquez could paint rapidly when he cared to. In working out his conception for *Las Meninas*, he accelerated the rhythm of creation, as seen in the absence of any fine, detailed use of the brush, turning instead to the sketch-like application of the colors.

There is another layer of meaning embodied in *Las Meninas* that might well have been understood by aficionados. This approach sets the painting within the context of a major theoretical debate of the time, namely which was the most important prerequisite for the creation of great painting: drawing or color?[13] Up to and including Velázquez's period, learned opinion had declared drawing as the victor, citing the work of Raphael and Michelangelo as proof of the argument. The appointed leader of the band of colorists was Titian, a great painter no doubt, but weak in the art of drawing and careless in his brushwork. In Spain, this judgment was questioned; works by Titian were considered to be second to none. This exalted position was secured by the patronage of the Habsburgs, especially by the emperor Charles V. His son, Philip II, was an even more enthusiastic patron of Titian. The dynasty's dedication to Titian and indeed to the practice of painterly painting was amplified by Philip IV, who avidly collected important paintings by the Venetian master. His other favorite painter was Rubens, who was believed to be Titian's legitimate successor.

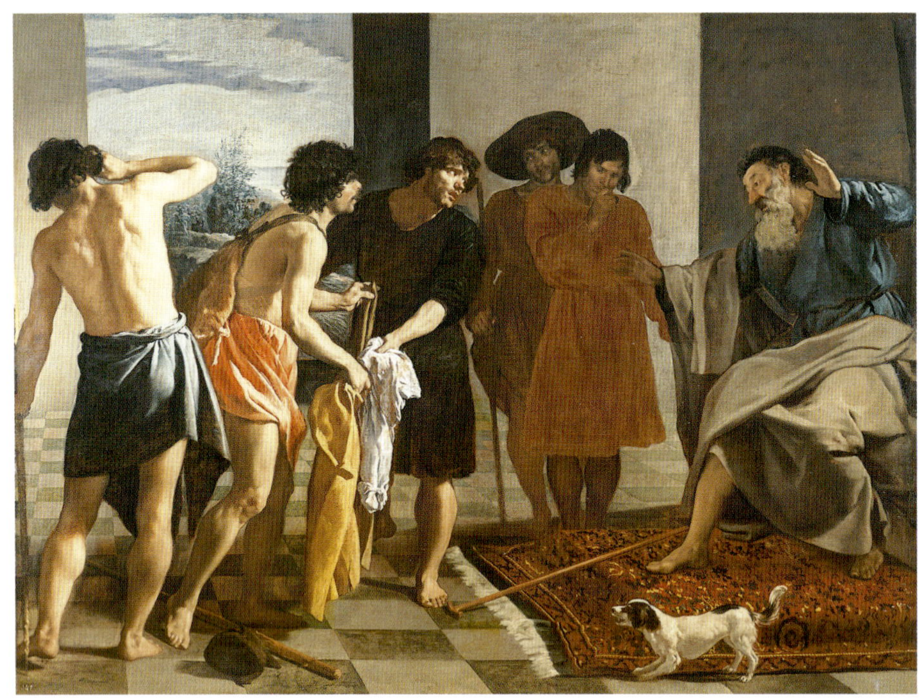

60   Diego Velázquez, *Joseph's Bloodied Coat Brought to Jacob*, Madrid, Patrimonio Nacional.

The precedence of drawing over color was known to Velázquez, whose interest in Italian art theory was certainly informed. In a painting done in Rome in 1630, *Joseph's Bloodied Coat Brought to Jacob* (pl. 60), he proved that he could master the rules of neo-classical painting, particularly the one known as *affetti*, or the use of gesture and gaze to externalize emotions. However, as we see in the remainder of his output, Velázquez threw his lot in with the colorists and their sketchy technique. Given the exalted status of Titian and Rubens at court, he had no choice. And once he had made the choice, Titian and Rubens became his rivals, as Vicente Carducho had been at a much earlier stage in his career. In *Las Meninas*, he rises to the challenge.

Las Meninas is a rebuttal to those who championed drawing as the standard of excellence and an affirmation of the power and potential of naturalist art, of painterly painting. Velázquez's involvement in this debate may now seem arcane. The contest between drawing and color is long since settled (neither wins) and of no consequence to the artistic production of today. However, in the seventeenth century, it was a burning issue. Unfortunately, Velázquez could not participate openly in the debate. Despite the praise later to be heaped upon this masterpiece, *Las Meninas* was a "prisoner" in the Alcázar of Madrid and was virtually unseen except by a few connoisseurs, among them the renowned Italian artist Luca Giordano, who was the royal painter from 1692 to 1702. As I have said, *Las Meninas* was hidden treasure until it was moved to the Prado in 1819 and "discovered" by French and English painters, who quickly grasped the implications of the picture and its challenge to the dominant tradition of Western art. One of the terms Palomino uses to describe the painting is as a "nuevo capricho." Nowadays "caprice" means "whimsy." For Palomino's epoch, the word carried a different meaning – "a judgment formed by an idea and generally outside the common and ordinary rules" ("Dictamen formado de idea y por lo general fuera de las reglas ordinarias y communes" – *Diccionario de autoridades*, 1726). In other words, *Las Meninas* breaks the rules; it is a figment of the imagination designed to demonstrate the painter's unprecedented virtuosity and originality.

The first stage was his rivalry with Titian and Rubens, whom he respected but had to surpass. Velázquez sunk them in the shadows. Deep in the background of the *Spinners* (pl. 61) is a tapestry; the composition is a partial view of Titian's *Rape of*

61   Diego Velázquez, *The Spinners*, Madrid, Museo del Prado.

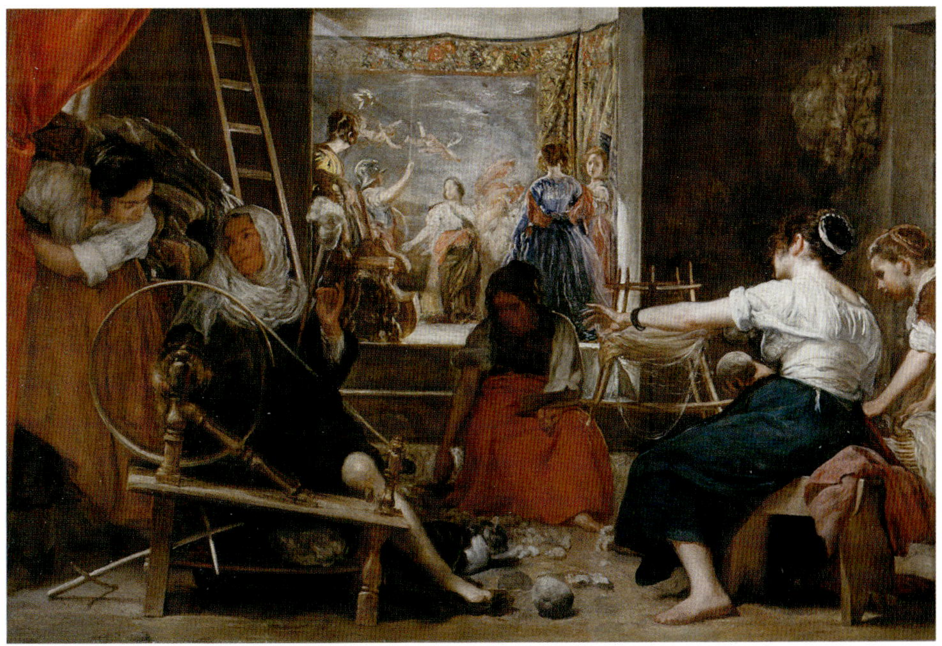

Europa, one of the masterpieces of the royal collection. This very painting had been copied by Rubens during his visit to the court of Spain in 1628–29. In *Las Meninas*, Velázquez again confronts Rubens. Installed on the rear wall of the workshop are two copies of paintings by Rubens, the originals of which were part of the commission for the Torre de la Parada, to which Velázquez had contributed. Titian and Rubens appear as footnotes in Velázquez's dissertation on the art of painting. Now he had to defend his thesis.

The best way to understand *Las Meninas* is to look at it for a long period of time, to scrutinize the surface part-by-part and then to take a few steps back and observe how the details come into focus. You will be following in the footsteps of every writer on Velázquez and the countless visitors who have seen it at the Prado. I daresay that only a few paintings of the time require this sort of bodily movement of the viewer to complete a work of painting. X-radiographs reveal an astounding fact; it appears that Velázquez painted directly on the canvas, without making a preliminary study. (This was his customary practice.) *Las Meninas* is what might be called a calculated improvisation, a deliberate tour de force. Velázquez's self-confidence borders on arrogance, a component of his personality already analyzed. The painting also carries the message that Velázquez had achieved his personal goals, despite the obstacles put in his path at every step of the way. He is a Knight of Santiago and has privileged access to the royal family.

Las Meninas is greater than the sum of its parts, but the parts need to be appreciated as much as the whole. The composition, particularly the sense of an interrupted action or intrusion, and the outward gaze of most of the protagonists have been understood by many, myself included, to posit that a specific event is occurring, involving the king and queen who are somewhere in the space or standing just outside it. As an alternative hypothesis, I suggest that the illusion of a moment suspended in time has no other purpose than to enliven and unify the composition and to provide a pretext for this demonstration of artistic brilliance.

Among other things, *Las Meninas* is a group portrait. Group portraits are often interpreted as hieroglyphs of social status, pictorial documents that happen to be works of art. They were especially popular in Holland during the seventeenth century, and tend to follow a similar formula. The subjects are frozen in time; their gazes fixed, their poses unmistakably contrived; each figure occupies its own space. To my knowledge, only one Dutch group portrait successfully broke through the barrier of artificiality into the promised land of verisimilitude, Rembrandt's *Sampling Officials of the Drapers' Guild*, 1662 (pl. 62). As in *Las Meninas*, the unity of action is

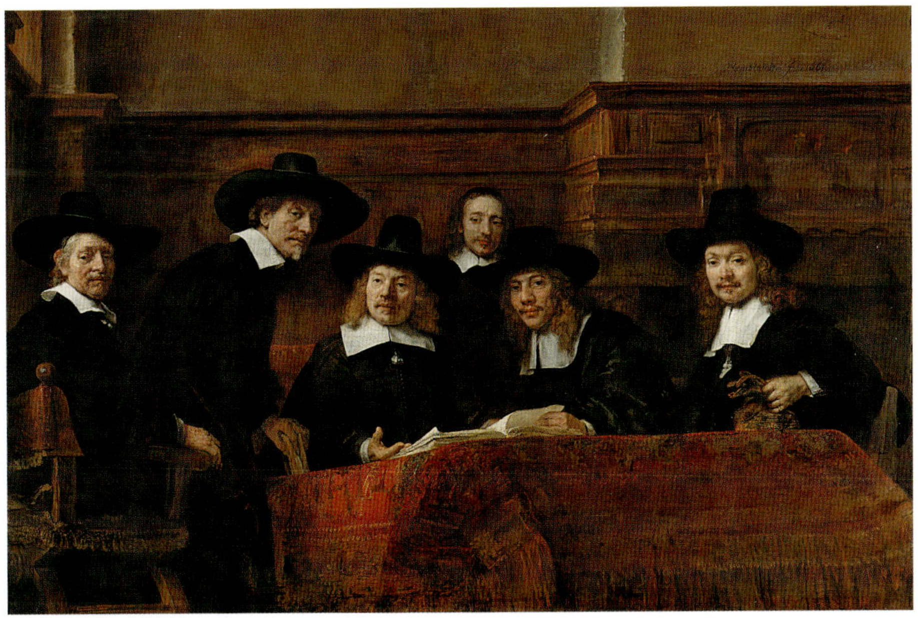

62   Rembrandt, *Sampling Officials of the Drapers' Guild*, Amsterdam, Rijksmuseum.

achieved by the simple maneuver of focusing all the gazes at some unspecified point outside the frame and subtly using gesture, expression, and pose to animate the reactions of the sitters.

As seen in the details, *Las Meninas* is executed with unsurpassed virtuosity. The profound complexity of the touches when viewed at close hand (pls. 63, 64), and the subtle interplay between the weave of the canvas and the colors are essential components of the genius of the painting. Velázquez, it seems, wished to devise a composition that would permit him to display his mastery of the widest imaginable variety of effects of light, shadow, and color. I have come to believe that *Las Meninas* was designed by Velázquez to display his infinite resources as a painterly painter (and, of course, to demonstrate his personal relationship with the monarch). There is no other painting of the seventeenth century that compares. At close range, the surface looks like a jumble of incoherent strokes of the brush, and then, miraculously, once you have taken those crucial few steps backward, everything snaps into place to represent a living, breathing gathering of the infanta and her entourage. The composition may seem to be unpremeditated; however, it was pondered like the moves of a master chess player.

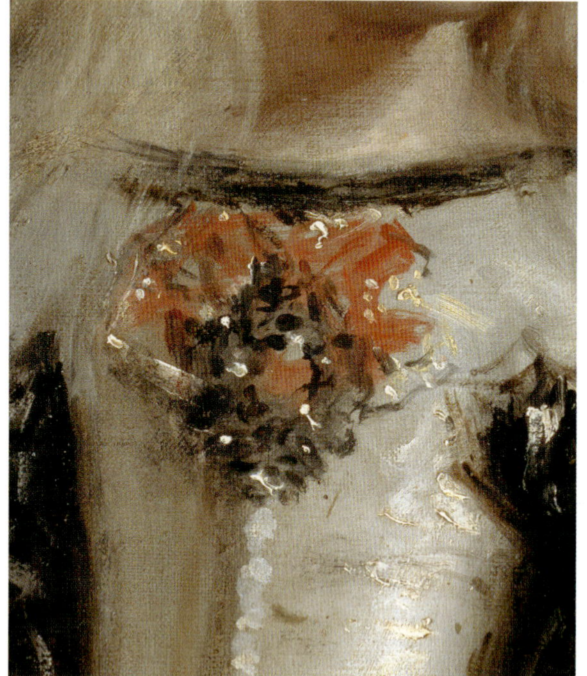 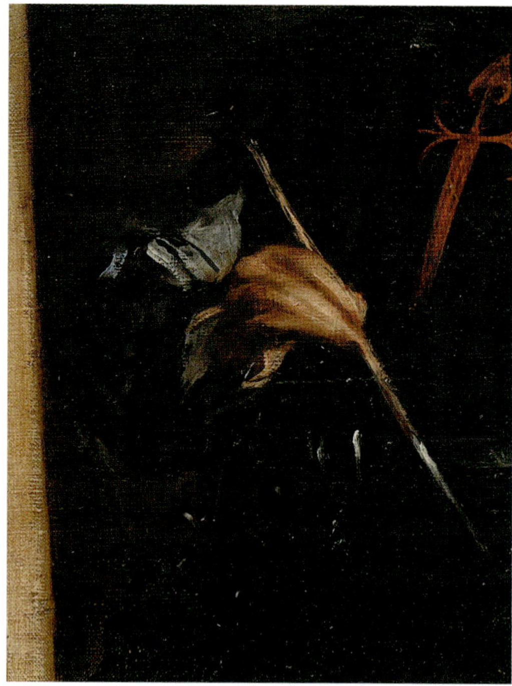

63 Diego Velázquez, *Las Meninas*, detail.   64 Diego Velázquez, *Las Meninas*, detail.

There are no mysteries of *Las Meninas*, no hidden meanings to uncover, no codes to be deciphered, no secrets to be revealed. Luca Giordano got it right when the king asked his opinion of the monumental canvas. "At first the painter was speechless. Then he proclaimed: 'This is the theology of painting.' By this he meant to say that, as theology is superior among the sciences, this picture is superior in painting."[14] *Las Meninas* is an unsurpassed example of pictorial mastery and a demonstration of the steely self-confidence required to challenge not only the social hierarchy of the Spanish court but also the canons of western art.

6

MY DISCOVERY OF

SPANISH AMERICA[1]

In 1994, I discovered America, or more specifically, painting in Spanish America, and more specifically still, seventeenth-century painting in the Viceroyalty of New Spain (Mexico). As a Hispanist, I had subconsciously believed that colonial painting was a poor relation to its sources in metropolitan Spain. Not to pull punches, I was ignorant.

It was in that year that I was invited by the Department of Art History at the Universidad Autónoma de México to offer a seminar on the Golden Age of Spanish Painting. The seminar met in the morning; in the afternoon I was taken by Mexican colleagues to admire the sights of Mexico City and Puebla. It was a thrilling experience! Although I was tactfully allowed to draw my own conclusions, it did not take long to see how rich and suggestive this material is. Furthermore, the colonialists I met at the Instituto de Investigaciones Estéticas, an institute for advanced study connected to the university, although few in number, had exhaustive knowledge of New Spanish painting and a restless curiosity about the theoretical problems it posed. On my return to New York, I was determined to insert the subject into our curriculum. I gathered $600,000 from donors and foundations as seed money for books, slides, and fellowships and we were underway.

I was under no illusion that this extension of my interest in Spain would require a lot of work. In order to get up to speed, I would have to read a mountain of material and see as many works as I could manage. In the meantime, I decided to bridge the gap via visiting professors. Two of the best accepted the offer – Clara Bargellini and Serge Gruzinski. Serge stayed for two weeks, but it could have been twenty, given the energy, knowledge, and accessibility he provided to our students. Clara, a researcher at the Instituto de Investigaciones Estéticas, made a bigger impact still, especially by way of the full-fledged academic courses she offered. Having been raised in the United States and earned her Ph.D. at Harvard, she was thoroughly familiar with the practices of higher education in this country. One of her professional goals was to encourage the study and appreciation of Mexican colonial art in the USA. As she had been for many other students, she was the *camino real* to Mexico. My ultimate ambition was to participate in the formation of a "youth movement," a cohort of young specialists who would help to advance the field as teachers and curators. So far, the Institute of Fine Arts has produced ten "colonialists", to use that hateful word, and more are on the way. Of course we are only one of a number of American universities that offer degree programs in Latin American art, some of which have been in existence for decades. However, the amazing upsurge of interest in Latin America in American universities and museums is approaching that critical mass of scholars needed for a new area to flourish.

As it happened, my involvement in New Spanish painting was accelerated by an unanticipated misfortune. One of my Mexican colleagues, Juana Gutiérrez Haces, had launched a major effort to bring New Spanish painting to a wider audience. Juana, one of the leading specialists, had initiated a project to study the relations between Spanish and Mexican painting from about 1550 to 1710. The goal was summed up in an influential article, in which Juana posed a question: Is Mexican painting Spanish painting in America or Spanish painting of America? I believe that neither is quite correct; I would prefer to call it New Spanish painting (i.e., painting in the Kingdom of New Spain). As a matter of fact, the unsettled nomenclature of these various terms are freighted with political connotations. One day, perhaps, as the field advances, a common name will be formulated.

After a rocky start, Juana and I became good friends. Juana mistakenly interpreted my call for more Spanish art historians to pursue the study of Latin American art as critique of the work then being done in the Americas. She went so far as to circulate a petition rebuking my supposed allegation. I was not so much depressed as distraught. My career in the study of colonial painting was over before it began.

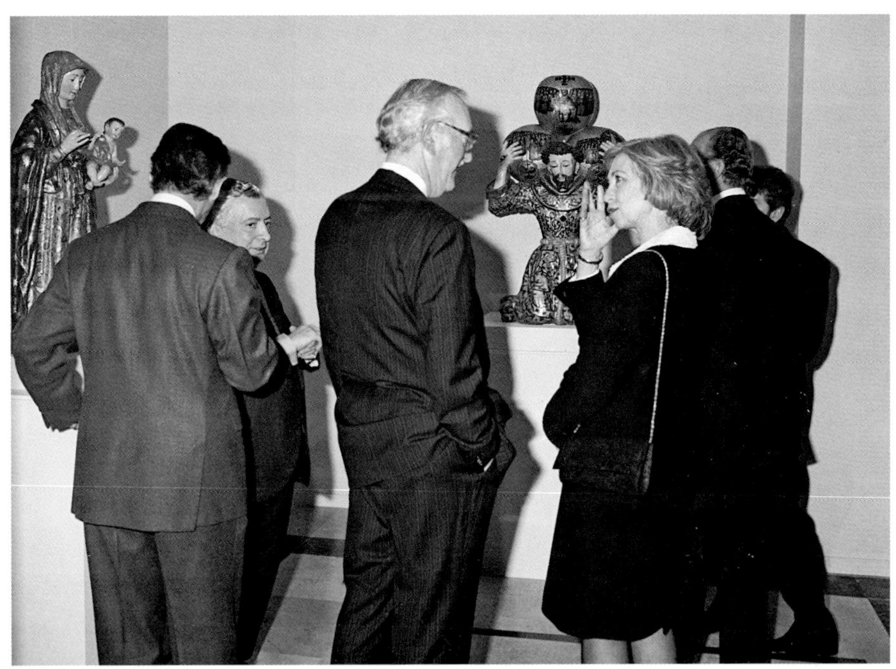

65   Jonathan Brown and Queen Sofía at the opening of "Los Siglos de Oro en los Virreinatos de América, 1550–1700" in 1999.

Fortunately, she recognized her error, and we subsequently worked harmoniously together. Sadly, Juana fell mortally ill and died in 2007. The sponsor of the project, Fomento Cultural Banamex, headed by the indefatigable Cándida Fernández de Calderón, asked me if I would take Juana's place and direct the completion of her two major projects, a charge I accepted. They were coupled under the title of "Pintura de los Reinos," a monumental, four-volume anthology of studies (2010) and a major exhibition of viceregal painting that was shown in Madrid at the Prado and the Palacio Real (October 2010–January 2011) and in Mexico City, at the seat of Fomento Cultural Banamex (2012).[2] This was the second large-scale exhibition of colonial painting that I promoted. (The first was "Los Siglos de Oro en los Virreinatos de America, 1550–1700," which took place at the Museo de América, Madrid, pl. 65.) My total immersion in Mexican colonial painting helped me to see as never before the complex history of the subject and to locate Mexican colonial painting within a broad global framework. Therefore, I begin with some speculative or theoretical observations.

117

The history of art has long been shaped by two ideas that have nothing to do with art. One emerged in the aftermath of the French Revolution, the formation of the nation-state, and the attendant rise of nationalism. The other was a consequence of the First World War, which started to fix the boundaries of European nations much as we know them today. These events, which roughly span the years of 1789 to 1919, coincided with the evolution of the history of art into an academic discipline and determined how it would develop. Knowingly or not, works of art were transformed into symbols of national character and achievement, incarnated above all by artists who were universally regarded as geniuses. Evidence of this observation is found in every library of art history in the USA; books on the history of painting are catalogued by national "school."

An alternative approach to the nationalist problematic has been articulated in the revival of the practice of artistic geography, the subject of a thoughtful recent essay by Thomas DaCosta Kaufmann.[3] In this range of ideas, the correspondence between the nation-state and artistic production is supplanted by what he calls a cultural field or, as I prefer, a cultural area. In the pre-modern world, cultural areas were coterminous with empires. A famous example is the Roman Empire at the death of Trajan in 117 AD, when it extended from Syria to Scotland. To govern this vast sweep of land and wide variety of peoples, the Romans created systems of transportation of goods and communication of ideas. The Romans interacted with their conquered subjects in what can be called a transactional relationship, which was conditioned by geography, climate, and local customs. Roman walls are found in Britain, Roman temples in Nîmes and Baalbek, Roman aqueducts in Segovia and Ephesus. All resemble the models created in Rome, yet all are as different from Rome as they are from each other. As Roman models were transported to places near and far, they encountered local conditions and materials that were used to refashion the prototype. This process has been called cultural mixing.

Other types of cultural mixing occurred along trade routes. One of the most important was the trans-Asian network known as the Silk Road, which linked the seaports of Tyre, Sidon, and Aleppo in the eastern Mediterranean to Xi'an (Shaanxi Province, China), some 8,000 km away. A branch of the Road passed through northern India. Religious pilgrimages created another path of communication between cultural centers; the Camino de Santiago is an example.

And, of course, there is Spain, whose history of art is perhaps best understood within a cultural area that is coterminous with the Habsburg monarchy. The empire stretched from Antwerp to Potosí and included territories in East Asia. In linking these distant places, Spain played the role of intermediary between Europe, America, and East Asia.

A second major factor in the understanding of Spanish–American painting is semantic. The history of painting in New Spain, from about 1550 to 1700, has long been plagued by misunderstandings and misapprehensions, some of which are the consequence of nomenclature. For instance, the use of "colonial," which was incorporated into the title of the most influential book on the subject, written by Manuel Toussaint, carries the burden of second-class status.[4] "Colonial" implies the domination and subordination of a territory and its inhabitants, who are dependents of the conquerors. Once started in this direction, the path is clear; the final stop becomes "derivative" and thus inferior. "Center" and "periphery" are also insufficient, with their implication of hierarchy. Equally, "hybrid" has its flaws, for the hybrid is set implicitly into opposition to the pure and unadulterated.

Rather than seeking solutions in nomenclature, it may be more useful to look at New Spanish painting as part of a universal artistic phenomenon – the diffusion of ideas and practices from one place to another, with all the attendant adaptations and changes. A prevalent mode of art-historical discourse privileges invention and innovation as the supreme determinants of quality. This idea, essentially formulated in the Italian Renaissance, is far too limited and exclusive. It is important to remember that there exists another history of art, one in which artistic ideas are ceaselessly bartered across political boundaries that are quite different today from those in the seventeenth century.

The trajectory of painting in Mexico City, the focal point of this chapter, is both unique and commonplace. As in many places in Europe, the painters in these New Spanish cities were open to a variety of artistic options which they adopted and adapted to suit local traditions and taste. Even the modes of transporting ideas from one place to another were comparable – they include itinerant painters, the use of prints as a source of motifs and compositions, the massive importation of visual imagery of all sorts – these components were put into play everywhere in the subcontinent of Europe. Mexico is distant from Seville, to be sure, but London and Rome are not next-door neighbors.

From this vantage point, then, Mexico City was not as different from European centers as might first appear. However, the differences need to be respected. When all is said and done, New Spanish painting developed its own identity as it picked and sorted a way through the variety of available options and helped to answer the needs of its society.[5] The dynamic process by which this occurred is analyzed in this chapter.

The transfer of the visual culture of Europe to New Spain was complex and efficient. However, the establishment in Seville of the monopoly of trade with Spanish America simplified the process and, to some extent, determined which sectors of European art would be shipped abroad. These sectors were Flanders and Andalucía, and specifically Antwerp and Seville. Seville, as the port of the Indies, was a logical choice; Antwerp, as a territory of the Spanish monarchy and the center for large-scale, industrialized production of prints and paintings, was an inevitable choice. Another, if lesser source of imagery was East Asia, via the Manila Galleon.[6] This term is applied to the fleet that sailed annually from Acapulco, bound for the Philippine Islands (part of the viceroyalty of New Spain), which served as an entrepôt for trade with Japan and China. The Manila Galleon would return to America, carrying a rich array of luxury merchandise, including painted screens and pictures made of inlay of mother-of-pearl. Once in New Spain, the former inspired the local production of *biombos*, the latter, of *enconchados*. It was in these media that the depiction of secular scenes often occurred.

During that time period, the demand for religious imagery was as vast as the territory conquered by the conquistadores. As in Catholic Europe, but on a larger scale, imagery was needed for instructional and devotional purposes. In addition to these traditional functions, images were contestants in the battle for the sacred space of the indigenous people.[7] Last and certainly not least was the requirement to provide aesthetic pleasure to the consumers of art, although this situation would slowly improve during the course of the seventeenth century.

The supply rose rather effortlessly to meet the demand. Despite the uncertainties of the transoceanic voyage and the dangers sometimes encountered on the overland routes, there was money to be made by providing religious images to consumers in the viceroyalty. Since the beginning of the sixteenth century, enterprising artists in the Netherlands had been manufacturing art for export markets, especially Spain. Of particular importance for New Spain were the engravings produced by the Plantin Press (later Plantin-Moretus Press) in Antwerp. During the later sixteenth century, the Plantin Press was the principal producer of illustrated books and individual prints in the Catholic world. The Press enjoyed the patronage of Philip II and its products were avidly acquired in Spain and New Spain alike. Equally important was the prolific output of religious imagery produced by the three Wierix brothers of Antwerp (Jan, 1549–c. 1618; Jerome, 1553–1619; Anton, c. 1559–1604).[8]

Despite an addiction to alcoholic spirits, they were, when sober, able to function as high-speed engravers for the Jesuits and other militant Catholic groups.

In the seventeenth century, a second, equally important source of religious imagery were prints that reproduced compositions by Peter Paul Rubens.[9] After his death in 1640, the production of prints after Rubens's works exploded. It has been calculated that between 1615 and 1800 over two thousand were produced, many of which were sent to the Spanish lands in America.

No less important were the works produced in the picture factories of Antwerp, knowledge of which is still emerging. One example is the husband–wife partnership of Chrisostomo Van Immerseel and Marie de Fourmenstraux, which operated a sophisticated system of providing paintings for the New Spanish market. Between 1623 and 1648, they sent well over six thousand works from Antwerp to America via Seville.[10] Not unexpectedly, religious images prevailed, but secular subjects such as landscapes, hunting scenes, battle scenes, and flower pictures were included in the shipments, which may explain the low rate of production of such themes in the output of New Spanish artists as it does in Spain itself.

A few works by recognized Flemish painters made it across the ocean. The most important were by Marten de Vos the Elder (Antwerp 1532–1603). A handful of his paintings are still in Mexican churches, including the *Archangel Michael* (1581; Cuauhtitlán).

Another major source of paintings was the workshops of Seville. Attention to this trade has tended to focus on the exports of a few famous artists, notably Francisco de Zurbarán and Juan de Valdés Leal. Their production for American markets is really quite small; in fact, as yet no documented shipments of paintings from the Zurbarán workshop to New Spain have come to light. A more characteristic example would be the obscure Juan de Luzón, whose surviving paintings are in inverse proportion to his documented production.[11] Between 1647 and 1665, the Luzón workshop is known to have sent 1,509 paintings to the New World, not one of which has been identified. He was probably just one of several artists supplying the markets in the Indies.

Although much remains to be known about the picture trade between Europe and New Spain, a few provisional conclusions can be drawn. The trade was enormous in scale and variegated in subject and constituted the wholesale transfer of a particular visual culture from Europe to America. This visual culture stemmed from two of the leading centers of the Habsburg monarchy, Antwerp and Seville, with Italy a somewhat distant third. A layer of complexity is added by the circumstance that Seville itself was continually absorbing fresh inspiration from Antwerp. Seville, Antwerp, and Mexico City thus formed part of a cultural area united by religion, sovereignty, and the resulting visual culture.

The effect of the imported works on local production is a complex and evolving story. One impact has already been mentioned, the monopolizing of secular subjects, except for portraiture, by European artists. New Spanish painters faced difficult competitive conditions because the cost of imported works could be very low; the flood of paintings from abroad tended to depress the market for all the participants. However, one area where the field was both open and lucrative was the production of altarpieces, which were site specific, and another, of course, was portraiture, which ideally required the sitter to be present. Still, for all the similarities, Mexico City was not Antwerp or Seville and in time would develop its own conceptions of the office of painter, its own way of interpreting the models, and therefore its own visual culture.

PATTERNS OF PRODUCTION

During the first hundred years after the conquest of Mexico, pictorial production in the viceroyalty seems to have been concentrated in the hands of painters from the European territories of the Spanish monarchy. The available information admittedly is incomplete; the roster of successful painters is largely comprised of Spaniards (Andrés de Concha, Alonso Vázquez) and the occasional Fleming (Simon Pereyns). Just offstage, and unfortunately nameless, were the numbers of indigenous artists who proved to be adept in mastering the modes of European painting. Their powers of imitation and assimilation were astonishing. According to one observer, they were always under a cloud of suspicion of heterodoxy. Another group was comprised of painters born in New Spain itself. Over the decades of the seventeenth century, the balance between Spanish and Creole artists shifted in favor of the latter, while the *indios* remained a shadowy presence, very active but unnoticed. If we add the imported images to the diverse production of local painters, a complex scene unfolds.

As in many parts of Spain and also in Flanders, corporations were founded to regulate the commerce of paintings, of which the most prominent was the guild.[12] The formation of the guild in Mexico City is thought to have been fostered by the dictates on sacred imagery promoted by the Church Council of 1555. Promulgated on August 9, 1557, the ordinances, comprised of twenty-one articles, were closely modeled on those of the guild in Seville (1527). In the main, they established basic requirements for obtaining a license by means of an examination that tested competent execution. These ordinances, it must be said, seem to have been observed in the breach, and by around 1600 the guild had all but ceased to function.

One reason for the demise can be attributed to the fact that the guild was pre-empted by the family dynasty. (They are also a familiar feature of European centers of production.) This informal institution was the by-product of the closed society of medieval and early modern Europe, which fostered only limited social mobility. There were also important economic advantages to be gained by keeping the business within the family – each new generation could capitalize on an established reputation and brand-name. A famous example is the dynasty founded by the immigrant Spanish painter Baltasar de Echave Orio (active in New Spain, 1582–1623), who passed the business to his son Baltasar de Echave Ibía (1625–1643/44), whose son and heir Baltasar de Echave Rioja (1632–82) kept the workshop going until he died. These dynasties served an artistic purpose by transmitting a "family" style from one generation to the next, across the decades of the seventeenth century.

Guilds had their uses, however, especially the regulation of commerce, which included keeping indigenous practitioners from surmounting the barriers of skin color and social class. When the guild was being reconstituted in 1686, the painters attempted to exclude *indios* from any participation, but were overruled by the viceroy. In the final version, native people were included and allowed to participate in the market of sacred images once they had passed the requisite examination. They were free to do landscapes, still lifes, and scenes of natural life, without having passed a test.

For all the commercial benefits, guild membership had one significant drawback. Guilds were trade organizations and thus fundamentally incompatible with the desire to elevate the social status of painters from craftsmen to artists. This was a battle that European painters had been fighting since the fifteenth century, with only partial success. In Spain itself, the issue was still alive at the end of the seventeenth century, although by then the claims of the painters had largely been validated. In New Spain, the pace of progress was even more sporadic. The conflict makes a deceptively early appearance in a well-known self-portrait by Baltasar de Echave Orio (pl. 66), which is the frontispiece to his treatise on the Basque language (1607). Echave's self-presentation as a man of letters, and thus a liberal artist, was to fall on fallow ground. We next hear of a painter's aspirations in a legal brief presented by Pedro de Benavides to the tribunal of Puebla on April 9, 1655.[13] Benavides was seeking exemption from the *alcabala*, a sales tax on manufactured goods. Deriving his arguments from Spanish sources, he pleaded his case in vain.

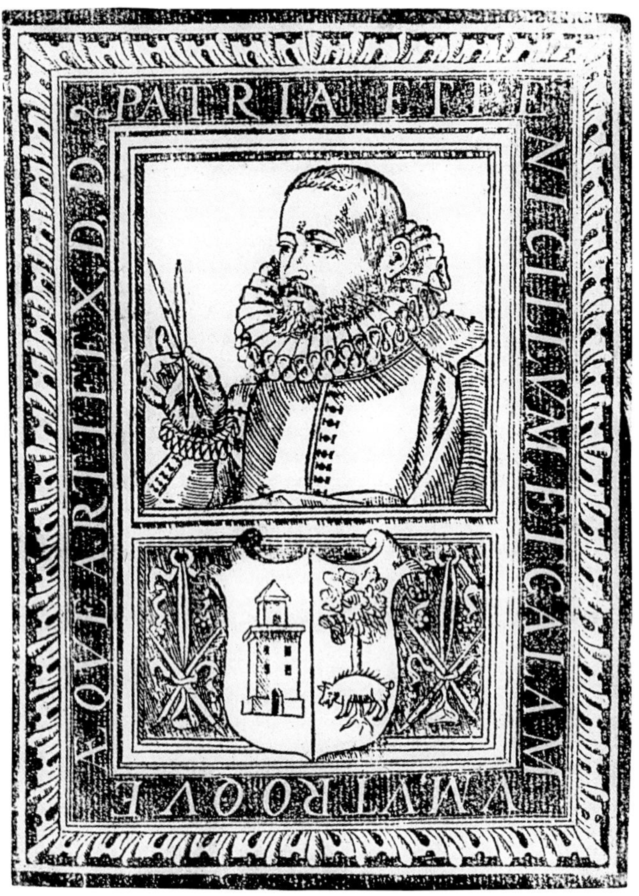

66   Baltasar de Echave Orio, *Self-Portrait*, Madrid, Biblioteca
Nacional de España.

In truth, the social and political structures in New Spain, although comparable
to the metropolis in certain respects, were notably different in important ways, and
these differences had a huge impact on the aspirations of the painters. One significant
factor was the absence of a permanent ruler. In Europe, the princely court was
instrumental in promoting the liberal status of artists. With the support of an enlight-
ened prince or prelate, the route to professional prestige was opened. In the Hispanic
world, the career of Diego Velázquez is exemplary. This gifted painter, born in Seville
in modest circumstances, made his way up the social ladder at the court of Philip
IV and became enriched and ennobled.

The ruler in Mexico City was only a tenant in the viceregal palace. Viceroys, who were members of the Spanish aristocracy and high clergy, seldom served for more than a few years and were thus unable to build a record of patronage and protection of individual painters. This circumstance left the field open for the ecclesiastical sector, which was a major if problematic component of patronage. Bishops, like viceroys, came and went with frequency. A few, notably Juan de Palafox y Mendoza (1600–1659), bishop of Puebla from 1640–49, made an impact.[14] The majority, however, were transient holders of the office. This placed power in the hands of the canons of the cathedral and the monastic and clerical establishments. These groups might or might not have artistic interests, but they shared a conviction in the power of images to teach and foment the spread of Catholic doctrine.

The impact of these patrons is everywhere to be found in New Spain and perhaps most tellingly and explicitly in the guild ordinances of 1686. The very first section aligns artistic skill with doctrinal correctness:

> First, no painter or gilder shall have a workshop or use his office publically or secretly, without first having been examined by the governors and overseers of said art, by which will cease the problems caused by people who are not knowledgeable, skillful, or sufficient to make paintings or other images of God our Lord, of his immaculate holy Mother and the saints, which cause irreverence and impiety.[15]

Painters were compelled to tie their fortunes to the church and its requirements for a successful work of art. Doctrinal correctness was paramount and was secured by copying approved compositional and iconographical models, often transmitted by engravings, etchings, and woodcuts.[16] These circumstances had a major impact on the production of sacred images in New Spain, particularly during the first hundred years after the conquest. However, with the passing of time, New Spanish painting used European formulas only as a point of departure for the significant inventions and elaborations which responded to the changing dynamic of local conditions and institutions.

FORMATS OF FAITH

Religious painting in New Spain closely adhered to models of Catholic art followed in Spain, which centered on instruction, devotion, and commemoration. In practice, these categories could overlap but each had a characteristic format. The most important in terms of scale and financial commitment was the *retablo* or altarpiece. At their grandest, the *retablos* consisted of an elaborate architectural framework made of wood, which was gilded and adorned with paintings and polychrome sculpture. The figurative components were customarily scenes from the life of Christ, with secondary emphasis on the Virgin Mary. Statues of saints were intercalated in the narrower spaces. Given their size and complexity, *retablos* of the sixteenth and seventeenth centuries were fabricated by teams of artists and craftsmen and aimed to present episodes from the Gospel narratives in as clear a way as possible in order to enhance their instructional efficacy. Consequently, the "personal" touch of the master was of secondary importance. Unfortunately, a great number of these monumental structures have perished, victims of neglect and, what is less pardonable, neo-classical taste.

More accessible to individual worshippers were devotional paintings, the hearty staples of Catholic art. In New Spain, devotional paintings carried the double burden of instruction in the tenets of the faith and inspiration to prayer. The Christianizing mission of the Spanish crown and church, two interrelated enterprises, necessitated a gigantic output of devotional paintings which were essential to the never-ending struggle against the native religions. Devotional paintings had another function in New Spain, which developed from the numerous cults dedicated to Christ and the Virgin Mary. Marian cults, of course, had proliferated in Catholic Europe, where they served as an essential link between mortals and deities. To this function was added another in New Spain, the assertion of cultural and political identity. In a system that foreclosed the possibility of political dialogue, the Marian cults provided one of the few available outlets for the political aspirations of the stratified society.

The most famous is the best example, the Virgin of Guadalupe.[17] Nowadays, Guadalupe symbolizes and glorifies the Mexican nation and its mixed-race population. However, this is only the latest (and possibly the last) incarnation of this potent Marian advocation. The origins of the cult are disputed; some authors date the miracle to December 8, 1531, a mere ten or so years after the Spanish conquest, while others believe that the miraculous event occurred around 1555. According to the story, the Virgin appeared to an indigenous man, Juan Diego, ordering him to have a shrine built at the place where the event occurred, the hill of Tepeyac, outside Mexico City. She spoke to Juan, a Christian convert, in his native language, Nahuatl. Juan made a fruitless attempt to convince the archbishop of Mexico City, Juan de Zumárraga, to comply with the Virgin's mandate. To corroborate the miracle, she pointed to a barren hill, which was suddenly covered with roses despite the fact that it was the winter season. Juan gathered the roses in his *tilma*, or cloak, and hurried back to Mexico City, where he obtained an audience with the archbishop. As they

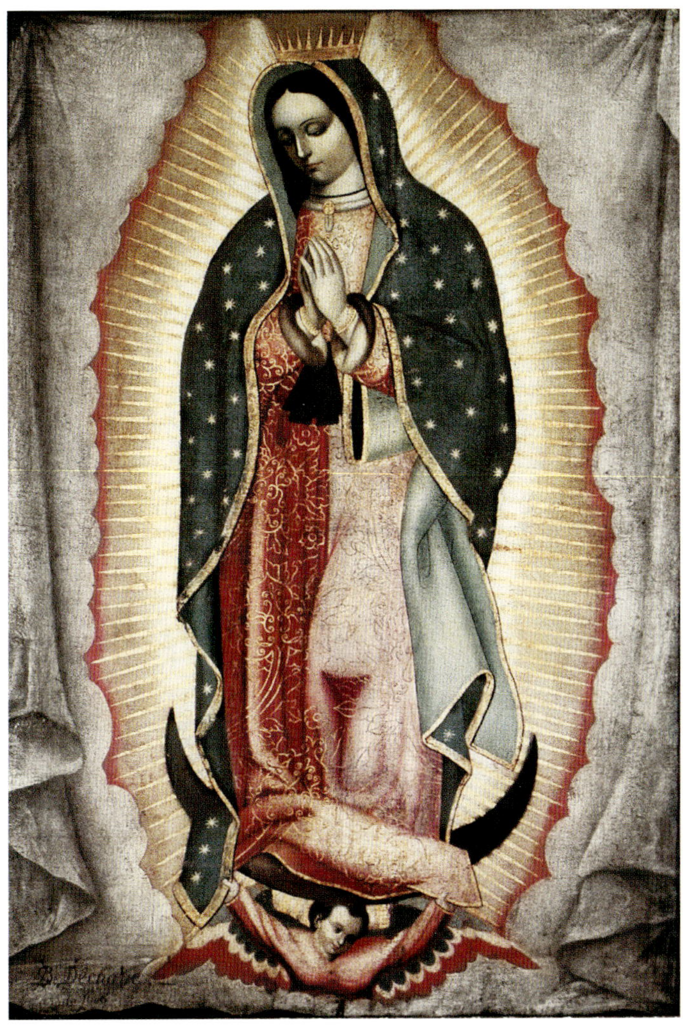

67   Baltasar de Echave Orio, *Virgin of Guadalupe*, Mexico City,
Private Collection

met, the roses cascaded out and were replaced by the likeness of the Virgin imprinted
on his outstretched cloak. After this convincing demonstration, the archbishop
ordered that the shrine be built upon the site of Juan Diego's visionary experience.

The earliest known depiction of the miraculous image was executed by Baltasar
de Echave Orio in 1606 (pl. 67), a good forty years before the image began to be
widely reproduced. Behind the expansive growth of images of Guadalupe is a major

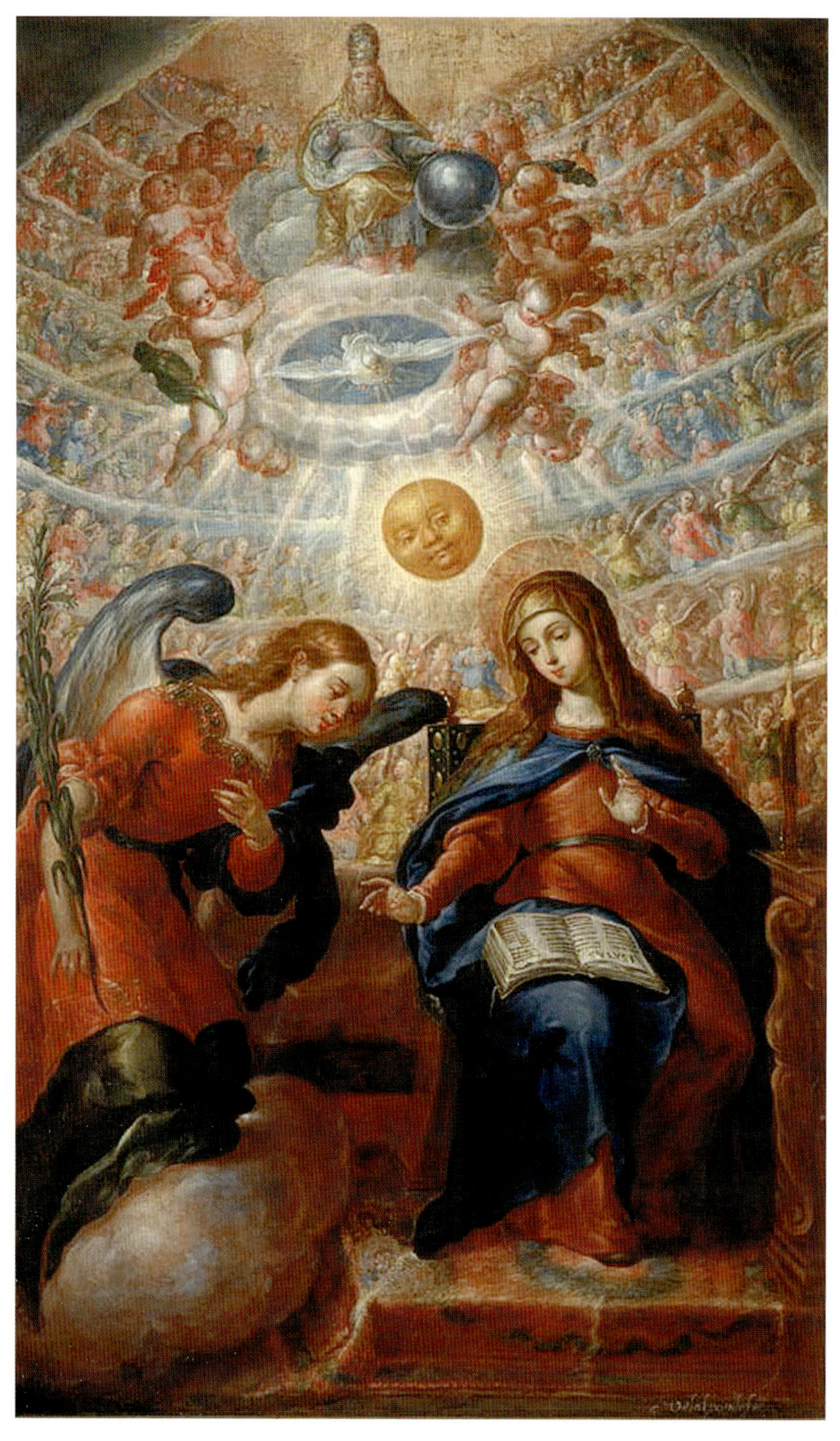

68 Cristóbal de Villalpando, *Annunciation*, Zacatecas, Museo de Guadalupe.

socio-political development. During the first hundred years after the miracle, the cult of the Virgin of Guadalupe was one among many local cults. Her fortunes changed dramatically in 1648, with the publication of a book that has since become renowned, *Imagen de la Virgen María Madre de Dios de Guadalupe milagrosamente aparecida, en la ciudad de México* by Miguel Sánchez. Sánchez, a Creole (a Spaniard born in America), appropriated Guadalupe as the patron of Mexico City and secondarily of the native people, who had inhabited the site before the arrival of the Spaniards. Sánchez and other apologists were opening a space between New Spain and Spain, and the pictorial image of Guadalupe was to become their battle flag. A new iconography proclaimed a new ideology.

Beyond the significance as a religious icon, the Virgin of Guadalupe epitomizes the singular iconographical inventiveness of New Spanish painters, long recognized as one of their distinguishing traits. This quality is illustrated by an *Annunciation* painted by Cristóbal de Villalpando (c. 1649–1714) in 1706 (pl. 68). Positioned behind a conventional representation of the Gospel narrative (Luke I, 26–38) sits God the Father enthroned on high, accompanied by the dove of the Holy Spirit and the beneficent face of the sun. Rank upon rank of kneeling angels, arranged as if in a stadium, fill the upper part of the composition. One source of this unusual composition has been identified as a mystical text by Sor María de Ágreda, a renowned Spanish nun whose works were admired in New Spain, not least because it was claimed that she had been transported bodily to various sites in colonial Mexico, including what is now northern Texas, where she was spotted by the Jumano Indians. The purpose of her aerial escapades was to convert the native populations to Christianity.

As a complement to the invention of new subjects and the embellishment of old ones was the use of non-traditional formats and materials, the latter of which will be discussed further on. The most impressive was monumental mural painting, executed in oil on canvas, of which the earliest example is the decoration of the sacristy of the Cathedral of Guatemala, signed and dated by Pedro Ramírez in 1673. The subjects derive from prints after Rubens's Eucharist tapestries, executed for the convent of the Descalzas Reales, Madrid, in 1628–32. They were followed by a similar set, done in 1675 by Baltasar de Echave Rioja for the sacristy of the Puebla Cathedral. Undoubtedly the best-known work in this format is the cycle of six in the sacristy of the Cathedral of Mexico City by Cristóbal de Villalpando (four) and Juan Correa (two), the largest of which measures 9.29 by 7.65 meters (pl. 69). On these vast surfaces, the painters, in collaboration with their patrons, composed what

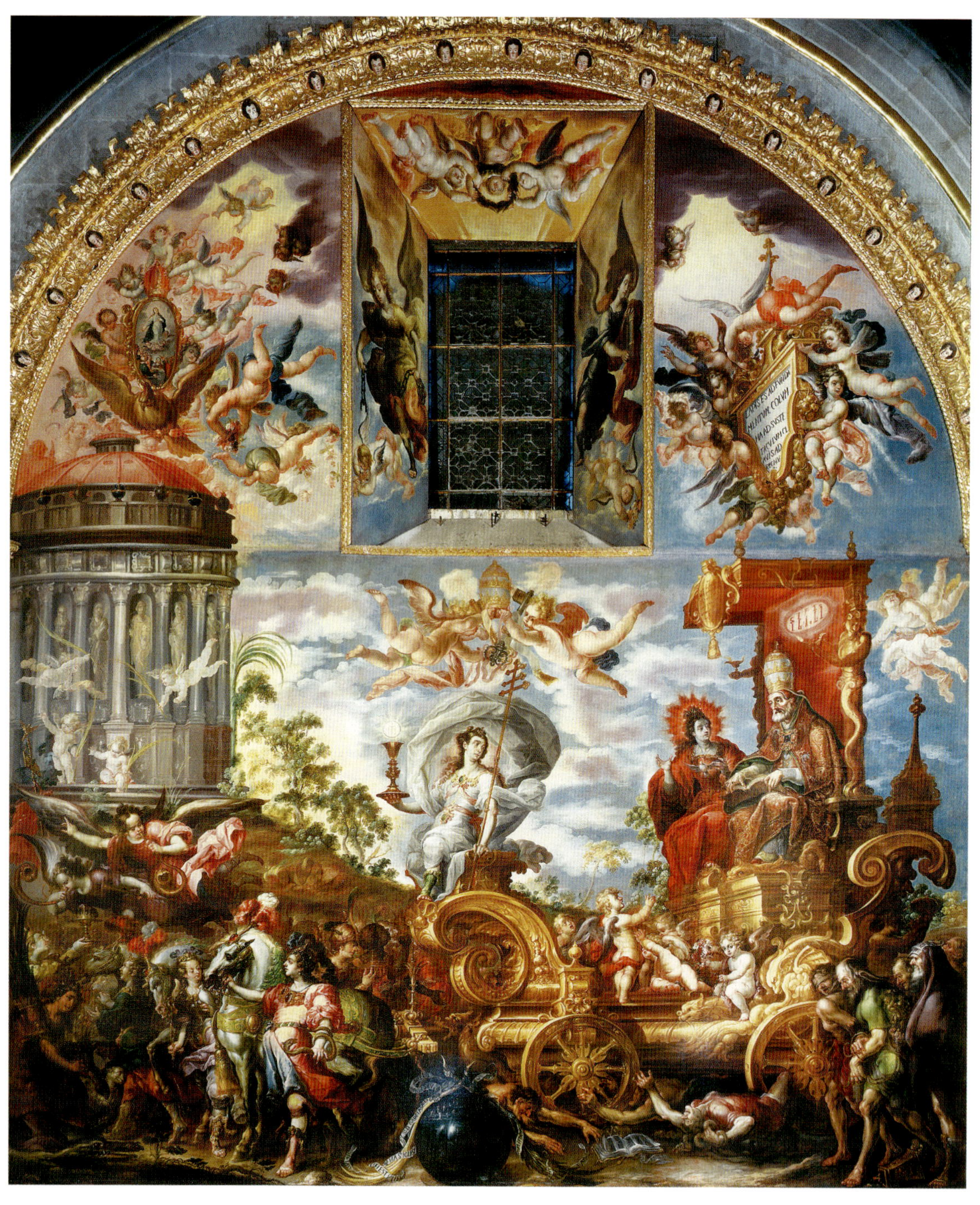

69   Cristóbal de Villalpando, *Triumph of Religion*, Mexico City, Cathedral, sacristy.

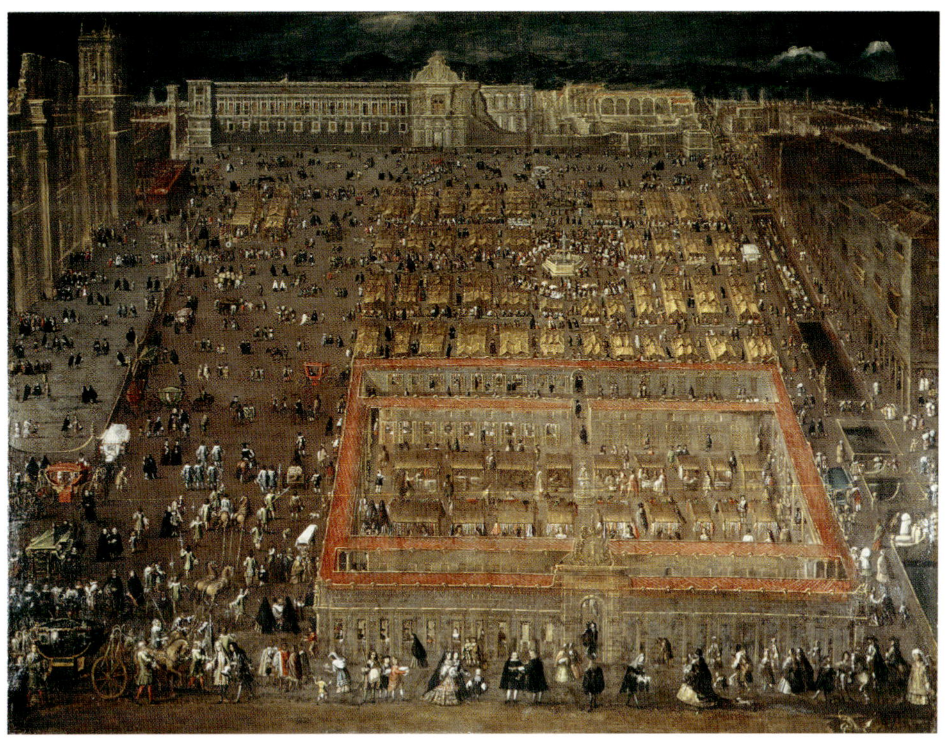

70   Cristóbal de Villalpando, *View of the Plaza Mayor of Mexico City*, Bath, Corsham Court, James Methuen Campbell.

may be called a symphonic iconography, based only loosely and in part on Rubens's prototypes. While paintings of this scale and complexity are uncommon, these examples constitute a noble chapter in the history of art in New Spain.

SECULAR PAINTING

Paintings of secular subjects during the seventeenth century are relatively few but fascinating. The paucity is probably to be explained by the massive imports of Flemish paintings. However small the corpus, they play a vital role in the history of New Spanish painting of the period.

The first category of these images consists of panoramic scenes of religious spectacles and spectacles of daily life. The most renowned is Cristóbal de Villalpando's *View of the Plaza Mayor of Mexico City* (pl. 70), painted around 1695.[18] The plaza is framed at the top by the Viceroy's Palace, which shows the damage inflicted by an uprising on June 8, 1692. To the left is the Cathedral of Mexico and, to the right, a row of houses resting on an arcade. The square thus formed is populated by innumerable merchants' stalls, including those within the red-roofed enclosure called the Parián. A diligent scholar, who counted the number of figures, arrived at the total of 1,283, most of whom appear to be members of the upper classes. As a slice of daily life in the viceroyalty, this painting has no peer.

A fertile subject for representation was the history of the conquest of Mexico. This was favored by Creoles seeking to establish their own "myth of origins" which, through the fabrication of a separate history, would place them on a par with peninsular Spaniards.[19] The best is a series of eight paintings by an unidentified artist that takes the viewer step-by-step from Cortés's landing at Veracruz to the capture of Cuauhtémoc (pl. 71). These large, spirited paintings translate the conventions of the European battle painting into the idiom of the Spanish Americas.

Easel paintings were but one of the options available for the depiction of everyday activities in New Spain. Another was the painted screen or *biombo*, which was

71 Anonymous, *The Encounter of Cortés and Moctezuma* (detail), Mexico City, Banco Naciónal de Mexico.

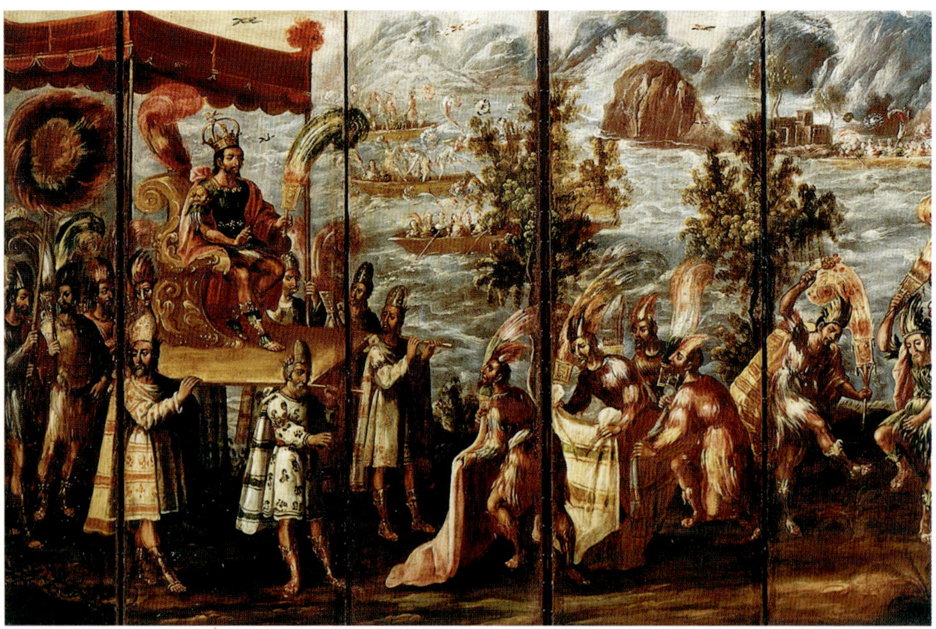

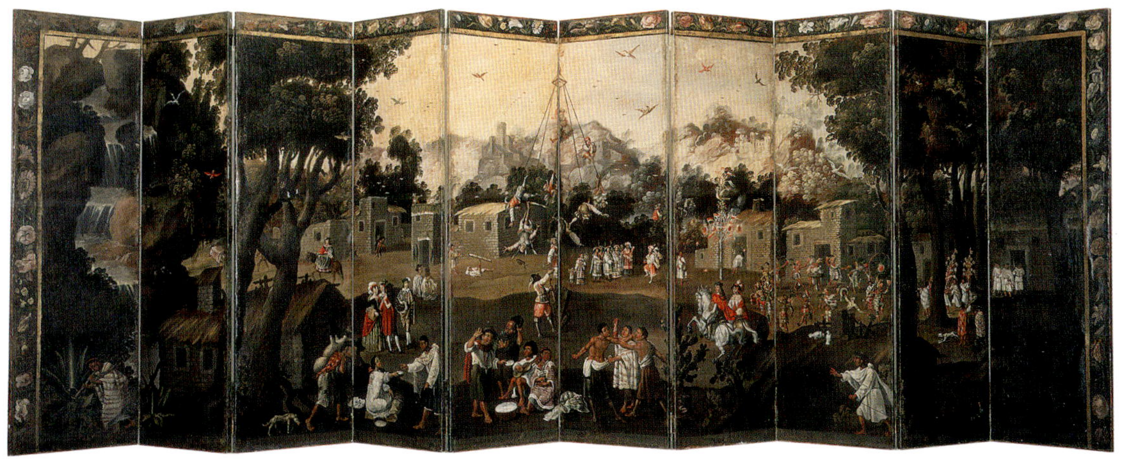

72   Anonymous, *Indian Wedding with Flying Pole*, Madrid, Museo de América.

inspired by Japanese screens known as *byobo*.[20] Painted screens were introduced into New Spain and Europe by a Japanese embassy that passed through Mexico City in 1585 en route to visit Philip II, King of Spain, and Pope Gregory XIII. A few examples may have arrived in 1573, when the Manila Galleon began to ply the Pacific Ocean. By the mid-seventeenth century, the *biombo* had become a fashionable item of household furnishing, more so in New Spain than in Europe. Comprised of several panels and often attaining a width of some six or seven feet, they were the ideal format on which to display some of the practices of colonial life, as filtered through a Creole lens. A representative example is the *Indian Wedding with Flying Pole* (pl. 72), datable to around 1690.[21] This *biombo* depicts in some detail the various stages of an Indian wedding condensed into a single composition. In the center is the *palo volador*, a kind of acrobatic performance. At the foot of the pole stand the bride and groom. To the right, a *mitote*, or traditional, pre-conquest dance, is performed by a group of Indians. An essential part of the ceremony was the consumption of *pulque*, an intoxicating drink made of juice extracted from the maguey plant. In the left-hand panel, an Indian manufactures the drink, which is then transported in an animal skin to the celebrants, who experience the intended effect.

Another *biombo* of comparable date depicts on one side a view and plan of Mexico City (pl. 73) as seen from the hill of Chapultepec.[22] In addition to supplying visual data, the plan encodes a political message as an expression of Creole pride in the achievements of their ancestors, who have "hispanized" the capital of the Mexica.

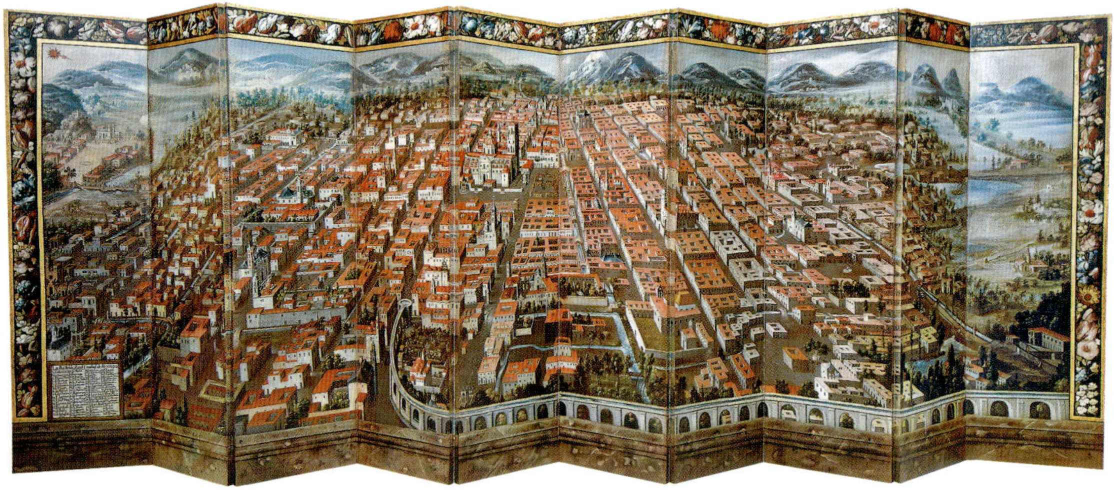

73   Anonymous, *View of Mexico City*, Mexico City, Museo Franz Mayer.

In fact, on the verso the conquest of Mexico unfolds from right to left, representing a series of events and battles that transpired over the year and a half required to subdue Tenochitlán. The subtext of the narrative is the Creoles' assertion of their identity as the founders of this realm of the Spanish monarchy. The conquest of Mexico thus was overlain with a new meaning and became a political statement of difference as well as an historical event.

This theme is taken up in a series of twenty-four scenes realized in another novel pictorial medium known as *enconchado* or mother-of-pearl inlay.[23] Like the *biombo*, the *enconchado* was a New Spanish adaptation of an east-Asian technique and was used to represent both secular and religious subjects. *Enconchados* were a luxury item and were acquired by the upper echelons of Mexican society. They were also prized in Spain; in fact, the set in question, dated 1698, was sent as a gift to Charles II by the viceroy, the count of Moctezuma.[24] These panels were executed by Miguel and Juan González, the leading specialists in the production of *enconchados*. The significance is a matter of debate. According to one line of thought, the panels were meant to be inscribed in the Creoles' project of creating a usable past, a past that would serve to distinguish them from the *gachupines*, as the Spaniards were derisively called. In fact, it has been suggested that the program of this series was devised by Carlos Sigüenza y Góngora, a scholar and writer who was a leading voice in the glorification of a Creole history. Recently, however, the series has been assigned exactly the opposite significance; they are intended to be a glorification of Hernán Cortés and, by extension, of the Spanish Habsburg dynasty. The identity of the giver and the recipient – viceroy and monarch – strengthens the latter interpretation.

The most common secular subject was the portrait, which is just now being seriously studied. One explanation for the neglect is the seeming uniformity of New Spanish production.[25] The sitters without exception belong to the upper class, with viceroys and archbishops at the top of the scale, followed by officers of the crown and members of the civil and ecclesiastical administration. The positions defined the individuals who held them, and thus the portraits represent them as members of a hierarchy and not as sentient human beings. This kind of "portrait of position" is by no means unique to New Spain; it was commonplace throughout early modern Europe. While it is true that masters such as Velázquez, Van Dyck, and Rembrandt made an art of portraiture, most painters were content to follow the prevailing fashion and satisfy the basic mission of the genre – to reproduce a credible, recognizable replica of the sitter and evoke his/her place in society. Similarly in New Spain the portrait was conceived as a document of status and achievement. It also functioned as a form of institutional memory. Series of portraits of the viceroys and archbishops were installed in official spaces, where they served as markers of stability and continuity.

These factors conditioned the evolution of the portrait during the seventeenth century. An early representative example is Baltasar Echave Orio's *Portrait of Fray Alonso de Montúfar* (pl. 74), the first in a series of portraits of the archbishops of Mexico City, which is installed in the vestry. Montúfar was archbishop from 1556–69; thus the portrait is posthumous. This excellent work displays all the features of the format. A full-length figure stands beside a table on which he rests his hand. He is accompanied by the attributes of his office, the mitre and the pastoral crozier. His coat of arms, a pedigree of his quality, is inserted in the upper left corner. In the lower left is an escutcheon – a sort of honor roll – with a text consisting of biographical data. As time went on, the list of honors was extended. Perhaps the transitory nature of these offices – the incumbents either died in office or returned to the metropolis – generated the use of a biographical text, which was soon being emulated by lesser officials and especially by Creole dignitaries who were permanent residents of the viceroyalty. (In the patriarchal society, portraits of women and children are rare.)

In a class by themselves are the imaginary portraits of Moctezuma, the best-known example of which is attributed to Antonio Rodríguez (1636–1691) (pl. 75).

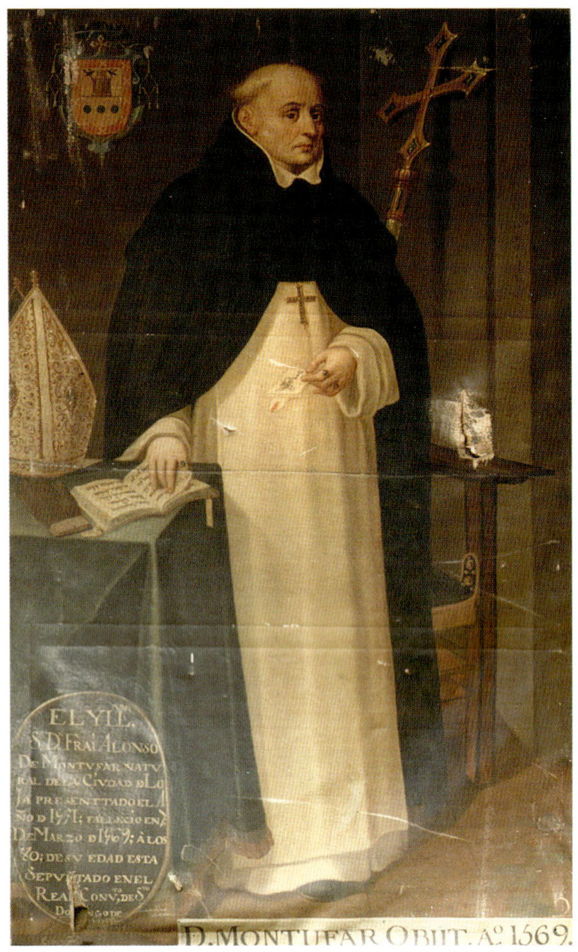

74   Baltasar de Echave Orio, *Fray Alonso de Montúfar,*
Mexico City, Cathedral.

It has been suggested that the painting was given to Cosimo III de Medici (ruled 1670–1723) by the New Spanish polymath Carlos Sigüenza y Góngora. Among his interests, Sigüenza y Góngora was an avid historian of the Mexica and an advocate for *criollismo*, the concept that American-born Spaniards were the social and political peers of Spaniards born in the homeland. In framing his argument, Sigüenza sought to demonstrate that the Nahuatl monarchy was similar to the Spanish monarchy and in fact deserved to be regarded as the founders of New Spain. In this order of things, the viceroys were the successors of the indigenous rulers.

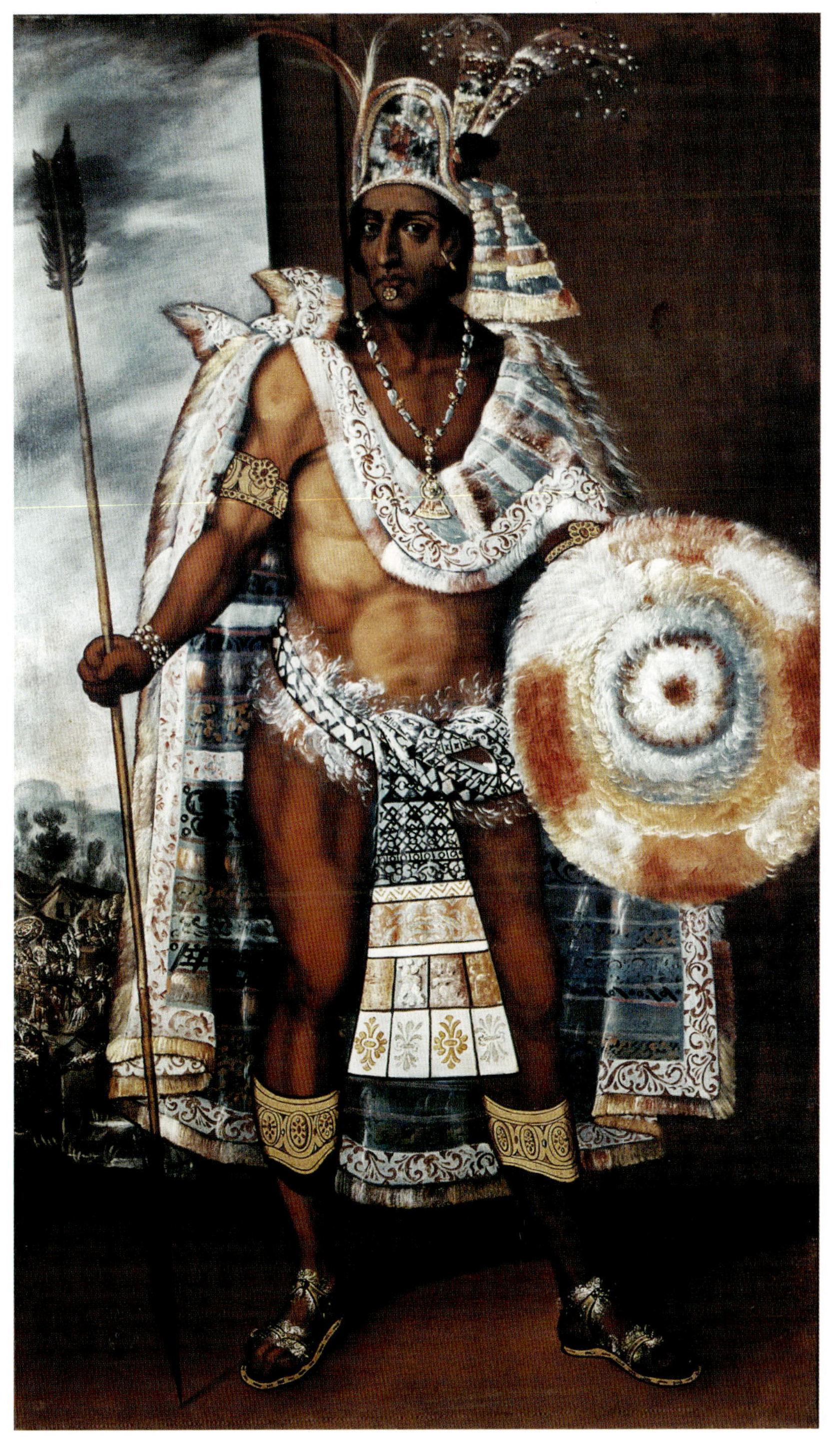

75   Antonio Rodríguez (attributed), *Moctezuma*, Florence, Museo degli Argenti.

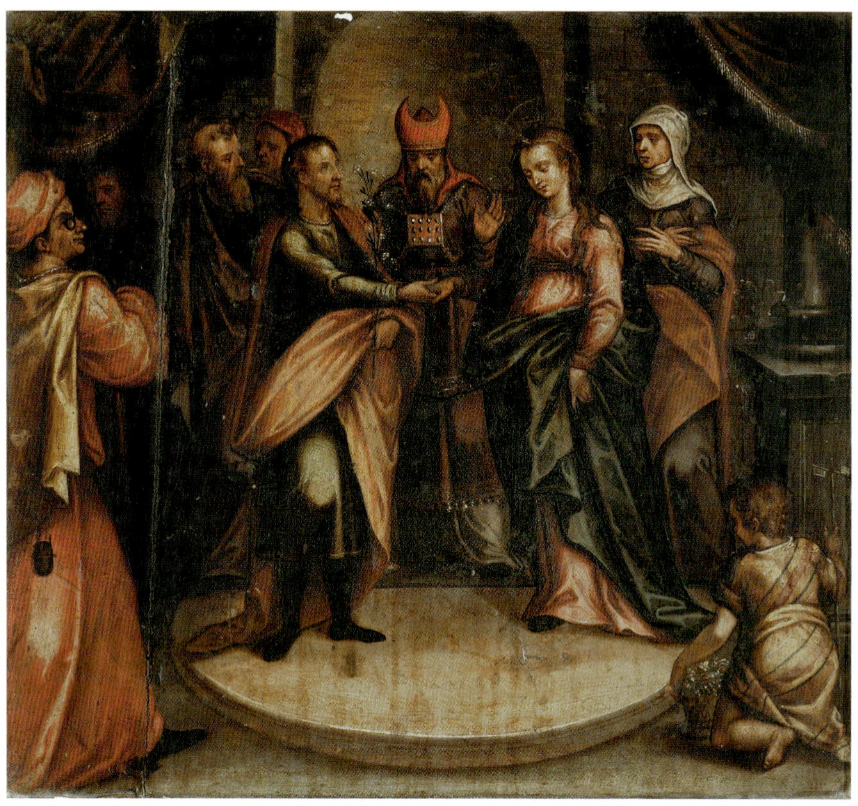

76   Francisco Pacheco, *Marriage of the Virgin*, Seville, La Anunciación.

RELIGIOUS IMAGES AND THEIR MAKERS

The use of Spanish models by the painters of New Spain requires no explanation; it is always taken for granted. Perhaps this explains why the phenomenon has not been carefully analyzed; it is always considered to be a matter of facile repetition whereas it is truly complicated. This point is most efficiently demonstrated by looking at the evolution of a single theme and composition as it developed over the course of the seventeenth century. The subject is the Marriage of the Virgin, an event that is not found in the Gospels and was based on the texts of the Apocrypha and the *Golden Legend*, a compilation of the saints' lives made in the thirteenth century.

In 1588, a leading Sevillian painter, Francisco Pacheco, illustrated the event in an altarpiece for the church of La Anunciación, Seville (pl. 76). The representation is cast in the form of a straightforward narrative. In the center is the rabbi who

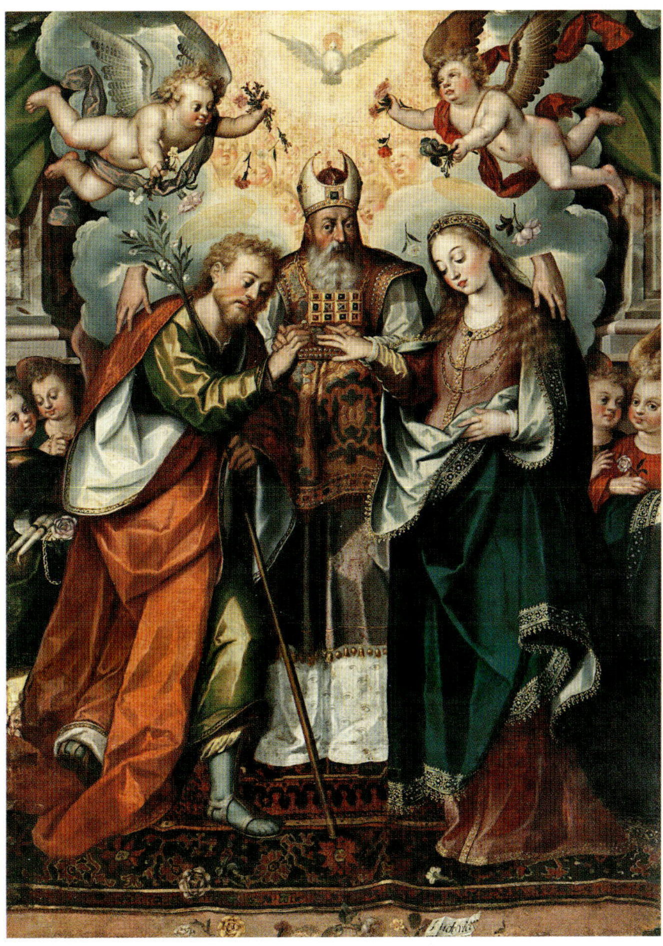

77   Luis Juárez, *Marriage of the Virgin*, Davenport (Iowa), Figge Art Museum.

performs the ceremony, flanked on either side by the holy couple. Joseph holds the flowering staff that designates him as the husband chosen by God.

Some years later, the New Spanish painter Luis Juárez (c. 1586–1639) produced a novel, lively version of the composition, which is marked by the addition of what might be called sacred grace-notes in the form of angels who flank the central group and hover above the protagonists (pl. 77). Most unusual is the appearance from the clouds of two disembodied hands, the hands of God, which have come to rest on the shoulders of the bride and groom and to bless their marriage.

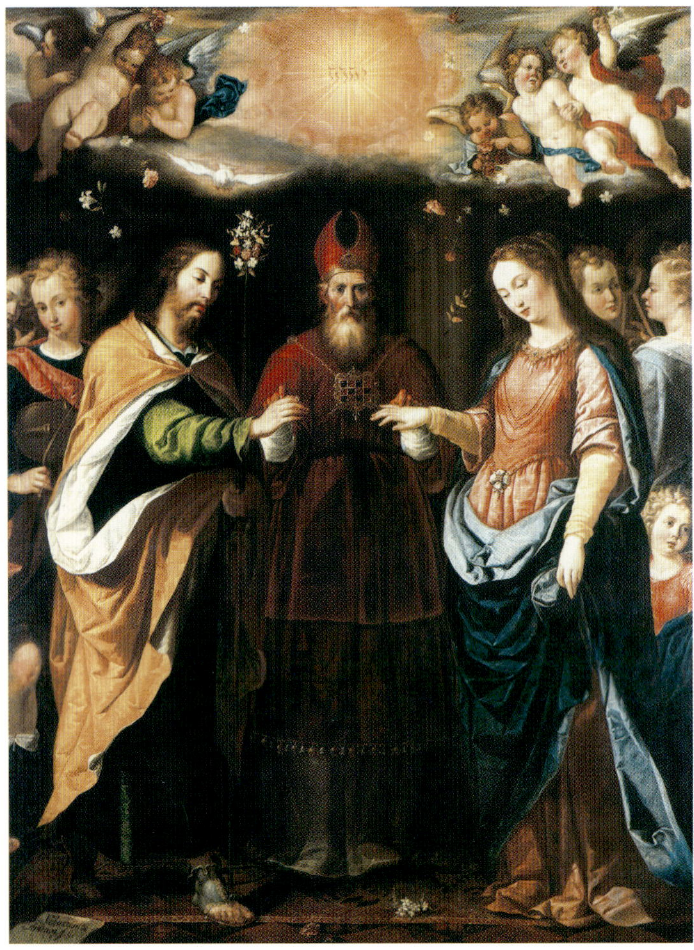

78   Sebastián López de Arteaga, *Marriage of the Virgin*, Mexico City, Museo Nacional de Arte.

The next stage occurs in the version of Sebastián López de Arteaga, executed around 1650 (pl. 78). López de Arteaga (1610–1652) had come to New Spain from Seville in 1640 and perhaps had seen the painting by Pacheco. Nevertheless, he follows the compositional model of Luis Juárez, although he diminishes the nervous energy of the prototype, and substitutes a mock Hebrew inscription for the dove of the Holy Spirit.

At the end of this line of representation and reinterpretation is the version by Cristóbal de Villalpando (c. 1649–1714), the leading painter in Mexico City in the

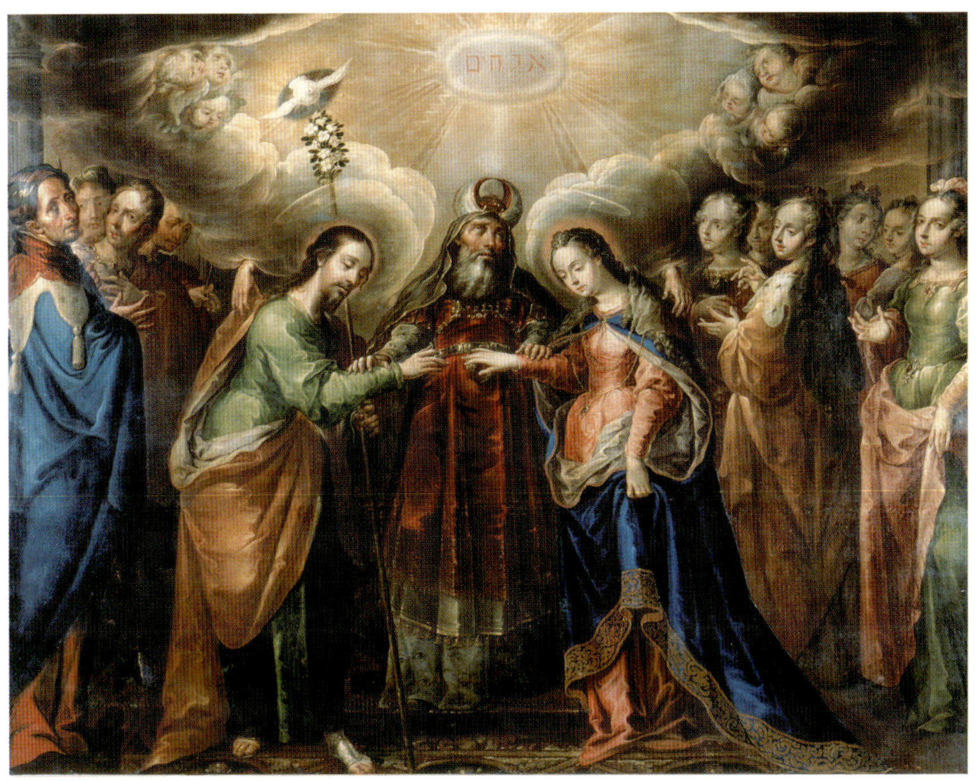

79   Cristóbal de Villalpando, *Marriage of the Virgin*, Jaén (Spain), Cathedral.

late seventeenth and early eighteenth century. In his painting of about 1700–14 (pl. 79), Villalpando once again preserves the arrangement of the central group. However, the horizontal format of the canvas compels him to amplify the scene by the inclusion of a group of female attendants at the right and male attendants on the left. Villalpando also has revised the formal vocabulary. He touches the canvas with a sketch-like brushstroke and introduces a range of gestures and facial expressions that provide a higher degree of animation to the scene.

These permutations of technique and iconography demonstrate the reworking of a Spanish model by New Spanish painters. The artists have enriched the narrative and revised the execution. Looking back from the work by Villalpando to the one painted by Luis Juárez around one hundred years earlier, it is possible to see the combination of tradition and innovation that characterizes New Spanish painting of the seventeenth century.

As I have tried to demonstrate, I believe that this is a field with a great future and it offers the potential to reshape our understanding of the diffusion of Spanish painting. If I could start over, this is where I would begin – not as a specialist in Spanish painting, nor as a specialist in viceregal art, but as a specialist in the arts of the Spanish Habsburg monarchy.

7

CLOSING REMARKS

As we draw to a close, I wish to summarize the principal themes of this book. Above all, I have offered the proposition that writing art history is more contingent on fate and personality than many might suppose. While historians strive to achieve objectivity, the truth is that they shuttle back and forth between the past and present, often without fully recognizing the degree of movement involved. This observation is by no means novel. In art history, the phrase "period eye" is often invoked to refer to this phenomenon. As I understand the term, it means that we see old works of art through the lens of the present, which is why painters go in and out of fashion or, at least, are subjected to periodic re-evaluation.

I have intermingled personal history with professional history by providing a peek at what goes on behind the scenes of an art historian's career and how his outlook is shaped by personality traits, family life, and by events near and distant in time. In keeping with this approach, I have raised the question of rivalry as a motivating force in art history. This characteristic can play a part in the tricky business of authentication, as I demonstrated by the discussion of my involvement in two controversial paintings assigned to Velázquez. These disputes occur somewhere almost every day. By following the current interest in workshop practice, I wanted to call attention to the fact that even the best painters – I used the examples of El Greco and Ribera, but Velázquez could be added to the list – recognized the advantages of multiplying their output by employing assistants. This practice needs to be kept in mind when considering the attribution of a painting to a great master.

Finally I have drawn attention to the phenomenon of the historical conditions that are prevailing when a person is born, what George Kubler calls the "point of entry." Was it a time of prosperity or plague? In my case, I found a propitious point of entry, that is to say *circa* 1964, the year I earned my Ph.D., although this would not become apparent until eleven years later. Had I entered the scene ten years earlier, I might not have been able to take advantage of the opportunities offered by the end of the Franco dictatorship or to find an audience outside Spain for my work. Nor perhaps would I have been able to participate to the same extent in the renovation of Spanish art history.

As soon as Franco was interred, the new democratic government confronted the problem of how to reintegrate the history and culture of Spain into its European context. Spain's long isolation had left it on the sidelines, a mere observer of how the world was being interpreted by the arts. Those with long memories will recall the forlorn Museum of Contemporary Art, located almost out of sight on the campus of the Universidad Complutense – a feeble and ultimately failed attempt to display contemporary art that was not "objectionable." The dictator's prolonged period of power had been particularly difficult for cultural initiatives and for preserving Spain's unique artistic patrimony.

A comparable problem, although on a much larger scale, was experienced by historians of the Golden Age, who had to hew to the party line and tread with care, lest they be ostracized or even imprisoned. Among this number was one of the most distinguished and respected historians of the twentieth century, Antonio Domínguez Ortiz, who did not have the confidence of the government and was made to pay by exclusion from the university. One of his observations made an indelible impression on me and validated the line of interpretation I had been slowly formulating. The words are taken from his book, *The Golden Age of Spain, 1516–1659*, published in 1971:

> Last but not least we must remember that this remote peninsula of Spain was never more united with the rest of Europe than it was in those days, by every kind of contact. There was a constant interchange of men and ideas, which acquired a particular intensity where Italy was concerned.

I draw attention to the adjective "remote." Domínguez was unconsciously externalizing the isolation experienced by Spanish intellectuals in the post-Civil War period. Spain as a geographical entity had not moved even one centimeter since the sixteenth century.

Otherwise his words describe my project as a Hispanist, although I would now include the art of Flanders, the Spanish colonies, and the other parts of the world in which Spaniards settled. In addition, I would reformulate the problematic of Spanish art to take account of its position at the center of a broad and dynamic cultural area. There is plenty of work to be done to take the full measure of Spain's leading role in the diffusion of European visual culture around the globe.

2 "SCIENTIFIC AND RIGOROUS"

1 Jonathan Brown, *Images and Ideas in Seventeenth-Century Spain*, Princeton, 1978.

2 Kathryn Brush, *The Shaping of Art History. Wilhelm Vöge, Adolph Goldschmidt and the Study of Medieval Art*, Cambridge, 1996.

3 Ibid., p. 192.

4 Diego Angulo Iñiguez, Enrique Marco Dorta, and Mario J. Buschiazzo, *Historia del arte hispanoaméricano*, 3 vols., Barcelona, 1945–56.

5 Diego Angulo Iñiguez and Alfonso E. Pérez Sánchez, "Historia de la pintura española." *Escuela madriléna del primer tercio del siglo XVII (Madrid, 1969); Escuela toledana de la primera mitad del siglo XVII (Madrid, 1972); Escuela madrileña del segundo tercio del siglo XVII*, Madrid, 1983. Pérez's devotion to the memory of Angulo can rightly be called filial.

6 Juan de Contreras, Marqués de Lozoya, "Preface," *Archivo Español de Arte*, n. 40 (1940), n.p.

7 Javier Portús, "Diego Velázquez, por Diego Angulo" in *Diego Angulo. Estudios completos sobre Velázquez*, Madrid, 2007, p. 21.

8 Elisa Bermejo, "Excmo. Sr. D. Diego Angulo Iñiguez (1901–1986)," *Archivo Español de Arte*, 59 (1986), 463–67.

9 Diego Angulo Iñiguez, "Algunos dibujos de Murillo," *Archivo Español de Arte*, 47 (1974), 97–108.

10 Diego Angulo Iñiguez, "Exposición de dibujos de Murillo en Princeton," *Archivo Español de Arte*, 50 (1977), 337–42.

11 Bonaventura Bassegoda, "Foreword," *Jonathan Brown. Collected Writings on Velázquez*, Madrid, 2008, pp. 26–28.

12 Kenneth Clark, *Civilization. A Personal View*, New York, 1969, p. xvii.

3 EL GRECO AND RIBERA

1 Jonathan Brown, *Jusepe de Ribera: Prints and Drawings*, Princeton University Art Museum, 1973. Spanish edition, Madrid, 1989.

2 Gianni Papi, *Ribera a Roma*, Soncino, 2007; *El joven Ribera*, Museo Nacional del Prado, 2011.

3 Nicola Spinosa, *Ribera. La obra completa*, Madrid, 2008.

4 Bernardo de Dominici, *Vite de' pittori, sculturi ed architetti napoletani*, ed. Fiorella Sricchia Santoro and Andrea Zezza, vol. 1, Naples, 2008.

5 Manuel B. Cossío, *El Greco*, 2 vols., Madrid, 1908.

6 Fernando Marías and Agustín Bustamante, *Ideas artísticas de El Greco. Comentarios a un texto inédito*, Madrid, 1982.

7 Jonathan Brown, "El Greco, The Man and the Myths," in *El Greco of Toledo*, Boston, 1982, pp. 75–147, and Richard L. Kagan, "The Toledo of El Greco," in *El Greco of Toledo*, Boston, 1982, pp. 35–72.

8 Fernando Márias, *El Greco. Biografía de un pintor extravagante*, Madrid, 1997. José Alvarez Lopera, *El Greco. Estudio y catálogo*, vol. 1, Madrid, 2005; vol. 2, Madrid, 2007.

9 Harold E. Wethey, *El Greco and His School*, 2 vols., Princeton, 1962.

10 Francisco Pacheco, *Arte de la pintura*, ed. Bonaventura Bassegoda, Madrid, 1990, pp. 440–41.

11 Fernando Marías, "El Greco y los 'originales' en su taller," in *El Greco's Studio*, ed. Nicos Hadjinicolaou, Iraklion, 2007, pp. 187–97.

4 ART AT THE COURT OF THE SPANISH HABSBURGS

1 Jonathan Brown, "Felipe II, coleccionista de pintura y escultura," in *Las Colecciones del Rey. Pintura y Escultura*. Madrid, 1986, pp. 19–31.

2 Hugh Trevor-Roper, *Princes and Artists. Patronage and Ideology at Four Habsburg Courts, 1517–1633*, London, 1976, p. 83.

3 Fernando Checa, *Felipe II: Mecenas de las artes*, Madrid, 1992.

4 Carmen García-Frías Checa, *Gaspar Becerra y las pinturas de la Torre de la Reina de El Pardo*, Madrid, 2005.

5 *Navarrete el mudo, pintor de Felipe II (Seguidores y copistas)*, Logroño, 1995.

6 For painting during the reign of Philip III, see Sarah Schroth and Ronni Baer, *El Greco to Velázquez. Art during the Reign of Philip III*, Boston, 2008.

7 Trevor-Roper, *Princes and Artists*, p. 83.

8 Ibid., p. 8.

9 Jonathan Brown and John H. Elliott, *A Palace for a King: The Buen Retiro and the Court of Philip IV*, New Haven and London, 1980; second, revised edition, 2003. For a virtual reconstruction of the palace, see Carmen Blasco, *El palacio del Buen Retiro de Madrid. Un proyecto hacia el pasado*, Madrid, 2001.

10 Brown and Elliott, *A Palace for a King*.

11 In general, the history of seventeenth-century Spain was neglected or shrouded in legend. See J. H. Elliott, *The Making of History*, New Haven and London, 2012, pp. 34–35.

12 J. H. Elliott, *The Count-Duke of Olivares: The Statesman in an Age of Decline*, New Haven and London, 1986.

13 For the most important series, see Andrés Úbeda de los Cobos, ed., *Paintings for the Planet King: Philip IV and the Buen Retiro Palace*, Madrid, 2005; and *Roma. Naturaleza e ideal. Paisajes 1600–1650*, Madrid, 2011. For the most recent contribution to the circumstances of the landscape commission, see Mercedes Simal López, "Nuevas noticias sobre las pinturas para el Real Palacio del Buen Retiro (1633–1642)," *Archivo Español de Arte*, 84 (2011), 245–60.

14 Jonathan Brown, "Felipe IV, el rey de coleccionistas," *Fragmentos. Revista de Arte*, 11 (1987), 4–19.

15 Yves Bottineau, "L'Alcázar de Madrid et L'inventaire de 1686," *Bulletin Hispanique*

58 (1956), 421–52; 60 (1958), 30–61, 145–79, 289–326.

16   Steven N. Orso, *Philip IV and the Decoration of the Alcázar of Madrid*, Princeton 1986; Bonaventura Bassegoda, *El Escorial como museo*, Barcelona, 2002.

17   Miguel Morán and Fernando Checa, *El coleccionismo en España: de la cámara de maravillas a la galeriá de pinturas*, Madrid, 1985.

18   Marcus Burke and Peter Cherry, *Collections of Paintings in Madrid, 1601–17. (Documents for the History of Collecting. Spanish Inventories 1)*, 2 vols., The Provenance Index of the Getty Information Institute/ Fondazione del' Istituto Bancario San Paolo di Torino, 1997.

19   Letitia de Frutos, *El templo de la Fama. Alegoría del Marqués del Carpio*, Madrid, 2009.

20   Jonathan Brown, *Kings and Connoisseurs: Collecting Art in Seventeenth-Century Europe*, New Haven and London, 1995.

21   Jonathan Brown and John H. Elliott, co-curators, *The Sale of the Century. Artistic Relations between Spain and Great Britain, 1604–1655*, Madrid, 2002.

5   VELÁZQUEZ

1   Ángel Aterido et al., eds., *Corpus velazqueño. Documentos y textos*, 2 vols., Madrid, 2000.

2   Antonio Palomino, *El museo pictórico y escala óptica. Tomo tercero:El Parnaso español pintoresco laureado*, vol. 3, Madrid, 1724; English edition, Nina Ayala Mallory, Cambridge, 1987.

3   For an excellent critical edition of Velázquez's biography with extensive notes, see Miguel Morán Turina, ed., *Vida de Don Diego Velázquez de Silva*, Madrid, 2008.

4   Francisco Pacheco, *Arte de la pintura*, Seville, 1649. For a detailed critical edition, see Bonaventura Bassegoda, Madrid, 1990.

5   Jonathan Brown, *Velázquez, Painter and Courtier*, New Haven and London, 1986; Spanish edition, *Velázquez, pintor y cortesano*, Madrid, 1990.

6   Pablo Pérez d'Ors, "New Information on Velázquez's *Portrait of Philip IV at Fraga* in The Frick Collection, New York," *Burlington Magazine*, 152 (2010), 652–59.

7   *Corpus velazqueño*, vol. 1, p. 283.

8   Ibid., pp. 469–538.

9   See the studies by Portús in Miguel Morán Turina and Javier Portús Pérez, *El arte de mirar. La pintura y su público en la España de Velázquez*, Madrid, 1997, and *Pintura y pensamiento en la España de Lope de Vega*, Madrid, 1999. For a concise account of this question, see Ángel Aterido, "The Culture of Velázquez: Reading, Knowledge and Social Connections," in Javier Portús, ed., *Velázquez's Fables. Mythology and Sacred History in the Golden Age*, Madrid, 2007, pp. 72–93.

10   *Corpus velazqueño*, vol. 1, p. 81.

11   Jonathan Brown, "Velázquez y lo velazqueño: los problemas de las atribuciones," *Boletín del Museo del Prado*, 18 (2000), 51–69. The last complete catalogue raisonée is that of José López-Rey, *Velázquez. A Catalogue Raisonée of his Oeuvre*, London, 1963. Later editions exclude copies and versions.

12   Benito Navarrete Prieto et al., *En torno a Santa Rufina. Velázquez de lo íntimo a lo cortesano*, Seville, 2008.

13   This observation is anticipated by Javier Portús Pérez, *Pinturas mitológicas de Velázquez*. Madrid, 2002, pp. 95–113, one of the best treatments of the subject.

14   Antonio Palomino, *El museo pictórico y escala óptica*, pp. 920–22.

6   MY DISCOVERY OF SPANISH AMERICA

1   For an expanded version of this chapter, see Luisa Elena Alcalá and Jonathan Brown, eds., *Painting in Latin America, 1550–1821*. New Haven and London, 2014.

2   Juana Gutiérrez Haces, ed., *Painting of the Kingdoms. Territories of the Spanish Monarchy, 16th to 18th Centuries*, 4 vols., Mexico City, 2008–09.

J. Brown, curator: *Pintura de los Reinos: Identidades Compartidas,* Madrid and Mexico City, 2012–13.

3   Thomas DaCosta Kaufmann, "*Pintura de los Reinos*: A Global View of the Cultural Field," in Gutiérrez Haces, ed., *Painting of the Kingdoms,* vol. 1, pp. 87–135.

4   Manuel Toussaint, *Pintura colonial en México,* ed. Xavier Moyssen, 2nd edition, Mexico City, 1982. The text was completed in 1934.

5   For a useful overview, see Rogelio Ruiz Gomar, "Unique Expressions. Painting in New Spain," in Donna Pierce, ed., *Painting a New World. Mexican Art and Life 1521–1821*, Denver, 2004, pp. 47–77.

6   M. Alonso Mela and C. Martínez Shaw, *El Galeón de Manila,* Seville, 2000, and Donna Pierce and Ronald Otsuka, eds., *Asia and America. Trans-Pacific Artistic and Cultural Exchange 1500–1840,* Denver, 2009.

7   Serge Gruzinski, *Painting the Conquest. The Mexican Indians and the European Renaissance,* Paris, 1992.

8   Zsuzanna van Ruyven-Zeman et al., *The Wierix Family. The New Hollstein. Dutch & Flemish Etchings, Engravings and Woodcuts 1450–1700,* 10 vols., Rotterdam, 2004–06.

9   See the exhaustive article by Helga von Kugelgen, "Painting from the Kingdoms and Rubens," in Gutiérrez Haces, ed., *Painting of the Kingdoms,* vol. 3, pp. 1009–78.

10   Neil De Marchi and Hans J. Van Miegroet, "Exploring Markets for Netherlandish Painting in Spain and New Spain," *Nederlands Kunsthistorisch Jaarboek,* 50 (1999), 81–105.

11   Duncan Kinkead, "Juan de Luzón and the Sevillian Painting Trade with the New World in the Second Half of the Seventeenth Century," *The Art Bulletin,* 66 (1984), 303–10.

12   Rogelio Ruiz Gomar, "El gremio y la cofradía de pintores en la Nueva España," in Elisa Vargas Lugo and Gustavo Curiel, eds., *Juan de Correa. Su vida y su obra,* vol. 3, Mexico City, 1991, pp. 201–22; and Paula Mues Ort, *La libertad del pincel. Los discursos sobre la nobleza de la pintura en Nueva España,* Mexico City, 2008.

13   Juan Miguel Serrera, "La defensa novohispana de la ingenuidad de la pintura," *Academia,* 81 (1995), 275–88.

14   Ricardo Fernández Gracia, *Iconografía de Don Juan Palafox: imágenes para un hombre de estado y de la Iglesia,* Pamplona, 2002.

15   Toussaint, *Pintura colonial en México,* p. 223.

16   Clara Bargellini, "Originality and Invention in the Painting of New Spain," in Donna Pierce et al., *Painting a New World. Mexican Art and Life 1521–1821,* Denver 2004, pp. 79–91, and "The Spread of Models. Flemish and Italian Prints and Paintings in America," in Gutiérrez Haces, ed., *Painting of the Kingdoms,* vol. 3, pp. 964–1005.

17   The literature on the Virgin of Guadalupe is vast. A good starting place for historians of art is Jaime Cuadriello, *Maravilla Americana. Variantes de la iconografía guadalupana. Siglos XVI–XIX,* Mexico City, 1989; and by the same author, "*Virgen potens.* Virgin Most Powerful. The Immaculate Conception or the Imaginary in the Spanish Realms," in Gutiérrez Haces, ed., *Painting of the Kingdoms,* vol. 4, pp. 1168–263.

18   Juana Gutiérrez Haces et al., *Cristóbal de Villalpando, ca. 1649–1714. Catálogo razonado,* Mexico City, 1997, pp. 274–76.

19   Jaime Cuadriello, "El origen del reino y la configuración de su empresa:episodios y alegorías de triunfo y fundación," in *Los pinceles de la historia. El origen del Reino de la Nueva España 1680–1750,* Mexico City, 1999, pp. 50–107.

20   Sofia Sanabrais, "The *Biombo* or Folding Screen in Colonial Mexico," in Donna Pierce and Ronald Otsuka, eds., *Asia & Spanish America. Trans-Pacific Artistic & Cultural Exchange, 1500–1850,* Denver, 2009, pp. 69–106.

21   Ilona Katzew, *Casta Paintings: Images of Race in Eighteenth-Century Mexico,* New Haven and London, 2004, pp. 174–76.

22   Jaime Cuadriello, "Vista de la ciudad de México y conquista de México," in *Los siglos de oro en los virreinatos de América*, Madrid, 1999, p. 153; and R. L. Kagan, *Imágenes urbanas del mundo hispánico 1493–1780*, Madrid, 1998, pp. 224–50.

23   María Concepción García Sáiz, "Nuevos materiales para nuevas expresiones," in *Los siglos de oro*, 1999, pp.135–39 and 384–89.

24   *Los siglos de oro*, pp. 384–89.

25   Michael A. Brown, "Image of an Empire: Portraiture of Spain and the Viceroyalties of New Spain and Peru," in Gutiérrez Haces, ed., vol. 4, pp. 1446–503.

Courtesy of the author: image on p. ix, 1, 2, 3, 4, 7, 8, 9, 10, 43, 44 (© Dalda), 65; © Estate of Nat Finkelstein: 5; Photograph © Clemens Kalischer: 6; Department of Art and Archaeology, Princeton University: 11; Courtesy of Gerda Panofsky: 12; Sara Krulwich / The New York Times / Redux / eyevine: 13; Bradley Marks for the College Art Association: 14; Madrid, Archivo Fotográfico del Museo Nacional del Prado: 15, 18, 19, 20, 21, 36, 40, 42, 51, 52, 59, 61, 63, 64; Hofphotograph Pieperhoff, Leipzig: 16; © bpk: 17, 22 (Jörg P. Anders), 24 (Elke Estel / Hans-Peter Klut); Photo © Antonio Sánchez Barriga: 23; Photo © Erik Cornelius: 25; The Bridgeman Art Library: 26, 27 (National Trust Photographic Library / John Hammond), 33 (De Agostini Picture Library), 45, 48, 49 (Giraudon); Image © 2014 The Barnes Foundation: 28, 30; Photo © National Gallery of Canada: 29; © The Frick Collection: 31, 46; Photography © The Art Institute of Chicago: 32; © Bruce Yuanyue Bi: 34; Photograph © Ricardo Gutiérrez: 39; © Carmen Blasco: 40; © Kunsthistorisches Museum, Vienna: 47, 53; © The National Gallery, London. Bequeathed by Sir William H. Gregory, 1892: 50; Samuel H. Kress Collection: 54; Leonard C. Hanna, Jr. Fund 1981.18: 55; © Luis Davilla: 56; Consejo Nacional para las Artes y la Cultura: 68, 69, 71, 73, 74; Archivo Fotográfico Manuel Toussaint, Instituto de Investigaciones Estéticas, UNAM: 74; Photo © Graphimag: 76; © Image courtesy of the Figge Art Museum, Davenport, Iowa. Gift of an anonymous donor, 1995.6: 77; Ciudad de México, Museo Nacional de Arte, Consejo Nacional para la Cultura y las Artes, Instituto Nacional de Bellas Artes. Reproducción autorizada por el Instituto Nacional de Bellas Artes y Literatura, 2013: 78; Photo © Tomás Antelo: 79

INDEX